# THE GAZA STRIP

## ITS HISTORY AND POLITICS

## The Cover Illustrations in Political Context

Persistence, indignation and a refusal to submit to an unjust fate are written on the face of this old woman from the Shaati refugee camp. Shaati began as a makeshift collection of tents on the seashore and has since grown into one of the larger urban centers along the eastern Mediterranean. The picture was taken in 1978, more than a generation after the *Nakba*, the Palestinian national disaster which led to the creation of a new square on the Middle Eastern chessboard – the Gaza Strip. When the author first began to work in the Strip in the 1970s such composed and dignified old-timers were part of the local landscape. Most courtyards included a grandparent in traditional dress quietly enjoying the shade of a fig tree, often consulted as living encyclopedias by their offspring. Their store of tales, knowledge and memories from the lost villages of Palestine was also a welcome resource for researchers and reporters.

Now, after another thirty years, the number of Gazan elders with clear and reliable memories of the old life is dwindling. Their patience and their pious confidence that a just and compassionate solution to their predicament would be found, is not a part of the younger generations' more militant mind-set.

After the upheavals and acute desperation of the first years of exile, the refugee asylums of the Strip were organized into rows of tents, which gave way to shacks and later to humble mud-brick housing. But life was too precarious ever to be termed "normal". Lack of work and opportunities fuelled emigration as thousands of Gazans left for the Gulf. In the absence of a political solution refugee life in the Strip settled into routines that had little in common with the previous reality, which had followed the seasonal rhythm of sowing and reaping. Life in the Strip took place in camp alleys and crowded streets. The four scenes on the back cover give an idea of workaday life in the Strip during its first decades: a busy market street near Medina Square in Gaza City in August 1971, when shopkeepers dared not observe a commercial strike declared by the PLO in protest against Israel's "dirty war" against Palestinian fighters; a bored Israeli soldier keeping guard outside the newly opened branch of the Leumi bank during the brief Israeli occupation of the Strip in 1956–57; women and children in a mud-brick alley of the Khan Yunes refugee camp in December 1956; and, lastly, the most crowded moment of any Gazan day – the end of school – when more than half a million pupils take over the streets and traffic comes to a near standstill.

The Gaza Strip, as a geopolitical unit, is only six decades old, but the portion of land covered by the term figures prominently in the annals of several civilizations. From time immemorial conquerors from near and far have set their sights on the city of Gaza and on the coastal highway leading from Egypt to the Fertile Crescent. No conquest along that route could be undertaken before securing the area's water resources and the junctions connecting the main caravan and marching routes. Napoleon, Samson, Alexander the Great, Saladdin and Richard the Lionheart are only a few in a long line of historical celebrities who have intervened directly in the history of Gaza. Pharaohs, Philistines, Persians, Greeks, Arabs and Ottomans all ruled Gaza before the modern era was ushered in by the British conquest in 1917, and the subsequent clash between the Jewish and the Palestinian national movements.

During the short existence of the Strip, it has been ruled by Egypt, Israel, the PLO and Islamist Hamas, whose masked "executive brigades" stunned the world when taking over Gaza in the summer of 2007. Its inhabitants have known little stability in recent decades, as the pendulum has swung wildly between peace-talks and hope – and then back to violence and despair. Not much remains of the deal struck between Yasser Arafat and Yizhak Rabin in 1993, but many still regard it as the only realistic blueprint for a solution. The latter part of this book is a detailed blow-by-blow account of the of the dramatic recent events, from the outbreak of the first Palestinian uprising in December 1987 until the Israeli invasion in 2008–2009, a campaign still generating intense polemics and political wrangling a year after it ended.

Better times will surely come to the Gazans, now squeezed between the Israeli embargo and the increasingly autocratic ambitions of its one-party regime. The photo on the cover showing war-shaken children from the Jebaliya refugee camp playing games during a therapy-session which took place during the Israeli bombardment, justifies the hope, if not the prediction, that such a change will come about in their generation.

"In *The History of the Gaza Strip* great and terrible histories are crushed into one small strip of land. With an unflinching critical eye, in which the follies of neither side are excused, this shrewd and seasoned reporter unravels the story of Gaza in its true role – as the crucible of the Israeli–Palestinian tragedy."

Alexander Linklater, *Prospect Magazine*

"Once I started reading *The History of the Gaza Strip*, I could not stop. It is a fascinating book, which takes no sides but makes good use of all kinds of sources: from personal experiences to official data to street gossip. Some of the protagonists occasionally behave decently, but mostly, they behave appallingly. Few stand for liberty or democracy. But the book makes me understand the reasoning of both sides, hostages as they are to ideologies and beliefs. I recommend it strongly to any reader who feels the need for an analysis of the Gazan tangle and of the spiral of senseless violence that defines the lot of men in this region. Gaza is shown here as a part of Palestine and the Middle East, in all its dependency on big power politics and on the good or ill will of its powerful neighbours, the Israelis and the Egyptians."

Jan Szeminsky, Professor of History, The Hebrew University, Jerusalem

"Nathan Shachar conveys his encyclopaedic knowledge of the Gaza Strip by means of a moving and entertaining narrative which escorts the reader through the turbulent annals of the Middle East's most cursed flashpoint. *The History of the Gaza Strip* puts Shachar right up there with masters like Orlando Figes, author of *A People's Tragedy, The Russian Revolution 1891–1924* – and sets him apart from those historians who pile on dates and names without ever stirring the soul of the reader."

Ramy Wurgaft, *El Mundo*, Madrid
(Middle East Correspondent 1991–2002)

# THE GAZA STRIP
## ITS HISTORY AND POLITICS
### From the Pharaohs to the Israeli Invasion of 2009

NATHAN SHACHAR

sussex
ACADEMIC
PRESS
*Brighton • Portland • Toronto*

2 4 6 8 10 9 7 5 3

*First published in hardcover and paperback, 2010, updated and reprinted in paperback July 2010, in Great Britain by*
SUSSEX ACADEMIC PRESS
PO Box 139
Eastbourne BN24 9BP

*and in the United States of America by*
SUSSEX ACADEMIC PRESS
920 NE 58th Ave Suite 300
Portland, Oregon 97213–3786

*and in Canada by*
SUSSEX ACADEMIC PRESS (CANADA)
90 Arnold Avenue, Thornhill, Ontario L4J 1B5



*British Library Cataloguing in Publication Data*
A CIP catalogue record for this book is available from the British Library.

*Library of Congress Cataloging-in-Publication Data*
Shachar, Nathan.
The Gaza Strip : its history and politics : from the pharaohs to the Israeli invasion of 2009 / Nathan Schachar.
p. cm.
Includes bibliographical references and index.
ISBN 978-1-84519-344-7 (hardcover : alk. paper) —
ISBN 978-1-84519-345-4 (pbk. : alk. paper)
1. Gaza Strip–History. 2. Gaza Strip—Politics and government. 3. Gaza Strip—Social conditions. 4. Social conflict—Gaza Strip—History. I. Title.
DS110.G3S49 2010
953′.1—dc22

2009032963

Typeset and designed by Sussex Academic Press, Brighton & Eastbourne.
Printed by TJ International, Padstow, Cornwall.
This book is printed on acid-free paper.

# Contents

# List of Illustrations

The author and publisher are grateful to the Government Press Office, Israel, and Paul Hansen, journalist and photographer, for assistance in sourcing and granting permission to reproduce many of the cover and internal pictures.

*Cover illustrations*:
FRONT: Refugee woman in her yard. Shaati refugee camp. Photographer: Sa'ar Ya'cov, August 1978; Prime Minister Yizhak Rabin and PLO Chairman Yasser Arafat meeting at the Erez checkpoint between Israel and the Gaza Strip, 1994. Photographer: Avi Ohayon; Pharaoh Thutmose III; masked Islamist Hamas executive brigade; Gaza ruins after the December 2009 Israeli bombardment. Photographer: Paul Hansen; children in the refugee camp in play therapy as a means to get over their war experiences, January 2009. Photographer: Paul Hansen.

BACK: Market street near Medina Square in Gaza City. Shopkeepers dare not observe the strike called by PLO to protest Israel's "dirty war" against Palestinian fighters. Photographer: Moshe Milner, August 1971; Israeli soldier keeping guard outside the newly opened branch of Israel's Bank Leumi in Khan Yunes. Israel hoped to retain control over the Strip after the conquest in October 1956, but was forced out by US president Eisenhower. Photographer: Fritz Cohen, November 1956; alley in Khan Yunes refugee camp. Photographer: Fritz Cohen, December 1956; masses of school children swarming along a street in the Shati refugee camp in Gaza. Photographer: Moshe Milner, 1975.

*Plate section (after page 114); photographers are acknowledged in plate captions.*

# Acknowledgments

The purpose of this book is to provide a brief historical account of the area known since January 1949 as the Gaza Strip. Here and there, during the account of earlier periods, I have allowed myself the anachronistic use of the term "the Strip".

My ambition, when writing on the controversial events of recent decades, has not been to apportion blame but rather to make the actions of the parties comprehensible, even when I find them reprehensible. Formal objectivity is at its most elusive when describing Gazan conflagrations, but that doesn't make it a less worthy goal to pursue. However, when the declared motives of the parties, notably the Palestinian Authority, the Israeli government and the Hamas movement, have obviously diverged from their real aims, I have not – in the interest of a purely formal objectivity – refrained from pointing this out. If our only explanations of why Israel denies basic goods to the Strip, or why Hamas fires rockets at Israeli towns, were those offered by the parties themselves, we would learn very little.

The main sources for the post-1975 events are my own notes, memories and contacts, collected during many years of reporting from the area. But I have shared my active years between the Spanish-American world and the Middle East, and there are large swaths of contemporary Gazan history that I have not witnessed personally and have had to piece together from newspaper archives. I wish to thank the staff at the Israeli National Library at the Giv'at Ram campus, and at the archives of the *al-Quds* newspaper in East Jerusalem, for their help and patience. The 1948–2006 photographs are published with the permission of the GPO archives at Beit Agron in Jerusalem and the ones from the 2008–9 war with the permission of Paul Hansen.

My two most valuable sources, both Gazans, have understandably declined to be named. One is a man, still living in the Strip and viewed with distrust by the authorities. The other is a woman, living outside the Strip, and facing great dangers directly related to the secular-Islamist struggle on which much of the Strip's future still turns. It is my hope that, one day, their courage will prove not to have been in vain.

NATHAN SHACHAR

*Jerusalem, November 2009/May 2010*

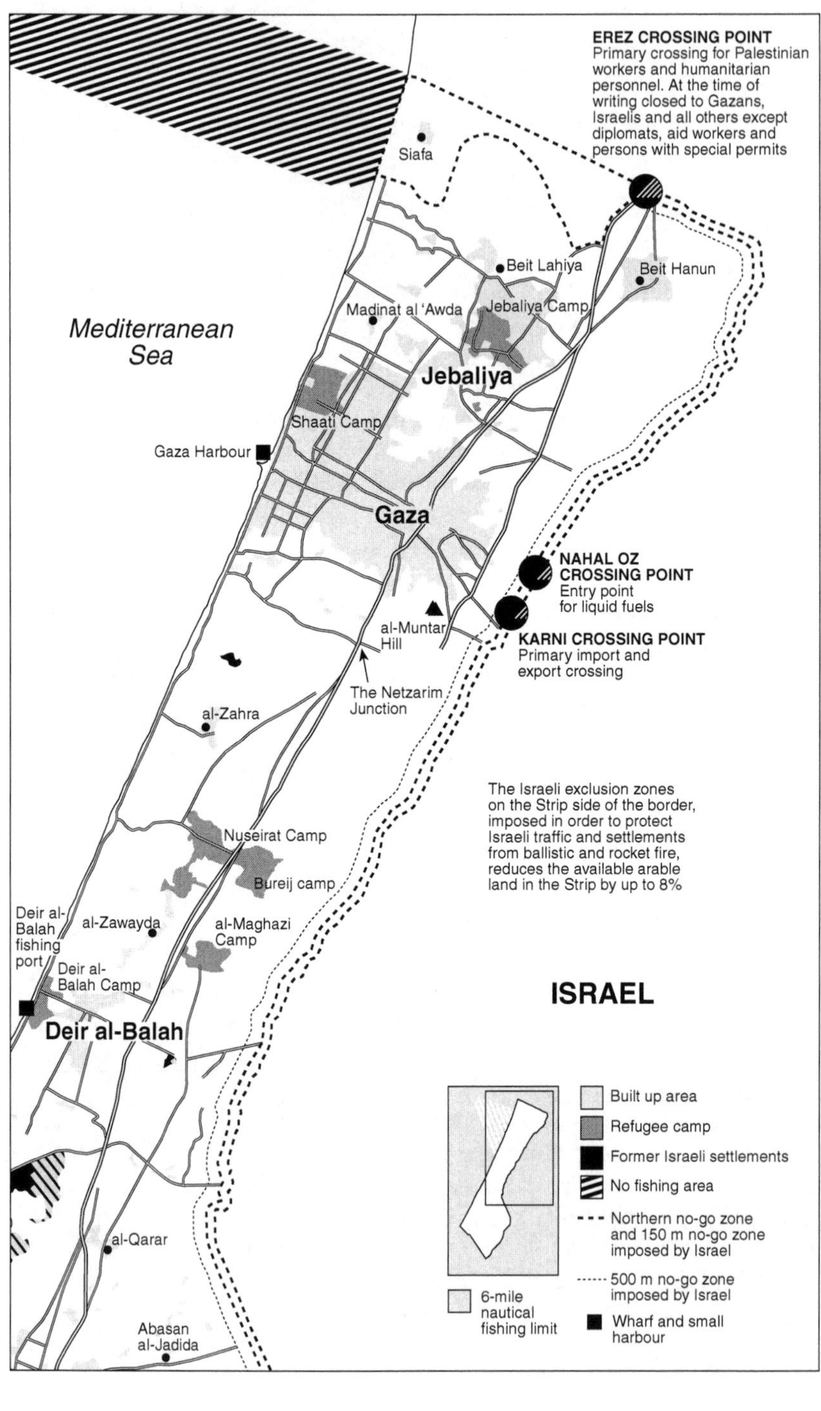
EREZ CROSSING POINT
Primary crossing for Palestinian workers and humanitarian personnel. At the time of writing closed to Gazans, Israelis and all others except diplomats, aid workers and persons with special permits
Siafa
Beit Lahiya
Beit Hanun
Madinat al 'Awda
Jebaliya Camp
Mediterranean Sea
Jebaliya
Shaati Camp
Gaza Harbour
Gaza
NAHAL OZ CROSSING POINT
Entry point for liquid fuels
al-Muntar Hill
KARNI CROSSING POINT
Primary import and export crossing
The Netzarim Junction
al-Zahra
The Israeli exclusion zones on the Strip side of the border, imposed in order to protect Israeli traffic and settlements from ballistic and rocket fire, reduces the available arable land in the Strip by up to 8%
Nuseirat Camp
Bureij camp
Deir al-Balah fishing port
al-Zawayda
al-Maghazi Camp
Deir al-Balah Camp
ISRAEL
Deir al-Balah
Built up area
Refugee camp
Former Israeli settlements
No fishing area
Northern no-go zone and 150 m no-go zone imposed by Israel
500 m no-go zone imposed by Israel
Wharf and small harbour
6-mile nautical fishing limit
al-Qarar
Abasan al-Jadida

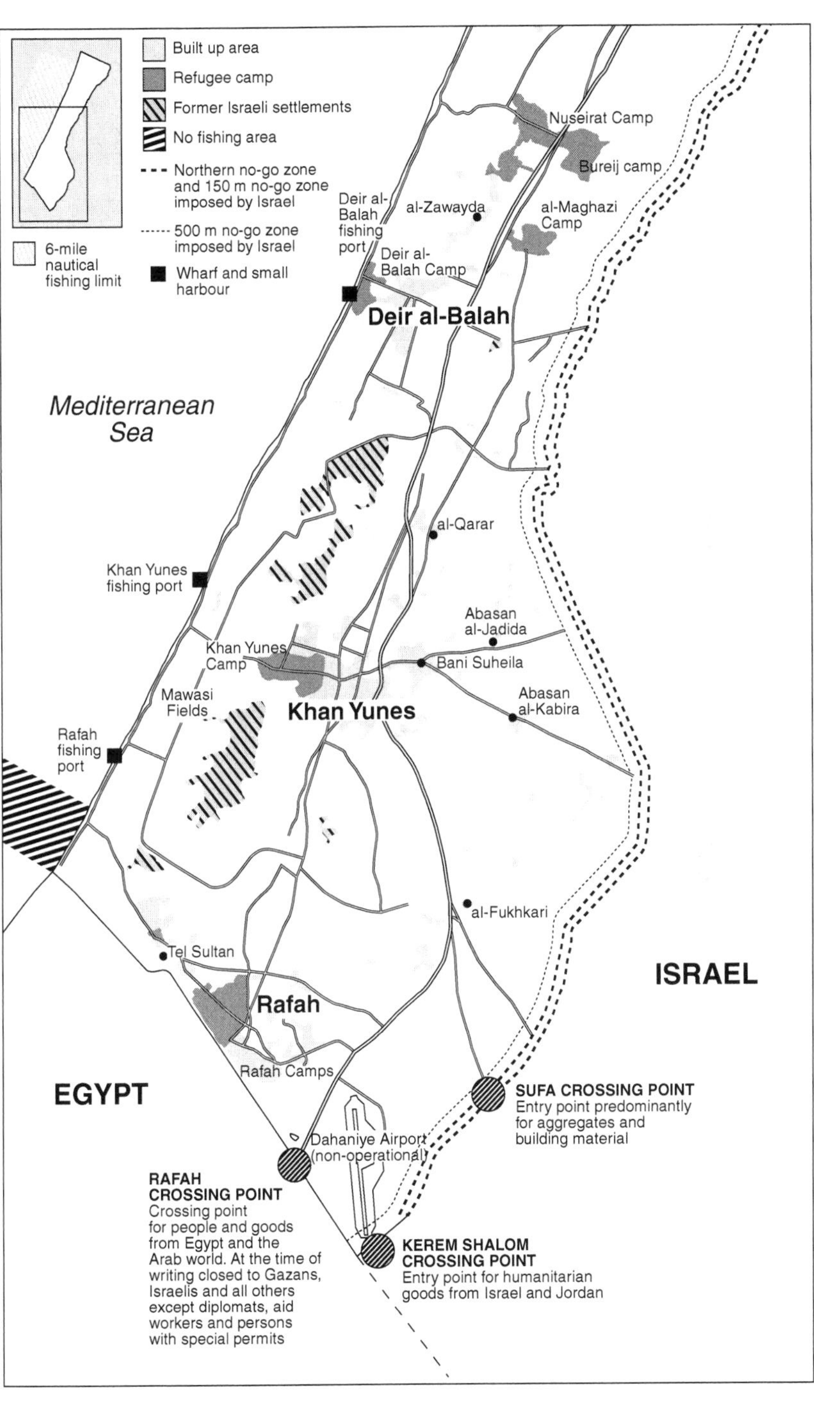

Built up area
Refugee camp
Former Israeli settlements
No fishing area
Northern no-go zone and 150 m no-go zone imposed by Israel
500 m no-go zone imposed by Israel
Wharf and small harbour
6-mile nautical fishing limit
Mediterranean Sea
Nuseirat Camp
Bureij camp
al-Maghazi Camp
al-Zawayda
Deir al-Balah fishing port
Deir al-Balah Camp
Deir al-Balah
al-Qarar
Khan Yunes fishing port
Abasan al-Jadida
Khan Yunes Camp
Bani Suheila
Abasan al-Kabira
Mawasi Fields
Khan Yunes
Rafah fishing port
al-Fukhkari
Tel Sultan
ISRAEL
Rafah
Rafah Camps
EGYPT
SUFA CROSSING POINT
Entry point predominantly for aggregates and building material
Dahaniye Airport (non-operational)
RAFAH CROSSING POINT
Crossing point for people and goods from Egypt and the Arab world. At the time of writing closed to Gazans, Israelis and all others except diplomats, aid workers and persons with special permits
KEREM SHALOM CROSSING POINT
Entry point for humanitarian goods from Israel and Jordan

*Along the road of Gaza the Pharaohs Shishak and Necho invaded Israel by the way of the Philistines. By that road, too, one Eastern despot after another – Assyrian, Chaldean, Persian and Syro-Grecian – marched to win the rich prize of the Valley of the Nile.*

H.B. Tristram

# Introduction
## Trauma and Violence

*Anything up to the size of a scooter or a cow can be imported into Gaza through the famous underground corridors dug along the "Philadelphi" road between the Strip and Egypt. Food, fuel and countless consumer items reach the Strip that way, but with each tunnel costing between 100 and 200 thousand dollars to dig, the rental costs and the logistics are prohibitive . . .*

"The Gaza Strip" is a young geopolitical concept, but the area has a history of millennia, much of it unearthed and neatly filed away by scholars and archaeologists. Like most of the ancient Holy Land it has been disputed and subdued by Egyptians and Assyrians, Philistines and Israelites, Greeks and Arabs, Mongols and Mamluks, Turks and British, Palestinians and Israelis.

The coastal strip between the Egyptian desert and the green Levantine heartland was fated to become a highway of armies. In itself it has not created much world history, but it has endured and absorbed heavy doses of it. Anyone wishing to wield intercontinental power in the region has first needed to secure the Gaza area as a deployment platform, a watering station and a shipping post. Rarely have the Gazans attacked their neighbours. Often – fifty-five times by the ancient Egyptians alone – they have been overwhelmed, plundered and burned by impatient conquerors on their way north or south.

But for all its notable annals, the Gaza Strip will not strike us with the same heady feeling of historical awe which overwhelms any visitor to Peru, Rome, Mexico or Cairo; places where a glorious past is visibly linked to a mundane present. Ancient Egyptian, Greek or even Ottoman Gaza offer little insight into current complications. At certain moments one gets the feeling that the crowded and tumultuous history of Gaza began only yesterday; or at least within living memory – in the last days of 1948, when angry British and American diplomats barked at the Israelis to call off their assault against Egyptian forces boxed in along a narrow coastal enclave in the south-western corner of Palestine. Trapped with the Egyptian soldiers, who had entered the country in May as the Jews declared independence, were close to two hundred thousand Palestinian civilians who had fled the fighting or been evicted by victorious Jewish forces. They hailed from many areas: the modern towns of Jaffa and Majdal on the Mediterranean coast, the Bedouin tribal areas around Beersheba in the Negev Desert and the agricultural lands of the *fellaheen* farmers in between. Their natural escape route would have led most of them into Egypt. But that was no option, for two reasons. The refugees would have risked perishing in the arid and empty Sinai desert before reaching their destination. More significantly, Egypt, alone among Palestine's Arab neighbours, refused to receive any fleeing Palestinians on its territory. And so it came about that all the refugees from the south-western parts of the new Jewish state set out towards the Mediterranean coast, hoping to find shelter and water in the last four Palestinian towns this side of the Egyptian border: Gaza, Deir al-Balah, Khan Yunes and Rafah.

None of the actors in that drama, neither the stunned local population nor the desperate refugees, the Quaker charities or the UN personnel that moved in to care for the needy, suspected that the emergency was anything but temporary. But it proved irreversible. Suddenly, as if by a sword-cut, the small coastal area around the four towns was severed from its previous history and its economical hinterland, and launched in a strange and unknown direction.

Until that moment the area to be called the Gaza Strip had scarcely appeared in any news-bulletins. Since then it has rarely been out of the news. Every TV viewer in the world has watched Gaza, but very few have been there. In fact, most people would decline an offer to make the trip with all expenses paid, for the reputation of Gaza is one of misery, danger and extreme violence. The only outsiders with any first-hand experience of it are journalists, diplomats, aid-workers and, before 1967, UN peacekeepers. Today, when its ports, its airspace and its southern and northern borders are sealed off by Israel and its western border by Egypt, the Gaza Strip is off the map for tourists.

Of all the geopolitical flashpoints on the international agenda in 1948, only Kashmir, Tibet and Gaza are still smouldering. And the Strip's miniscule borders coincide with several of the most volatile fault-lines of our time: between Islam and Arab secularism; tradition and modernity; East and West; Israel and the Arab world – and between the affluent first world and the indigent third one.

I first saw the Gaza Strip in 1975. I was twenty-three and I went there to write a feature about a new housing project in Sheikh Radwan near Gaza city, sponsored by the Israeli authorities. The purpose was to offer the refugees permanent housing, in the hope of dampening their hostility and driving a wedge between them and their exiled leaders. The PLO roundly condemned the idea, and its broadcasts from Beirut and Baghdad carried grim warnings against anyone who agreed to move into, or even to help construct, the new buildings. Some bricklayers were attacked and some homeowners were shot. But the allure of modern plumbing, watertight roofs and running water proved stronger than any threats. The refugees scrambled to register for the project, and the PLO gave up opposing it. Contrary to Israeli hopes, the joy of the beneficiaries barely dented the growing popular support for the PLO.

I had lived in several countries, rich and poor, as I grew up. But I had never been anywhere like Gaza. Toddlers with their clothes in ribbons played amid open sewers, but the schoolgirls in their ironed green-and-white striped uniforms were impeccably neat. Except for a ceremonial tea-session at the imposing divan of the powerful al-Shawa family, I saw need and hardship wherever I looked, even if UN food rations and the expanding Israeli labour market kept misery from sliding to Latin American levels.

The trauma and the violence had not ended with the 1948 exodus. Egyptian rule, between 1948 and 1967, had been cruel, racist and corrupt. For a quarter of a century, at the time of my first visit, all refugee hopes of returning had foundered on gridlocked regional and global power constellations. Many buildings were pockmarked by gunfire, some of it fresh. Recently, in one of the region's many forgotten wars, the Israeli general Ariel Sharon had crushed Palestinian armed resistance in the Strip with shocking measures, including the razing of hundreds of homes. It was not the first time that Sharon had burst onto Gaza's stage – nor would it be the last.

All those afflictions should, logically, have added up to an atmosphere of sullen resentment. Instead, Gazan society radiated vitality and openness, and each time I returned to work there I did so in high spirits. Today's Gaza, in Western minds, is almost synonymous with hidebound, anti-Western jihadism. In 1975, to be sure, many elders still donned traditional village dress, the abbayas and pantaloons of the farming fellaheen they had been until 1948. But rather than demonising and denouncing the West, everyone I spoke to – and back then one did not speak to men only – yearned to join the modern world. Most men my age were dressed like me; they were Marxists – unlike me – and they eagerly discussed progress, education, revolution and independence. All the bright lights on their ideological firmament were decidedly Western. The popular fronts, the DFLP and the PFLP, were financed by Eastern Bloc countries. But, geopolitics permitting, they would much rather have aligned with Paris and London than with Moscow. We had fish and beer on the beach and watched the girls – local, Palestinian girls, nota bene – in their diminutive swimsuits. At the homes of my hosts I was proudly shown translations of Sartre and gramophone records by Moustaki, "a Jew from Egypt who has taken our side against Israel".

A decade and a half later, the Gaza I had first known was on the wane. The crushing gloom after the failure of the first Palestinian uprising of 1987–91 was chiefly a disappointment with the Western concepts that had inspired it: with democracy and nationalism, if not with politics altogether.

The tenacious secularism that had struck me had begun its long retreat. A week after the outbreak of the first Intifada, which occurred in Gaza on December 10, 1987, Ahmad Yassin, a local leader of the Muslim Brotherhood, changed the name of his local charity from al-Mujamma' al-Islami to the more defiant Harikat al-Muqawme al-Muslamiya, the Muslim Resistance Movement, acronymed Hamas – a word meaning "enthusiasm" in Arabic.

Through my acquaintance with Samira, a student from the Shaati refugee camp, I watched the steady demise of the Western core beliefs of human rights, democracy and equality between the sexes. Those ideals had never been realised, to be sure, but they had animated a generation. Now the tide turned with distressing speed. There was little in the way of extreme Islamism in Palestinian tradition, but the Saudi and Qatari governments gladly assumed the responsibility for directing and financing the ideological shift. (The Saudis would come to regret this intervention bitterly, just as Israel would later regret having, for reasons of its own, groomed sheikh Yassin and smoothed the path of Hamas.) Samira was a brave young woman who starred in a book I wrote at the time. Her losing battle for the right to study and to dress as she pleased was a graphic tableau of the metamorphosis. Dress was the least of it. After the first round of battle, Samira sacrificed her blue jeans in the hope of carrying on with her anthropological research. But that too was denied her, and the final stab in her vitals came when all her hopes were reduced to the one choice: remaining at home or studying Sha'aria, Islamic law, considered a "safe" subject for women.

Secularism made a sudden and tumultuous comeback in July 1994. As the world watched Yasser Arafat – the emblematic 20th century refugee – crossed the Egypt–Gaza border, enter Palestine and put an end to his long exile. For a few years the foreign-sponsored fundamentalist tide was held in check, as al-Fatah recouped some of the lost ground. Hefty injections of foreign aid allowed the PLO–Fatah to compete with Hamas' free-lunch methods. Aid also remodelled the Gaza skyline. Broad, tree-lined avenues, high-rise apartment blocks, streetlights, sewage treatment (now largely broken down for lack of fuel and spare parts) and even an airport, gave the shack-ridden strip a veneer of normality, at least when viewed from a distance. For a few short seasons the secular optimism of old returned. Perhaps, it seemed, the Western dream of progress and justice would deliver after all. Bars and hotels flourished as NGOs and foreign aid delegations embraced the long-neglected causes of Gaza. Expectations reached a Messianic pitch as Israelis and Palestinians launched joint ventures in business, science and – amazingly – security.

But PLO rule bore within it the seeds of its own demise. The young PLO fighters who had confronted Israel in 1987 and done time in its jails were also the ones who took to the streets in the autumn of 1993 in order to win over sceptical Gazans for the wholly unexpected Oslo peace process. Some of those idealistic neighbourhood leaders were given executive posts under Arafat, but the system which replaced Israeli military rule essentially consisted of those same client–patron configurations which had served the PLO in exile. It was administered by upper-class Fatah bureaucrats, commonly known as "the Tunisians". Democratic façades were kept up, largely for the benefit of the donors. Western-style institutions were set up with great fanfare, but those in charge of them soon realised that theirs was to be a spectator role. Trouble-making journalists, parliamentary watchdogs and human rights activists who took their jobs too seriously were liable to lose them – and even to find themselves in Palestinian jails.

Many courageous social critics fought hard against the trend, but as Yasser Arafat and the Tunisian old-boy network emasculated the control mechanisms the flow of foreign aid became a breeding ground for graft. The revelations were, as always, kept out of the local press, but the horror stories of waste and shameless favouritism soon became common knowledge, closely covered by Internet sites and by the al-Jazirah TV-channel, whose patrons in the royal palace of Qatar kept sponsoring Hamas long after other Arab governments had turned away from the organisation.

Hamas was allowed to operate in Yasser Arafat's state but not to bear arms. Its suicide attacks against Israeli targets were more effective than any weapons in threatening Arafat's project. The explosions were followed by closures that hit the Gazan economy hard. After the most intense wave of Hamas bombings, in early 1996, Arafat stepped up his crackdown against the Islamists. Apart from two dramatic suicide attacks in Jerusalem in the summer of 1997, the Hamas and the Islamic Jihad were kept firmly in check by Arafat's many security services until the summer of 2001. But in other ways time worked for the Islamists. The graphic contrast between the well-run Hamas schools and charities and the bloated and nepotistic PA (Palestinian National Authority) state organs could not be papered over by the ubiquitous Arafat-posters, and the unavoidable comparisons began to grind his popular base in the Strip to dust.

Arafat died in November 2004 and Mahmud Abbas, his replacement as Fatah leader, was elected president in January 2005. In September the same year Prime Minister Ariel Sharon stupefied his own party, the hawkish Likud, by actually carrying out his unilateral decision to evacuate the Israeli settlements in the Strip. Those colonies, largely a result of Sharon's influence with Prime Minister Yizhak Rabin in the 1970s, occupied a third of Gaza's territory, the only available space in the Strip for large-scale agricultural development. Sharon had to leave the Likud and wreck time-honoured Israeli political constellations to get his way on Gaza. By leaving the Strip without a formal accord with the post-Arafat leadership, Sharon weakened the PA and handed a huge prize to Hamas. The Islamists cheered and celebrated, playing up the Israeli exit as the result of

Hamas rocket fire against Israeli settlements in the Strip. The claim was baseless, but Hamas presented it well. Once more, the impression of Hamas as daring doers, as opposed to the bloated *al-Sulta* ("the regime" as the PA government is commonly known), was brought home. Soon afterwards George W. Bush, driven by his vision of a democratic remodelling of the Middle East, twisted the arm of the Israelis to let Hamas take part in the upcoming Palestinian elections. The PA, while outwardly committed to democracy, practically went down on its knees to dissuade the Americans, but both it and the Israelis were steamrolled. After Hamas' stunning election victory in January 2006 Washington, in an acrobatic turn of policy, denounced Hamas as terrorist and began to apply enormous pressure on President Abbas to depose the Hamas government. Abbas is a prudent man, and he knew that his own environment was much less tolerant of impulsive gambling than Bush's. He promised the Americans he would deal with Hamas but, aware of the unfavouable conditions on the ground, kept putting the confrontation off. Abbas's Fatah party expected to continue to run the show from behind the scenes, above the heads of the Hamas government, through its control of the treasury and the tangle of security agencies. As Israel, the Americans and the donor community cut off funding to the Hamas government, the Fatah hoped to reduce Hamas ministers to pliable puppets.

But Hamas did not play along with this scenario, and secured its own financial backing, chiefly from Iran and Qatar. Under the diligent direction of Interior Minister Said Siyam it began to give its wild armed gangs a unified command structure. Up until the winter of 2007 Hamas forces avoided confrontation with official Palestinian security organs in the Strip, most of them under the direct command of Muhammad Dahlan, a local Fatah veteran and a key figure during the peace process with Israel.

If Abbas was unwilling to confront Hamas, Dahlan shared the Americans' sense of urgency. He knew about the Iranian money, arms and training, and he also knew that his own forces had not recovered fully from the recent 2000–2003 confrontations with Israel. The Americans egged Dahlan on and promised him arms and money on a scale to match Iranian largesse. In one of the many absurdities of this tragedy, the money never arrived. It was blocked by congressmen concerned about Israeli security. The Americans now pleaded with the Gulf states, many of whose donations had helped build up Hamas in the past, to step in and pay. Some did. And the Israelis looked the other way as Egyptian army trucks brought in arms for Dahlan's forces. All the while President Abbas was trying his best to stave off bloodshed. In March 2007 the Saudis stitched up a Fatah–Hamas deal which led to a unity government. But it was too late. The PLO felt that it should have the upper hand in the partnership, or at least that Hamas should call off its military build-up. Hamas, sensing that militarily the scales were tipping, was in no mood to bow.

During the spring of 2007 the tension often erupted into full-scale Hamas-Fatah fighting, with bombs, missiles, drive-by shootings and murders tearing neighbourhoods and families apart. For several weeks a veritable civil war raged, as residents scurried from doorway to doorway, dodging snipers and cross-fire on their way to shops and markets. Schools closed down. When someone in either camp was abducted, the first place his family went to look for him was the morgue, not the hospital. The end-game was short and brutal. Dahlan had foreseen the outcome and left the country for "medical treatment". In a few days of fighting the PLO defences crumbled before the disciplined and ferocious onslaught of a much smaller force.

The unity and brotherhood of all Palestinians is an axiom in Palestinian public life. In his historic speech upon returning to Palestine in 1994, Yasser Arafat showered his rival, Hamas founder Ahmad Yassin, with compliments. But that tradition meant little to the Hamas commanders. To them the PLO and the Fatah were venal and godless sellouts, American and Zionist collaborators, betrayers of their own faith, heritage and national pride.

Many of the victorious Hamas fighters had been tortured and humiliated by the men now at their mercy. But during previous skirmishes the prospect of retaliation and escalation had tempered both camps. Now, in a classic example of civil war psychology, Hamas vengeance was given free reins. Palestinians everywhere – most Western media decided not to broadcast the footage – gasped as the pictures of shackled Fatah prisoners, shot in the neck, proliferated on the internet. Wounded Fatah fighters were whisked to the Egyptian and Israeli border crossings, away from certain death. Towards the end even healthy Fatah fighters fled, mostly in fishing boats.

The Hamas victory created two hostile Palestinian political entities, thereby hugely confounding future negotiations and dividing thousands of companies, government agencies, civil organisations and families. Israel, claiming that Hamas now bore the whole responsibility for rocket fire across the border, in effect presented it with an ultimatum: recognise Israel, accept previous peace agreements and put an end to Qassam rocket attacks. If not, the ebb and flow of supplies into the Strip would faithfully reflect the intensity of the rocket fire. Certain materials, especially metals, chemicals and fuel, were severely restricted by Jerusalem even during quiet periods. The measures had little effect on the rocket producers, but they swiftly put Gaza's vulnerable private sector out of business.

The abduction, by groups close to Hamas, of Israeli soldier Gil'ad Shalit in June 2006 silenced the Israeli voices who advocated a modus vivendi with Hamas. Shalit was on Israeli soil when he was taken away and the reaction in Israel was furious. Hundreds of Palestinians died in the air attacks which followed, and Shalit became – and remains – a litmus test for the determination of both governments. Hamas would not release him for less than many hundreds of high-profile security prisoners, and Israel – without declaring it openly – would not lift restrictions on Gaza-bound goods until Shalit is returned. (In August 2009 the Israeli Prime Minister finally did declare this policy openly.)

Thus the importance of the tunnels from the Egyptian part of Rafah to the Palestinian part. Anything up to the size of a scooter or a cow can be imported into Gaza through the famous underground corridors dug beneath the "Philadelphi" road between the Strip and Egypt. Food, fuel and countless consumer items reach the Strip that way, but with each tunnel costing between 100 and 200 thousand dollars to dig, the rental costs and the logistics are prohibitive for businesses operating with cement, metal bars and other bulky materials.

Considering the mounting outside pressure, including a marked lack of support from most of the Arab world, the fuel cuts, the Israeli bombings and the endless supply-emergencies, Hamas has done an impressive job. Not only of staying in power, but of successfully engaging Israel politically while shooting rockets at it. Part of Hamas' confidence comes from the knowledge that it can only be unseated by a huge fighting force prepared to sacrifice hundreds of soldiers in the alleys and tunnels of the refugee camps. The only candidates, Israel and Egypt, would welcome the end of Hamas rule, but they both have their own good reasons to avoid such an adventure.

Discounting outside intervention, the only other possible threat to Hamas rule is the discontent of the local population. In private conversations many Gazans lay the blame for hardship and economic collapse on Hamas. For them, the thrill of launching rockets and mortars against Israeli targets is not worth the sacrifice of their own economy, especially when the myriad of rockets launched have killed very few Israelis, less than two a year on average. The rocket campaign, in the view prevailing among non-Hamas Gazans, is a case of cutting off one's nose to spite one's face. But a significant sector of the Strip's population regards its tribulations in a different light, as an endurance test where divine grace and history will be on the side of those who do not flinch.

This view is the only one aired in public. Compared to the present regime, the harsh PLO rule of the past appears almost pluralist in retrospect. Hamas keeps a tight lid on its internal affairs. No details of aid received, arms traffic or the regime's connections with smugglers and profiteers appear in the Gazan press. Formal censorship is not necessary. All journalists know the rules. Freethinkers, feminists and democrats keep a low profile. But the mobile phone and the internet have changed the game, and details of Gazan life regularly slip through to foreign media, not least to the PLO papers in Ramallah, which eagerly pounce on unsavoury data about life under Hamas.

The cult of Yasser Arafat is, needless to say, a thing of the past in Gaza. The dead leader is not taunted and ridiculed in the Hamas media, but any attempt, on his birthday or on PLO anniversaries, to light candles or invoke his memory is promptly foiled. (Just as anyone waving green Hamas flags during demonstrations in Ramallah will be apprehended by the official gendarmes there.)

Gaza's Christians are a small minority, but have always been in the forefront of new plans and projects. Traditionally they have been protected by the PLO, which always made a point of appearing as a national, not a Muslim, body. Indeed, the Christians did not need any protection until the spread of violent Islamism. They have suffered heartbreakingly under Hamas. Businessmen and booksellers have been murdered, mixed-sex schools attacked, Bibles confiscated and – perhaps unique in Islamic history – an alcohol ban has been imposed on non-Muslims. Hundreds of Christians have fled, mostly to Bethlehem. On Christmas Eve 2008, as 150 Christians with special permits huddled at the Israeli border crossing on their way to Christmas celebrations in Bethlehem, mortars were fired at them by Islamic Jihad fighters.

In the summer of 2008 both Israel and Hamas reneged on their vows never to negotiate with the arch-enemy, and agreed to an Egyptian-brokered truce lasting six months. The Israeli government was exhausted, not so much by the actual damage caused by Hamas rockets and mortars hitting its civilians in the south, as by the toxic political fallout. After each attack the Israeli press and the nationalist right would lash out at Prime Minister Ehud Olmert and Defence Minister Ehud Barak for their failure to defend the country's sovereign borders. It was an impressive prestige victory for the banned and isolated Hamas government to be able to show the Israelis – and the Gazans – that no matter how many air attacks Israel launched against their artillery units, they could still keep the residents of Sderot and other Israeli settlements in shelters for days on end. After the truce went into effect Hamas had some difficulty explaining why rocket attacks should be suppressed against an enemy which continued its embargo, total or partial, on fuel, medicines, building materials and even toilet paper.

But the Hamas leadership misjudged the dynamics of interior Israeli politics. They believed that the end of the truce would mean a return to the *status quo ante*, with rocket attacks and Israeli retaliation in predictable doses. When the rockets started to fall over Israel in December 2008, and the nationalist opposition made the most of the government's "kowtowing to terrorism", it became obvious to Olmert, Barak and Foreign Minister Tsipi Livni that any return to "normal", pre-July conditions would not be tolerated by the general public, set to vote in a few weeks.

The Israeli strike against the Gaza Strip was expected, but its intensity, scope and duration were not. Just before noon, December 27, 2008, nearly a hundred Israeli combat aircraft attacked fifty targets in the most comprehensive Israeli attack ever on Gaza. In three minutes and forty seconds most Hamas bases and offices lay in ruins. At least 250 people lost their lives during the first wave of bombings, many of them police cadets at a graduation ceremony.

The war, whose course will be treated in detail below, again put Gaza in the focus of international diplomacy, media coverage and debate. The protests against Israel were massive, in Muslim and European capitals, but the diplomatic storm was still much less severe than feared by the Israelis. Several Arab governments, fearful of Hamas' role in Iran's expanding regional schemes, were obviously supportive behind an official veil of harsh criticism.

The reality of the Gaza strip in late 2009 bears little resemblance, in terms of daily life, fears and ideological constraints, to the one of 2005. And that one, in turn, was worlds apart from the conditions before the second Intifada broke out in the autumn of 2000, and which had been thoroughly transformed time and again since 1994, 1987, 1967, and 1948 – usually in a plume of smoke.

The word "change" is barely adequate to describe these violent shifts. Each time the Gazan stage has revolved, the script has been rewritten. Rules, living conditions, and political options have been reshuffled in a flash, usually with those in control losing their influence to new and unexpected actors. Even if we take 1948 as our year zero, the Gazan chronicle is epically rich in eruptions, suffering and table-turning calamities. In view of this, any attempt to cover the totality of Gazan history from Samson and Pharaoh Amenhotep to Ariel Sharon, Yasser Arafat and the Hamas in one pocket-sized volume would seem reckless. Few areas of comparable size – around 362 square kilometers, a fifth of the Greater London Area – are more densely packed with human history. The half-hour car-ride between Erez in the north and Rafah in the south would give you no more than a glimpse of the tragedy, the vitality and the volatility of the Gaza Strip. But such a trip would still be better than nothing. It is my hope that this book, a compressed journey along the entire known time-axis of the Gaza Strip, will provide signposts to a history that is disproportionate in its scale to the diminutive scope of its borders.

# 1

# The Setting

## *Geography, Climate, Wildlife and Ecology*

> *"Gaza is quite embowered in . . . great olive groves, which stretch . . . the whole four miles to Beit Hanun . . . The luxuriance of the gardens and orchards, remarkable for the scarlet blossoms of the pomegranates, and the enormous oranges which gild the green foliage of their groves, is due to the abundance of water, drawn from twenty wells of fresh water bursting from the sandy soil."*
> (the British missionary Theodore Dowling, 1891)

Having heard so much about the tininess of the Gaza Strip – a mere 1.33 per cent of historical Palestine, itself a small country – it comes as a surprise to find that its 362 square kilometres do possess three dimensions, real distances, sweeping vistas and seemingly endless beaches. There is even enough road, 43 kilometres between Beit Hanun in the north to Rafah in the south, to exasperate a driver during rush hour. The German traveller K. B. Stark, who, in the 1850s, wrote one of the first scholarly monographs on Gaza, shuddered as he remembered the gruelling six-hour camel passage from Gaza City to Rafah at the southern extreme of the Strip. The first car, introduced by a German in 1908, covered the distance in two hours – without a road. In the 1960s, before anyone but Egyptian officers, UN personnel and rich citrus merchants owned cars, the same ride, in eight-seater collective taxis, was a smooth half-hour affair.

The highest point in the Strip is Jabel al-Muntar, a hill about three kilometres southeast of Gaza City, near the Karni crossing-point into Israel. Napoleon, on his way north, camped below it and used it as a lookout. On a clear day the ninety-metre summit commands a wide arc of coastline, from central Israel to the Egyptian desert. The shoreline is a perfect curve, except for two minor irregularities, the port at Gaza City and some cliff formations near Deir al-Balah. The view from the Muntar hill also encompasses the Hebron mountains to the east, the first undulations of the Sinai highlands and the chimneys of the coal-driven power plants in the Israeli coastal towns of Ashdod and Ashkelon to the north.

The contours of the Gaza Strip are, like those of most political territories, arbitrary. They were shaped by events, not by topographical common sense. Their outline is the result of the first Arab–Israeli war, formalised in the Egyptian–Israeli armistice agreement on the island of Rhodes in February 1949. Geographically, the Gaza Strip is a compound of two quite different landscape types, roughly separated by the stream Wadi Gaza (*Wadi Ghazza* in Arabic; *Nahal Besor* of the Bible). The north-eastern part of the Strip belongs to the southern Palestine coastal plain, which is usually fertile 30–40 kilometres inland, with a thin band of shifting dunes along the beachfront. The south-western part of the Strip, almost two-thirds of its territory, belongs to the desert. In the Bible, the Besor stream marked the limit between the habitable parts of southern Palestine and the dreaded Wilderness of Zin.

The Gaza Strip thus stands with one foot in the vast Afro-Asian desert system, and the other in the Mediterranean world of farming and high culture. Around Gaza City, vegetation grew higher and more lush than anywhere else along the coastal plain, due to the profusion of wells. During antiquity, and well into modern times, the fertility of the fields and olive forests surrounding Gaza City stirred chroniclers and travellers to outbursts of lyrical praise.

Today the Strip, at its bisection by Gaza City, is built up almost continually from the ocean to the crossing point into Israel at Nahal Oz, but here and there between the concrete blocks a pastoral allure lingers on. As in European capitals of a century ago, small islands of countryside dot the outskirts of the sprawling city. A flock of sheep, driven by a minute shepherdess, brings traffic to a noisy halt; the clucking of chicken around a carpet-sized field of skye-blue lupinus, whose yellow beans, the *turmuz*, are the typical snack of poor Gazans; the pink blossoms of a backyard apricot grove or the cool relief under the canopy of a majestic mulberry tree, all remind you that this land, and its people, is a farming one.

The water supply, abundant until the population of the Strip broke through the half million barrier in the 1960s, is no longer sufficient for large-scale irrigation. Israeli agriculture is also heavily taxing the common groundwater resources, and Gazan agriculture has been forced into drastic adaptations. But until the 1960s, fields of grain and even cotton, the thirstiest of all cash-crops, literally reached the gates of the city of Gaza. According to research published during the British mandate, 17.5 million cubic metres of water could be drawn yearly from the aquifers under Rafah, Khan Yunes and Gaza, without depleting their sources. A measure of the privileged water-conditions is the following animal inventory, from an Ottoman count in 1912, covering Gaza City and the surrounding villages: 6,700 camels, 171,000 sheep and goats, and 10,000 oxen. Horses and donkeys were few. A few years later, when the Turco-German army camped in Gaza on its way to the Suez Canal and amassed a supply train of thirty thousand camels, the water supply was still sufficient.

The rising population of Gaza and the resulting pressure on arable land has set a vicious circle in motion, threatening several areas with degradation and even desertification. Growing food-demand has led to over-pumping from the natural wells (i.e. pumping at a rate higher than the replenishment rate of the aquifer). This, in turn, has increased the salinity of the water, and hence of the soils irrigated by it. The increase in salinity continues to bring down the productivity of the land. In addition to this danger, there is another, equally alarming development at work. There are two water-carrying strata below the Strip's surface: an upper one which carries fresh water, and a lower one of brackish water. The over-drawing of sweet water from the more superficial layers has tempted farmers to pump brackish water from the deeper reserves. But the brackish reserves, it now appears, had acted as a vital barrier against the seepage of sea-water into the system.

The geographer Shams al-Din al-Ansari visited Gaza in the late thirteenth century. He was born in Damascus, perhaps the world's largest oasis. Even so, Gaza's green expanses, probably viewed from the al-Muntar Hill, impressed him: "What profusion of trees around the town, as a cloth of rich fabric spead out!". When the German traveller Johan Helffrich summed up his impressions from a journey to the Orient in the 1570s, he gave Gaza the all-Mediterranean prize for fertility. His countryman K.B. Stark echoed that enthusiasm three centuries later: "In all directions, vast fields stretch out towards the horizon. We saw the largest olive forests of all Palestine north of Gaza, as well as serried rows of date-palms. The gardens abound with the succulent fruits of the apricot, fig, pomegranate, vine and cactus." The British missionary Theodore Dowling first visited Palestine in the summer of 1891. When describing his first encounter with Gaza, his somewhat dry account becomes almost lyrical:

> "Gaza is quite embowered in . . . great olive groves, which stretch . . . the whole four miles to Beit Hanun . . . The luxuriance of the gardens and orchards, remarkable for the scarlet blossoms of the pomegranates, and the enormous oranges which gild the green foliage of their groves, is due to the abundance of water, drawn from twenty wells of fresh water bursting from the sandy soil."

(The king-size oranges were of the large Shamuti kind, later marketed by Israel under the "Jaffa" brand name. The Shamuti trees have their fruit concentrated among the upper branches; its name comes from a Gazan word meaning "to climb". In our time, when the Communist bloc countries became an important export market for Gaza´s citrus growers, the smaller and less sweet Valencia orange was planted in large areas.)

A few years earlier, in the 1880s, Dr Chichester Hart explored Gaza at the request of the Palestine Exploration Fund. He marvelled at the spectacle of plenitude: " . . . fig, vine, pomegranate, almond, apricot, date, mulberry, palm, apple, orange and banana are all grown, besides vegetables of all kinds, of a size rarely met with in Great Britain." In and about the olive-groves Hart found a teeming bird-life of "sparrows, swallows, buntings, goldfinches, black redstarts, chaffinches, stonechats, willow-wrens, chiff-chaffs, blackbirds, hooded crows, Egyptian kites, buzzards, owls, red-breasted Cairo swallows, pelicans, cunlins, calandra and crested larks, bulbuls, pied-chats and Menetrie's wheat-ear . . . ".

In the wetlands around the mouth of Wadi Gaza there is still a remarkably varied reptile and bird-life, with several kinds of kingfishers, terns, snipes, pipers, plovers, flamingos, ibises, stilts and herons. Buzzards, kites, the grand imperial eagle and many other raptors can be seen circling overhead. The biotope around Wadi Gaza is unique in Palestine, and is really an offshoot of the magnificent Bardawil Lagoon in northern Sinai, where population pressure drives many aquatic birds eastward in search of nesting space. The struggle to protect the polluted and ravaged Wadi Gaza is the most urgent challenge for the under-funded but heroic Palestinian wildlife services (www.wildlife-pal.org). The campaign is led by Imad Atrash from Beit Sahur in the West Bank, the founding father of Palestinian ecology, who has spent years sleeping out in the open among the reeds of Wadi Gaza, taking photographs and notes.

The sources of Wadi Gaza originate in the hills above the village of Samu'a in the Hebron hills, 105 kilometres to the east. Travellers of old describe it as a substantial watercourse, impossible to ford during the rainy season. In the Bible, many of King David's soldiers, in hot pursuit of the Amalekites, are too tired to cross the stream and stay behind to rest (1 Samuel, 30:21). But today, having been tapped by Israeli farmers, polluted by Israeli factories, used as a sewage outlet by the refugee camps of al-Bureij and Nuseirat inside the Strip and as a land-fill by Gazan builders, the agreeable swamp has become a stagnant and foul-smelling cesspool during the dry months. Its putrid contents are mercifully being diluted by seawater pushing into the mouth of the river, and many of its flying inhabitants still manage to survive and procreate there. Formally the wetlands constitute a nature reserve, but since the peace process collapsed and foreign aid dried up in the wake of the Hamas takeover, local ecologists are helpless. In the PLO government there were few decision-makers with a heart for ecology. In the Hamas government there seem to be none at all.

There is one bird all Gazans, from time immemorial, recognise. It is the common quail, *coturnix coturnix*, the catching and eating of which is documented on Pharaonic friezes. It is written (Numbers 11:31) that during the desert wanderings of the Israelites, a divine wind "brought quails from the sea, and let them fall by the camp . . . ". This sounds fanciful, but it is precisely what happens every September, as swarms of quail arrive from

Europe on the way to their African winter quarters. The Gazans tie nets along the beach to trap the birds as they land, eager to rest after the long stretch from Cyprus. British, Israeli and Palestinian authorities have forbidden this kind of hunting, but it still goes on. Each fall, wrote the American clergyman H.E. Fosdick in 1927, "the markets of Jerusalem are glutted with Gazan quail". At a count held in 1900, British naturalists observed "millions of netted quails".

Gazan ecologists are trying, without much official encouragement, to combat the quail-netting excesses and the more serious hazard of blast-fishing. With the general decline of Mediterranean fishing and the drastic fishing limit of six nautical miles enforced by the Israeli navy since late 2006, only about a third of the Strip's 3,000 fishermen now scrape their livelihood from the sea. In their desperation to make ends meet they are carrying out a race to the bottom, depleting the stocks of clams, crustaceans and fish.

The Gaza Strip south of Wadi Gaza belongs to a very different physiographical unit. In accounts of old, Gaza City is routinely called "the gates of the desert". The city was the last, green outpost of the Mediterranean world before it curves south-westward and tapers out into the North African desert. Going south there is no need to carry provisions until Gaza; but after Gaza there is no forage and no water until the Nile. When the British came from Egypt to conquer Gaza in 1917, the only way to do it was to build a water pipeline and a narrow-gauge supply railway across the Sinai desert.

The verdant glories around Gaza City, extolled by visitors, receive more than double the rainfall, often three times as much, as the towns in the south-eastern part of the Strip. The drier part, comprising two-thirds of the area, belongs to the Negev–Naqab coastal plain and is mostly sandy desert of the storybook kind. The glorious postcard dunes are mainly made up of quartz blown from the Nile delta during the winter storms. The abundance of sand, nowadays an expensive raw material for the cement industry, covers not only beaches but forms shifting dunes several kilometres inland. Until not very long ago Rafah, Khan Yunis and Deir al-Balah – the main urban centres of the southern Strip – had to be dug out after desert storms had set the dunes in motion.

Still today, with the imprint of man everywhere, the brief trip from Gaza City across Wadi Gaza and into Khan Yunes, with its dunes and its old Mamluk seraglio, spans two very distinct worlds. But even in the southern, drier part there has always been agriculture, thanks to the wells. The mouths of those wells, reports Stark in 1852, were a well-kept secret and only through the assistance of an Arab guide would a stranger get a drink. Date-palms, not a few rows but veritable forests of them, almost reach the sea-shore. They have produced a cash-crop for the tribes around Deir al-Balah ("House of Dates") from Biblical times until this day. In the 18th century, tobacco became the main export of the south, while greenhouse farming dominates today. The 19th century boom in rye and bitter melons will be described in a later chapter.

The inordinate access to water in an area with uncertain rainfall, straddling two deserts, has been the key to Gaza's importance throughout the ages. Possession of Gaza and its water was a prerequisite for the conquest of Syria and Palestine from the south, or the conquest of Egypt from the north. Moreover, the water was a precondition for the agriculture and growth of the city of Gaza into an intercontinental entrepôt thousands of years ago. The water also played a part in the creation of the Gaza Strip in early 1949. In no other part of southern Palestine could two hundred thousand refugees have survived. If not for the water and agricultural capacity of this easternmost corner of Palestine, Egypt would have been forced to let them continue their flight, and there would have been Palestinian refugee camps around Cairo today, like around Beirut, Amman and Damascus.

After the Oslo agreements of 1993, when it seemed that the 1949 armistice line between Israel and the Gaza Strip would turn into an internationally recognised border, a 60-kilometer fence was erected by the Israelis. Large stretches of that fence were torn down by Palestinians during the opening stages of the second Palestinian uprising, which began in September 2000. Between December 2000 and July 2001, the Israeli Southern Command put a new fence in place, this time with more elaborate electronic support and early-warning systems. Palestinians have dug tunnels under this fence, notably during the abduction of the Israeli soldier Gil'ad Shalit in the summer of 2006. Rabbits and red foxes are also known to have squeezed under it, but the larger mammals who used to roam the southern deserts of Palestine without any political considerations have become hermetically sealed off from pastures, prey and mating opportunities on the Israeli side. A century ago the cheetah and several species of large antelopes were occasionally observed in the Gaza Strip, but in recent years the wolf, the hyena, the boar, the jackal and the mountain gazelle have been the only larger mammals with a stable presence inside the territory. All but a few of the boars and gazelles caught inside the Strip by the new fence have been shot and eaten in recent years, resulting in an unavoidable decline of their predators.

# 2

# Egyptians, Hebrews and Philistines

*The Israeli attack, later expanded into the biggest ground operation ever directed at populated Palestinian areas, was named "Cast Lead" after a line in a children's poem by the Hebrew national poet Chaim Nachman Bialik (1873–1934) – a man of peace.*

As I begin to write this, on the last day of 2008, two kilometers from the outskirts of Gaza city, the heavens loom like some latter-day rendering of Biblical prophecy. Plumes of dark smoke billow up from the earth and the sky is crisscrossed by the trails of red tracer bullets. Every now and then, when a blockbuster bomb hits an ammunition depot in Gaza city, the ground shifts under our feet. The missiles of the Israeli F-16 fighter-bombers are of the fire-and-forget kind, and the pilots do not have to dive anymore. But they still do, to deafen and to impress. Their targets are north of the village of Beit Lahiya, a favoured position of the Hamas artillery. A Soviet-style Grad rocket shrieks by on its way towards Ashkelon, and an instant later two glowing points appear above, as a Cobra helicopter activates its Hellfire-missiles and steers them towards the launching site of the Hamas rocket.

The Israeli attack, later expanded into one of the the biggest operations ever directed at populated Palestinian areas, was named "Cast Lead" after a line in a children's poem by the Hebrew national poet Chaim Nachman Bialik (1873–1934) – a man of peace. Before Cast Lead was over large parts of the Tel al-Hawwa, Sabra and Zeytun quarters around Gaza city were shot to pieces by Israeli artillery, and more than 1300 Palestinians, including several hundred civilians and children, had been killed.

But in the end the Israelis, after agonising internal debates, decided not to attempt the conquest of the city on the hill. As we shall see, the amassing of overwhelming force outside the gates of Gaza promises nothing in terms of the outcome. The scenario has been played out over and again throughout the centuries, and some of the greatest conquerors in history have been held up for months trying to break the spirit of Gaza's tenacious defenders. Some, like Saladdin, Islam's greatest warrior, had to give it up altogether. In ancient times Gaza's prosperous port and its role as the hub of vast trade networks made it a mouth-watering prize.

But during the latest conflagration, Hamas' fighters were defending one of the poorest corners in the region. Neither they nor their Israeli enemy were in it for the spoils but for reasons of vengeance, hate, faith, dignity, and national security.

The first time we hear of Gaza in the Bible, is in Genesis 10:19, where the Canaanite country is delineated: "And the border of the Canaanite was from Sidon, as thou goest toward Gerar, unto Gaza; as thou goest toward Sodom and Gomorrah and Admah and Zebboim, unto Lasha." Through the ages, and right up to the present day, Jewish sages and ideologues have been split over whether the Strip really belongs to "Eretz Israel", the Land promised Abraham in Genesis (12:1–3).

But our oldest sources on Gaza predate the Bible by many centuries. There are some signs that the city of Gaza was first founded as a depot by frankincense traders from Southern Arabia. We know of Egyptian military movements through the Gaza area as early as the twenty-third century BC, but the first concrete date in the annals of Gaza hails from the eighteenth Egyptian Dynasty. The event, not surprisingly, was a battle. In the spring of 1457 BC, Thutmose III set out to quash a rebellion by one of his Canaanite vassals, the King of Kadesh. Geopolitically, if not spiritually, Thutmose was one of the great Pharaohs, an Egyptian Alexander or Napoleon who expanded the empire all the way to Asia Minor and Ethiopia. On his way north, bound for the battle of Megiddo, Thutmose overran Gaza, made his camp there and held a sumptuous banquet to celebrate the 23rd year of his accession. He let it be chiselled into the wall of chronicles at the Amon temple at Karnak that "Gaza was a flourishing and enchanting city".

For centuries after that, with pendular regularity, the Egyptians lost Gaza to its indigenous inhabitants, the Canaanites, and then regained it. When the Egyptian state was weakened by drought or internal strife, Gaza wriggled out of its grip. As soon as a resolute pharaoh united the country and got his tax-collection in order, he would take it back again. It would have been careless not to: The historian Mordechai Gichon has calculated that Egypt has been attacked by regular armies forty-seven times throughout its history. Forty of those attacks were carried out from bases in the Gaza Strip. (The Egyptians themselves, according to the same count, have launched fifty-five military campaigns against objectives to the north by way of the Strip.)

In the 18th century BC those geopolitical routines were suddenly upset by the arrival of a new people on the scene, the mysterious Hyksos, who ran most of Egypt during several centuries. They turned the towns of Sharuhen in the southern Gaza Strip, and al-Ajul by Wadi Gaza into massive fortresses. These Hyksos strongholds, in Gichon's words, were "the vital links between the Asiatic and the African colonies of the Hyksos empire", while also serving as bases of supplies and spare parts for the feared Hyksos war chariots. Sharuhen was also the last stand of the Hyksos after they had been driven out of Egypt in the late sixteenth century.

The Egyptians, intent on preventing further designs on its Eastern frontier, now turned the city of Gaza into a mighty fortress, impressive enough to be showed off on royal friezes at the Seti temple at Karnak. Gaza, although populated by Canaanites, remained firmly within Egyptian control for several centuries, until the arrival of the most famous, or infamous, of antiquity's Gazans. After the "Sea Peoples" had been thrown out of Greece and Asia Minor they tried their luck in Egypt. After a series of epic battles along the Nile estuary their fleet and their army were crushed by Pharaoh Ramses III. One of the Sea Peoples, the Philistines, fled north along the coast in the direction of Gaza, where they struck root and remained for half a millennium.

The Philistines gave the Gaza Strip area a name, "Philistia", in use by travellers until modern times. Philistia, of course, became "Palestina" and then "Palestine". Possibly the Canaanites and the Egyptians had heard of the Philistines when they first appeared in their ships, for they arrived after a spell of several generations at Crete, fragments of whose culture they carried with them. (Only in 402 AD, with much bloodletting, did the Christians manage to destroy the temple of the Cretan god Marnas in Gaza and suppress his cult.)

The ravages of the Philistines were not unlike those of the Vikings in Western Europe two thousand years later. They sailed and fought and endured hardship like no others, but their intellectual aims were modest. When they found beautiful cities of high culture, as they did in the extraordinary and loveable city-state of Ugarit, they gutted the treasuries, grabbed the women and torched the libraries. The chronicler of Pharaoh Ramses III (1184–1153) commented wistfully:

> "The . . . [Philistines] made a conspiracy in their islands. All at once the lands were removed and scattered in the fray. No land could stand before their arms . . . "

When the Philistines arrived somewhere, the scribe noted, they first "desolated its people", and when they moved on the area left behind was "like that which has never come into being". As the Philistines settled along the coast, today's Gaza Strip became part of their heartland, the coveted southern coast of Palestine. It was a good stretch of coast to hold; at once the land bridge between Egypt and the Semitic empires of Mesopotamia, the redistribution point for several rich caravan trails and, in the days of flat-bottomed sea-craft, an excellent maritime location.

One reason that we happen to know so much about the Philistines, who disappeared from the scene without a trace around 600 BC, is that they became the scourge and arch-enemies of the Canaanite tribe whose writings have survived best, the Hebrews. The Biblical account of the Philistines is biased, to say the least. Even though they soon adopted the local Semitic language and many customs, the surrounding peoples always took a dim view of their doings. Their most deplorable trait, in Canaanite and Israelite eyes, was their refusal to circumcise their sons. The Philistines are the perennial bad guys of the biblical narrative. In the sources Hebrew–Philistine relations appear as one long brawl. But human reality is less clear-cut. Until the breakdown of the Oslo process and the electronic fence drawn around the Gaza Strip in 2001, a wide gamut of economic, pragmatic and human relationships connected the Gazans with the Israelis of the nearby towns. In spite of Israeli control and mutual animosity everyday life, as always, continued to defy generalisations. Something very much like it went on three thousand years earlier. The land was small, Philistine and Hebrew fields and towns were interspersed and borders in our sense did not exist. The Bible provides ample evidence of non-martial Hebrew–Philistine interaction. King David was a proverbial slayer of Philistines and, at least in the Bible, the ultimate Nemesis of their kingdom (II Sam 8:1). But David had plenty of dealings with Philistines, some of them rather unbefitting of a national hero. Not only does David accept asylum from the enemy when he is out of favour with his own king, Saul. He also joins the Philistines, serving as a mercenary with one of their kings, Achish. As Achish prepares for war against Israel, David does not flinch. His treason is averted, not by any contrition on his part, but because the other Philistine leaders don't trust him. Later, as king of Israel, David picks his bodyguards from the *Cheretim and Pelethim* – namely the Cretans and the Philistines, both terms referring to the same people.

The most revealing account of the ambivalent Hebrew–Philistine relationship appears in the story of Samson, one of the least sympathetic of the Hebrew heroes. Samson is a bad-tempered, cruel lecher with few redeeming qualities. (He cuts a very different figure in Milton's play, *Samson Agonistes*, where he faces death with a soul-searching, just about existentialist, monologue.) Samson fights the Philistines and kills them in great numbers, but he is strangely drawn towards them, especially to their women, one of whom he marries. The most famous of these, Delilah, is really in the pay of the Philistine secret service. She manages to lure Samson to Gaza, where she sweet-talks him into revealing his two vital secrets: Where his magic bodily strength resides (in his hair) and how he is to be tied up (with seven twigs, still green).

Bound, blinded and hairless, the vanquished Samson pleads with the Lord to restore his strength for one last feat of vengeance. As three thousand Philistines gather in Gaza's great temple of Dagon to feast and celebrate his capture, Samson breaks his fetters and tears down the building over himself and the Philistine nobility. That image, of a prostrate victim who pulls his enemy along with him into the abyss, has exercised a powerful influence over poets ever since. Lately, it has been used as a metaphor for the seemingly self-defeating Hamas policy towards Israel – but also for Israel's apocalyptic nuclear program, as in Seymour Hersh's 1991 book on that subject, *The Samson Option*.

# 3

# Persians, Greeks and Romans

*Ptolemaic Gaza was prosperous enough to strike its own coins, which bore the confident legend "The People of Gaza". Plutarch called the city* aromatophora, *"the bringer of perfume", referring to the trade in precious scents brought from the East and marketed in Gaza.*

The Philistine state was constructed around their five main cities – Gaza, Ashdod, Ashkelon, Gat and Ekron. In normal times they ran their own affairs, sometimes paying tribute to some larger, regional superpower. But a couple of times each century some colossal imperial army, usually Assyrian or Egyptian, would sweep up or down the coast, burn, plunder and set up new tributary arrangements. When this happened the people of Gaza usually hunkered down and let it pass.

But as Gaza grew richer and linked together more and more international trade networks, she had more and more resources to spend on her defenses – and more to lose to looters. When the Persian Emperor Cambyses tried to overrun Gaza in 529 BC he failed. Only after a long siege did the Gazans hoist the white flag. The Persians turned the city into a vast fortress, which is mentioned with awe by the Greek historian Herodotus, who calls Gaza *Kadytis*, "one of the greatest cities in all Syria".

When Alexander the Great got his global blitz into high gear few cities in his way put up any resistance. Gaza was the only place in Palestine to upset his schedule (332 BC). Alexander was on his way to conquer Egypt and he was in a great hurry. But the ruler of Gaza, the eunuch Batis, refused to yield, and the soon-to-be master of the world was forced to lay a siege, a thing impatient world-conquerors do unwillingly. In order to get the right angle for the catapults used to pierce the city walls, the Greek forces had to spend two months constructing an artificial hill. The Greeks also managed to dig tunnels under the city walls. Alexander was usually mild and forthcoming towards his new subjects, but the Persian garrison and the Arab mercenaries of Gaza had exasperated him. After the city fell he put the defenders to the sword and sold their families into slavery.

That would not have been difficult, for Gaza was, and remained for centuries, the principal slave-market of the area. In his furious anti-Gazan foretellings the prophet Amos quotes the Lord as promising "a fire on the wall of Gaza, and it shall devour the palaces thereof". This shall be the punishment, Amos declares, for having sold Jewish POWs into slavery. After the failed Jewish rebellion against the Romans in 132–135, Emperor Hadrian sold some of his Jewish prisoners as slaves, for the price of one horse apiece, while the rest were thrown to the lions at the new arena of Gaza, built to celebrate the victory. (As late as the 1880s slaves, mostly black Africans, could be bought in Gaza.) The Greek historian Strabo even claims that Alexander was so irked by the insolence of the Gazans that he "razed Gaza to the ground". That appears an exaggeration, because soon afterwards new contenders were at each other's throats for the sake of the desired city. After Alexander's death his generals tore the swiftly won empire to shreds. Gaza was claimed by both sides in the intra-Greek struggles of the Levant between the Ptolemies (Greeks based in Egypt) and the Seleucids (Greeks based in Syria). The Ptolemies, according to Polybius, saw Gaza as their chief port and its "most strategic fortress . . . Preparation for an eventual war meant first of all the military reinforcement of Gaza". The income from the caravan trade was essential to Ptolemaic Palestine. It was the terminus for the Nabatean camel trains from their great cities Palmyra, Petra and Aila (today's Aqaba) and traders arrived there regularly from Egypt, Phoenicia and far-away Greek islands. Ptolemaic Gaza was prosperous enough to strike its own coins, which bore the confident legend "The People of Gaza". Plutarch called the city *aromatophora*, "the bringer of perfume", referring to the trade in precious scents brought from the East and marketed in Gaza. This trade was the mainstay of Gazan prosperity and, like its envied position on the *Via Maris*, the road between Egypt and Phoenicia, it was a mixed blessing. The first impulse of any ascending power in the region would be to lay its hands on Gaza, in order to control the coastal trunk road and tax its trade in luxury items.

The Jewish king Alexander Yannay tried in vain to storm Gaza in 96 BC, and then spent a whole year on a costly siege. When he finally broke through the bulwarks he murdered the members of the Gaza senate and gave the city over to plunder. Instead of rebuilding it the Jews developed and settled the port area, called Mayoumas, where excavations have recently laid bare some exquisite mosaics. After Alexander Yannay's death (69 BC) his heirs of the Hasmonean dynasty fell out over the succession. When the Romans got word of this they seized the opportunity to put an end to Jewish statehood. Pompey took Jerusalem in 61 BC and annexed the whole country, including Gaza, to the new Roman province of Syria. Pompey's general Gabinus was charged with the rebuilding of Gaza and the other towns destroyed in the Jewish–Roman war. From then on the Gazans reckoned the year of their annexation to Rome as the year zero of their calendar. During the last chaotic years of the Roman republic the land around Gaza changed hands as if it had been a marker in a betting game. After Pompey it went to Caesar, Cassius and Brutus; then to Persian invaders and then to Anthony, who included it in his lover's gift to Cleopatra in 34 BC The senate annulled the gift and in 30 BC the Emperor Augustus gave it as a present to Herod, the Jewish–Edomite king who ruled in Jerusalem as a Roman vassal after the end of Jewish independence. But when Herod died in 4 BC Augustus broke off "the Greek cities", Gaza among them, from the province of Judea and made them part of Syria again.

Beyond this bewildering succession of rulers a momentous force was at work, transforming Gaza and all the peoples and cultures of the Levant: Hellenisation. The attractions of Greek culture and the example the Greeks had set in politics, warfare and art proved irresistible to individuals and to whole societies. Even those who resisted Greek ideas ferociously, such as the Jews, were changed forever by the experience. The Hellenisation of the peoples of the Eastern Mediterranean was as thorough as the globalisation, westernisation and modernisation of non-European peoples today. And, in several ways, it was a happier event. Only decades after Alexander and his armies raced through the old world, people in towns all over the Middle East were speaking Greek, wearing Greek dress, sending their children to Greek schools and playing, sometimes dangerously, with Greek ideas. To the Jews the encounter with the Greeks would be dramatic in the extreme, because it exposed their monotheism to a new and formidable menace: secularism.

Assimilation to Greek life proceeded with breakneck speed. As early as 290 BCE the Jews of Alexandria – just forty years after the foundation of that city – are reported to have been struggling with their own holy texts. That was the motive behind the Septuagint, a translation of the Bible into Greek, commissioned by Jews. It was the first of the thousands of non-Hebrew versions that would broadcast the ideas and beliefs of the obscure Hebrews around the world. Still today, ultraorthodox Jews in Jerusalem fight Israeli police and curse their secular adversaries with 2,300 year-old terms of abuse: *Mityavnim*! (Those who who take up Greek manners) *Epikorsim!* (Those who follow the philosopher Epicurus). This process was not disturbed when the Romans took control over the Levant and incorporated Gaza into their empire. Of all the ancient peoples the Romans were the most eager zealots for Greek culture, and almost all the great non-Roman writers of the Roman world, like Strabo and Josephus Flavius, wrote in Greek.

We know Gaza was thoroughly Hellenised, because the Gazan schools of rhetoric and philosophy, Sophist and Neo-Platonic, attracted aspiring young intellectuals from near and far. The academies of Gaza, along with those of the island of Rhodes, enjoyed Ivy League status during the first centuries of the common era.

# 4

# Freedom of Religion and the Rise of Christianity

*The abstruse doctrinal disputes of the first Christian centuries required vast amounts of Neo-Platonic, Sophist and Stoic manpower, and the Gazan doctors contributed heroically to the rapidly swelling theological corpus. The ban of the Athenian schools – emperor Justinian's formal closure order against Hellenist culture – was ignored in Gaza, where philosophy was taught throughout the century.*

In terms of religious variety Gaza at the beginning of our era was a little like Brazil of today. It had a vibrant but amorphous and permissive spiritual life. Its temples were dedicated to many gods, but their domains were not mutually exclusive. Someone with important business ahead would have been prudent enough to appease both Zeus and Isis, and then consult the oracles of Tyche. There were also those in the Greek cities who did not believe in or practise any religion at all, and they faced no inquisition.

The most popular Gazan god was Marnas, the Cretan Zeus. Other highly venerated deities were Isis, the Egyptian goddess of life, Tyche, the Greek goddess of fortune, Artemis, Io, Apollo, Nike, Minos and Bes, all represented on local coins. Sources also report Gazan rites in honour of Helios, Aphrodite, Persephone, and Hecate. There were Samaritans, Zoroastrians and Jews, and all along the coast flourished the growing cult of Sarapis, a new god born of the Greek–Egyptian cultural fusion. The Arab Nabatean traders worshipped their gods, not least She'a al-Qawm, the protector of caravan traffic, and Allat, the moon goddess. By all accounts these cults coexisted peacefully. There was one religion, however, which was excluded from the famous tolerance of Rome, and that was the new Jewish sect of Christianity. The church of Gaza was one of the first in the world, founded only years after Jesus' crucifixion. In Acts 8:26 the angel of the Lord instructs the evangelist Philip to go down through the desert and preach the gospel to the people of Gaza.

From the beginning, writes Martin Meyer, "the city became a veritable storm centre in the struggle between heathendom and the new faith . . . ". Many famous Gazan martyrs were mutilated and beheaded by the authorities under Trajan and Diocletian, apparently with the approval of the local population. The Gazans did not take kindly to the Christians, perhaps because they sensed that they sought not only freedom to worship, but monopoly. They feared, with reason, that Christianity, once in power, would ban the other cults and shut down Gaza's celebrated fairs, races and gladiator shows.

Even after the tables were turned in 313, when Emperor Constantine made Christianity legal, popular hostility prevailed. The Roman authorities stopped their persecutions of the Christians, but the Gazans continued to lynch and murder them, even "old men and young girls were killed and their mangled remains were thrown to the beasts". The saint Gregory of Nazianzus wrote in despair: "Who does not know of the madness of these Gazeans?"

In 379 the Spanish Caesar Theodosius began his eventful reign. The year before, near death from an illness, he took the sacraments and after his recovery he became a fervent Christian. In 391 he outlawed the pagan cults and ordered the destruction of the greatest heathen temple of all, the Serapeum of Alexandria. After that only one important non-Christian temple still stood in the Levant, the shrine of Marnas in Gaza, the Marneion. But in Gaza there was no scramble to join the new victorious faith. The number of Christians remained low – 280 people – and the Gazans did not even permit them to hold public office.

In church history the demise of Gazan heathendom is ascribed to a miracle. During a drought in 395 the pagans blamed the new bishop Porphyry for the delay of the rainy season. Porphyry dared the priests of Marnas to ask their god for rain, but they failed. The Christians then offered their prayers for rain, and were promptly rewarded. There followed, according to the Christian chronicle, an impressive rush of ex-idolaters queuing by the baptismal fountain. In 398 all pagan creeds were outlawed.

But in eight or nine pagan temples the old sacrifices and oracle séances were kept up. The non-Christians retained considerable power, and bishop Porphyry went to Constantinople, hoping to convince the emperor to put some earthly force behind the heavenly claims. He convinced empress Eudoxia that the Gazan unbelievers must be destroyed, along with their abominable sanctuaries. But the emperor, Arcadius, lacked the crusading spirit. He was a Christian, but unlike his resolute father, the great Theodosius, he did not mind diversity. In his dramatic study on the obliteration of Hellenism, *Der Untergang des Hellenismus*, Ernest von Lasaulx gives a moving account of the diffident emperor as he tried to evade violence. The Gazans, Arcadius argued, were faithful subjects who paid their taxes punctually. Their desert trade was a blessed source of income. Instead of being threatened, they should be reasoned with.

But when Porphyry returned to Gaza with a company of soldiers in tow, it was his interpretation of the imperial decree, not Arcadius', which applied. The closure order for the temples was read by a herald and demolition squads went to work right away. The site of the great Marneion temple was purified and a large church, dedicated to the empress Eudoxia, was erected in 406. Its courtyards were paved with flagstones from the old temple and, writes Meyer, "the women of Gaza refused to walk in it because of their strong attachment to the old cult".

Once in power and relieved of its competition, Christian rule became more relaxed and consolidated itself by incorporating old customs into the new faith. The games and festivals of Gaza, famed all over the East, were resumed, purged of their indecent elements. The philosophical heritage, another source of Gazan pride, was also given a new lease on life in the service of the new religion. The abstruse doctrinal disputes of the first Christian centuries required vast amounts of Neo-Platonic, Sophist and Stoic manpower, and the Gazan doctors contributed heroically to the rapidly swelling theological corpus. The ban of the Athenian schools – emperor Justinian's formal closure order against Hellenist culture – was ignored in Gaza, where philosophy was taught throughout the century.

One of the foremost intellectuals of the Gaza school was the bishop Marcianus, who was born and raised in the city and whose extended family kept tabs on all major institutions. Under Marcianus' direction Gaza grew splendidly. A new wall was raised, a moat was dug and games were held with great pomp. Magnificent theatres, baths and stoas were erected without raising taxes and at night – like in Byzantium itself – the streets were illuminated.

# 5

# Arabs and Crusaders, 634–1193

*"In the development of Gaza, we see all the characteristics typical of European urban growth: the fortress, surrounded by a semi-agricultural, semi-urban community. This is the burgus of western Europe, that eventually enclosed itself . . . and started along the path of internal urban expansion."* (Joshua Prawer)

At the onset of the 7th century, this proud Christian city, with its sturdy fortifications, buoyant commerce and high-flown diversions had become the main urban centre of southern coastal Palestine and large areas of the interior. Merchants, artists and ambitious youngsters of all trades were drawn from near and wide towards its bright lights. Many of them struck roots in the city, and Gaza kept growing in importance and population. In his *Gaza in the Early Sixth Century*, Glanville Downey evoked Byzantine Gaza on the eve of its disappearance: "If Gaza was historically an old Philistine city, it was now a metropolis in which the principal language was Greek, supplemented by Latin and the various tongues spoken by sailors and traders. If there were any descendants of the Philistines left in the city, they now spoke Greek or perhaps Aramaic."

One of the young men drawn to Gaza by the tales of quick wealth and urban splendour had come all the way from Mecca in Arabia. There was nothing exceptional in this, for the caravan links between the Hejaz and Gaza were ancient even then. His name was Omar Ibn al-Khattab, he hailed from the Qureish tribe and he had made a name for himself as a wrestler before he grew wealthy from the bustling Gazan wholesale trade.

Omar himself would have gasped in amazement at the suggestion that Byzantine Gaza, now at the peak of its influence and prosperity, was doomed, and that he himself would become its nemesis. The Arab conquest and the spread of Islam were events that even in retrospect seem barely believable. And Omar's role in this metamorphosis is perhaps the most fabulous. When he returned from Gaza to Mecca he was first taken aback by the new religion, and is even said to have plotted against Muhammad's life. But after becoming a believer he was accepted into the Prophet's inner circle and soon became indispensable. Omar was really the power behind the scenes when Abu Bakr was named Caliph in 632 and chosen to succeed the Prophet. But it was not until 634, when Omar became Caliph, that the Arabs from the Hejaz and their new faith became a world affair. In a few short years of lightning campaigns the Arab armies under the command of Omar and his generals crushed Christian opposition in all the lands of the Eastern Mediterranean and then pushed further eastward and westward.

But before setting out on their glorious Egyptian, Mesopotamian and Persian campaigns, the Arabs marched on Gaza. The city was the first significant conquest of Islam outside Arabia. Omar knew its value first-hand. In addition to its abundant supplies and its fresh-water springs, Gaza was the obvious place to drive a wedge between the northern and the southern parts of the Byzantine Empire. If the hill city could be taken by surprise, without destroying its fortifications, the Arabs would have secured a perfect bridgehead at the very doorstep of the Christian world.

As we know, Gaza was a defensive strategist's dream and a conqueror's nightmare. Some of the greatest military geniuses had wasted months there. Now, in 634, the city was defended by a regular Byzantine army under general Patricius. The Arabs were led by two of their most able commanders, Amr ibn al-As and Khalid ibn Walid. They first sent an embassy to parley with Patricius, who declined the offer to march off in peace. The Christians met the Arabs on an open field outside the city, near a village called Dathin. The Christians were scattered and lost the opportunity to barricade themselves in the castle of Gaza, and the Arabs received the city intact.

It is known that some Christians and Jews stayed on, as Gaza became an Arab city. A legend that the Prophet's great-grandfather Hashim had died there served to tie the new conquest to the Arabian past of its new masters. Since the Arabian clans became the aristocracy of the new Empire, many dubious Arab genealogies were invented by recently converted Palestinians. But the Hashim legend is quite plausible, since the commercial bonds between Mecca and Gaza went far back into the pre-Islamic era.

The bigger churches were turned into mosques, a permanent garrison was established in Gaza and the Greek-speaking Christian urban majority gradually became Muslim and Arabic-speaking. In the countryside the Christian faith and the Greek and Aramaic vernacular of the peasants lived on until the Crusades. Municipal life during the first Arab centuries was bedevilled by factional bickering, often related to the heated doctrinal disputes of early Islam, and sometimes superimposed on existing tribal rivalries. But the rich trade was never disrupted, and Gaza remained an indispensable outlet for several caravan systems. Throughout the 466 years until the Crusaders took Gaza in 1100, Arab and Christian travellers heaped their superlatives on Gaza, its "great markets", its ocean-views and its scholars and thinkers. Gaza's port, Mayoumas, was protected by a system of towers, to discourage a

Christian re-conquest. The port grew at the expense of the hillside city of Gaza, 3–4 kilometres inland. The Palestinian geographer al-Muqaddasi describes how Byzantine ships would arrive at the port in order to ransom Christian prisoners of war. The going rate was three captives for a hundred dinars – a lucrative business.

With time Gaza's impressive ramparts fell into neglect, for reasons unknown to us. Perhaps the growth of Mayoumas as a port drained Gaza city's resources; perhaps the district's secure position at the very bosom of the only contemporary superpower, removed from all frontiers, made defensive works redundant. But as the great Arab empire began to fragment, Gaza again found itself exposed and at the crossroads of strong and conflicting geopolitical ambitions. The leading Muslim states of the tenth century, the Egyptian Fatimids and the Turkish Seljuks, somehow settled the matter of Gaza peacefully. But in the years leading up to the next stunning change in Gaza's history, both Fatimids and Seljuks were rent by internal strife and raging epidemics. Their weakness became the main resource of the Crusaders, when they moved their forces into Palestine and "liberated" Jerusalem in an orgy of blood in 1099. It appears that when the first Frankish knights arrived at the gates of Gaza in 1100, they found the city almost defenceless. The Muslims and the Jews seem to have fled or been murdered.

The whole land was now under the cross once again, with one exception. Just north of Gaza, her sister city of Ascalon (Ashkelon) remained in Fatimid hands. For the Christians this Muslim bulge in the middle of the country was a sore headache for more than half a century. Each summer the Muslims of Ascalon made forays into Christian lands, often reaching the outskirts of Bethlehem and Hebron and plundering the Gazan caravans. In 1149 the fourth Crusader king of Jerusalem, Baldwin III, told his brother Amaury to give Gaza's tumbledown bulwarks an overhaul and turn the city into a forward base for a final assault on Ascalon. In 1153 Ascalon fell after a gruesome siege, and the entire coastline, from Antioch to the Sinai desert, became Christian for another short spell.

The conquest of the land by European knights was, in the words of Israeli historian Moshe Gil, "a revolutionary change" for Muslims, Jews and all other local groups. In Gaza a French style *chateau* was built at the summit and, after the conquest of Ascalon, the driving force behind Gaza's development became civilian. In Joshua Prawer's words:

> "Around the fortress, a new settlement blossoms . . . ordinary people seeking a measure of security . . . farmers . . . from the vicinity, but also traders and artisans to supply the needs of the castle, the new settlement and the neighbouring villages . . . In the development of Gaza, we see all the characteristics typical of European urban growth: the fortress, surrounded by a semi-agricultural, semi-urban community. This is the

*burgus* of western Europe, that eventually enclosed itself . . . and started along the path of internal urban expansion."

Not only the leading Christian chronicler of the times, bishop William of Tyre, but also his Muslim counterpart al-Idrisi, extolled the graces of crusader Gaza. Those who dwelled inside the *bourg* of Gaza were often European soldiers or pilgrims who had been tempted to remain by jobs or grants of land. But there were also native Christian Palestinians from the countryside, who had stuck to their faith and survived by tilling Byzantine church lands. The Arabs had confiscated some church lands, but left much of them alone.

Crusader control was thorough and intense, but short. (Its brevity has often been a source of hope for the Palestinians of our time, as they contemplate the similar intensity of Israel's presence.) Christian rule would have endured longer if the weakened and divided Muslims had not been blessed with the arrival of one of their greatest heroes. During the twelfth century, the Fatimid Caliphate, Gaza's neighbour to the south, was enfeebled by internal strife and by revolts in North Africa. As it lost more and more of its possessions around the Mediterranean and in Arabia and withdrew into its Egyptian heartland, Crusaders, Byzantines and the Turkish Seljuk rulers of Damascus drew ominously close. By cleverly playing out these threats against each other – sometimes with *both* Crusaders and Turks at the very gates of Cairo – the Fatimids tried to postpone the inevitable. They managed until the spring of 1169, when the Turks forced the beleaguered Fatimid caliph to appoint one of their own officers to the post of vizier. This officer was a young, unknown Kurd whose father was a crony of the Turkish–Syrian Sultan Nur al-Din. His name was Salah al-Din ibn Ayub, and he is known to Europeans as Saladdin.

The following year Salah al-Din took his armies northward, towards Crusader Jerusalem. The first enemy strongholds on the way were Darom and Gaza. He took Darom by storm but Gaza, defended by the Templars, the elite Crusader corps, defied all his efforts. The Christian civilians pleaded with the Templars to let them into the fortified city, but were turned down. The burghers were killed, but Salah al-Din could not overrun the citadel.

A year later, however, Salah al-Din became the sole ruler of Egypt, and he spent the next two decades uniting the Muslim states and rewriting the map of the Middle East. The decisive moment came in the summer of 1187, by the Horns of Hittin in lower Galilee, just next to what today is the shrine to the prophet Jethro, the holiest of holies of the Druze people. The Crusader armies were bogged down in internal squabbling and do not seem to have realised what was at stake. They were routed. The news broke the spirit of most of the other Christian garrisons in the land. The Gazans seem to have laid down their arms without a fight. In

October Salah al-Din destroyed the Kingdom of Jerusalem and marched into the Holy City.

The feats of Salah al-Din caused shock and horror in Catholic Europe. It was not only a question of all the efforts and investments spent during the previous century. Jerusalem had already become a spiritual touchstone, in the sense that its possession had deep religious implications. The loss of the city – poor and insignificant in commercial or military terms – was felt as an acute failure by all Catholics, and the clarion call was sounded once more: “To Jerusalem!”. Few of Europe’s great fighters failed to heed it. This Third Crusade was a strange and incongruous conflict, not unlike Napoleon’s Russian campaign – a series of glorious victories which together added up to a lost war.

Richard the Lionheart took Gaza in 1191, restored it to the Templars and hurried on towards Jerusalem. Salah al-Din’s armies, beaten and decimated, began to poison the wells and burn the fields along the road to Jerusalem. All through history the principal challenge has not been to seize Jerusalem but to keep its only, highly vulnerable, supply-route open. Richard realised that he lacked the resources to do it. Back in Europe his political rivals were taking advantage of this absence, and after a year of barren skirmishes he made a deal with Salah al-Din: Jerusalem would be opened to Christian pilgrimage, and in return the Crusaders would knock down the defensive works at their coastal strongholds, foremost among them Ascalon and Gaza.

# 6

# Tartars, Mongols and Mamluks

> *"It is a good and worthy land, yielding fruits of the highest repute. The finest bread and wine can be had there. The latter is made only by Jews. The circumference of the city is four miles; but there is no wall. It is six miles from the sea, built partly on a hillside and partly in a valley. The dwellers are many, among them sixty Jewish and four Samaritan families."* (Rabbi Meshullam of Volterra)

The razing of Gaza's citadel spelled more trouble for its inhabitants, who would be sorely tested all through the coming century. In those times a city without defences attracted less trade, less investment, fewer dynamic artisans – but more pirates and more Bedouin raids. On top of those immediate concerns the ongoing retreat of the Crusaders created a regional power vacuum which only deepened with the decline, after his death in 1193, of Salah al-Din's Ayyubid dynasty. Geopolitical players from ever further away took an interest in Gaza and its position as a springboard towards Egypt.

To those present the voracious thirteenth century grab-and-scramble of foreign armies around Gaza must have appeared less confusing than it does to us. We know too little of the realpolitik, the fears and the material motives behind the depredations let loose upon the city. During little less than a generation Gaza passed between Fatimids, Turks, Franks, Syrian Muslims, Caspian Tartars, the Mongols of Hulagu Khan and Egyptian Mamluks. Many of those uninvited visitors destroyed it, wholly or partly, and with the help of earthquakes, an outbreak of bubonic plague and the flooding of the normally staid river Sha'ria they managed, for a time, to reduce Gaza to a shadow of her former greatness.

The single most significant event during that geopolitical carousel was the epic collision between the Mamluks of Egypt and the Mongols. The waves of Turkic migrations from Central Asia brought large numbers of Turkic (those speaking Turkish or kindred languages) warriors into the Mediterranean world – more than their own tribes and leaders had use for once they had settled. The temptation to sign up as contracted fighters in the service of other kings, usually Muslims, was obvious. Sometimes such mercenaries were bought as slaves and trained as soldiers as the ruler's property. *Mamluk*, the Arabic word for "ruled", became the generic, and not very precise, term for this group of soldiers. Their *lingua franca* was a kind of Turkish and most of them were Turks, although many were Circassians or Slavs. Capable mercenaries rose through the ranks, and it was not long before the Mamluks wielded decisive influence. Their take-over of Egypt in 1250 was not their first, but it was their most important achievement to that date. A year later they threw Salah al-Dins successors out of Gaza.

If this was a curious and unexpected development, it was complemented by an even stranger one. For half a century medieval towns had reverberated with blood-curdling rumours about a people of horsemen from the East, the Mongols. They were reported to be kind to towns which waved the white flag and let down their drawbridges – and merciless to those who wasted their time with futile resistance. In 1258 shocking news reached Gaza and Palestine: the half-mythic Mongols were real, in fact they had just conquered Baghdad, formally put an end to the Abbasid empire and dyed the river Tigris crimson with Arab and Seljuk blood.

This struck fear into hearts far and wide, and there was a flurry of hurried realignments. Some Christians teamed up with the Mongols, other ones settled their differences with the Mamluks and prepared jointly for the Mongol demons, who were said – correctly – never to have lost a battle. In early 1260 Hulagu, grandson of Genghis, the first Great Khan, entered Palestine after destroying all the Muslim kingdoms in his way. But just then Hulagu was called back to Mongolia to take part in the nomination of his brother Kublai as Great Khan. Hulagu left his friend and first general Kitboga in charge of the army in Gaza, where they rested and watered their horses before the assault on Egypt.

The Mongols had seen the world, and were used to seeing it grovel before them. They had not yet met anyone like the Mamluks. Unlike those Chinese, Indian, Christian and Arab rulers swept off their thrones by the Mongols, the Mamluk had not – not yet – been weakened by soft court living. They were, like the Mongols, professional fighters. When the Mongol messenger from Gaza arrived at the Mamluk palace in Cairo with the customary offer to surrender and march off in peace, the Mamluks simply cut off his head and sent it back.

One of the commanders in chief of the Mamluk army was Baibars, later one of the legendary Mamluk sultans. He was a Kipchak Turk from the Caucasus, who had been seized in infancy and sold as a slave – by Mongols, according to some rumours. Baibars took the Mongols by great surprise in Gaza – they were used to preparing themselves in peace while the enemy said his last prayers.

Rather than fight in Gaza, the Mongols retreated and regrouped further north, in the Jezreel Valley. At the battlefield of Ayn Jalut – the site of today's kibbutz Ein Harod – Baibars achieved the first-ever victory over the Mongols. (When the Palestinian Liberation Army was set up in 1964, its Gaza-based brigade was named Ayn Jalut.) A few years later the Mongol empire began its long demise. Baibars went on, in a series of campaigns, to rub out the remaining fragments of the Crusader kingdom and create a large unified Mamluk empire.

Under the Mamluks Gaza enjoyed several centuries of comparative peace. In order to frustrate Crusader reconquests the Mamluks destroyed Acre, Caesarea and other coastal cities to the north, which won Gaza a larger share of many trades. But rather than stimulate commerce and production, the Mamluks were intent on taxing such efforts, and the city no longer generated wealth and investment on the scale it had during Byzantine and early Arab times. Much of the land was held *in absentia* by nepotistic Mamluk officers and dignitaries, who took little interest in the subtler aspects of running an estate. Under the Mamluks the Gazans were, except for Bedouin raids, spared the ravages of war. Jews and Christians were kept firmly in their place. Non-Muslims were banned from carrying arms and they were often stoned by gangs of small boys as they entered Gaza – preferring, therefore, to arrive at night. Meyers quotes a French traveller on his way to Jerusalem who was arrested in Gaza for wearing his sword in public. Some of the most famous medieval travellers report favourably on the city during the 14th and 15th centuries, among them the fantastic John Mandeville, who found it "fair and full of people". Both Meshullam of Volterra and Obadia of Bertinoro, two famous travelling rabbis from Italy, had plenty to say about Gaza. Meshullam's account puts the importance of the caravan trade into sharp relief. Intercity travel was always collective, never individual. When Meshullam arrived in Gaza he was told that Bedouin raiders were making the road north unsafe: "We were told we could not leave Gaza till a company of 4,000 or 5,000 men should have been gathered together with whom we could travel." A few hundred Bedouin could encircle and cut down a much larger force. At the time of Meshullam's visit the Mamluk Emir of Gaza set out with 23,000 men to assist the Emir of Ramle. They were all – save the Emir himself and a hundred of his horsemen – killed in one lightning Bedouin assault. Of Gaza, Meshullam said:

> "It is a good and worthy land, yielding fruits of the highest repute. The finest bread and wine can be had there. The latter is made only by Jews. The circumference of the city is four miles; but there is no wall. It is six miles from the sea, built partly on a hillside and partly in a valley. The dwellers are many, among them sixty Jewish and four Samaritan families."

The preposterous claims of the tourist trade, well known to future generations of Holy Land pilgrims and travellers, were already in evidence. Meshullam's company was taken by some Jews to see the house of Delilah in Gaza. A few years later the Dominican friar Felix Fabri was taken to the inn where Samson was seduced by Delilah, and then to a heap of rubble said to be the city gates, carried there by Samson. Fabri reported that Gaza was twice the size of Jerusalem, abounding in merchandise, all at good prices.

At the beginning of their two-and-a-half century long rule over Gaza the Mamluks possessed a notoriously fearsome cavalry. But with time their control came to depend more on the simultaneous decline of rivals. Neither Arabs, Turks nor Crusaders – now dug in behind the walls of their colossal fortress at Rhodes – caused the Mamluks much trouble. Most of their headaches came from within; precious Mamluk energy was spent on the bloody palace plots which was their only system of government. But during the 15th century two peoples appeared, each at opposite ends of the known world, who offered the feared Mamluks challenges to which they could not rise. After almost a century of intercontinental navigation and exploration, the Portuguese defeated the Muslim fleets at the battle of Diu in 1509. The Muslims fought to retain their monopoly on the spice trade, the most lucrative global business, in which desert caravans carried cloves, pepper, cardamom and cinnamon through Central Asia and Arabia from the tropical islands of the Indian Ocean to the markets of Cairo and Venice – much of it via Gaza.

The battle of Diu marked the beginning of the four century long European supremacy over the oceans, which lasted until the Japanese defeated the Russians at Tsushima in 1905. As the Portuguese, and soon the Dutch, began to ship the spices around Africa and set up their own outlets in Western Europe, Mamluk revenue plummeted. While this problem became more and more acute, the Mamluks were faced with a more immediate menace.

# 7

# Ottoman Conquest and Rule, 1517–1918

*"At a distance [Gaza] has an imposing appearance. It is a place of considerable wealth, derived from traffic with caravans, but the inhabitants live in the meanest and most sordid way. Notwithstanding its population of fifteen to twenty thousand, Gaza is emphatically a place of ruins . . . The roofs of squalid hovels are supported by fragments of beautifully sculptured capitals . . . "*
(John Fulton, 1890)

The Ottoman Turks had been expanding their realm slowly for two centuries, when one of the their most forceful rulers, Selim I, took over in 1512. He turned the Ottoman state into an empire, approaching the dimensions of the legendary Muslim empires of the early conquests. In late 1516, after an inconclusive attack on the Shi'ites of Persia, and having crushed the Mamluks in Syria, Selim reached Gaza. The Mamluks tried in vain to stop the Ottomans outside Khan Yunes, the new town the Mamluks had founded in the Strip. Selim left a small garrison at Gaza, and pushed ahead with his main force to Cairo, where state-of-the-art Ottoman mortars, considered ungentlemanly by the Mamluk fighters, sank the Mamluk empire. (Though Mamluks would continue to constitute the ruling class of Egypt for another three centuries.) Rumours from the battle soon reached Gaza, spreading a message that the Ottomans had been soundly defeated by the Mamluks. The Gazans failed to verify the news. Eager to display their loyalty to the Mamluks, they attacked and killed the Ottoman soldiers stationed in their midst. When the victorious Selim returned to Gaza in early 1517 and learned about the treachery he was merciless and ordered a terrible massacre of Gazan civilians.

The four centuries of Ottoman rule over Gaza is the longest ever recorded in its annals, and elude all generalisation. The Ottoman period, 1517–1917, covers the whole spectrum of imperial management, from peaks of exemplary, imaginative and forceful government to abysses of neglect and misrule. The foremost authority on Ottoman Palestine, Amnon Cohen, describes the initial sea-change:

"The new government was resourceful and energetic, and from the first took a great interest in the progress of the land and its people. During its nadir Ottoman rule reversed the trend of decline from the Mamluk times and embarked on a policy of development. It ran a just and orderly administration, put an end to Bedouin pillaging and brought them under centralised control . . . instilling a sense of security which greatly stimulated agriculture and the crafts."

Under the Ottomans Gaza became the centre of a *sancak*, an administrative district stretching from Rafah in the south, Ramle in the north and Beit Jimal at the western slopes of the Hebron hills. In later redrawings of the administrative hierarchy Gaza's status fluctuated. At times it was placed under the Ottoman governor in Sidon on the Lebanese coast, at other times under Jaffa or Acre. Sometimes Gaza's direct jurisdiction reached all the way to el-Arish in the Sinai desert, but sometimes only to Khan Yunes. Many Jews – most of them from Spain or Portugal – and Christians made Gaza their home. One of them, Nathan of Gaza, created a bizarre imbroglio in the 1660s, when he endorsed the messianic claims of one travelling preacher from Izmir, Shabtai Zvi. For the Ottomans the Shabtai Zvi affair was a passing nuisance, for the Jews one of the most traumatic events in their history. As large numbers of Jews all over Europe came to accept Shabtai Zvi as their saviour, he confounded them by converting to Islam, which gave rise to the fascinating judeo-muslim *dönmeh* religion which has survived – until 1912 in Salonica, and then in Istanbul – into modern times.

Christian and Jewish accounts during the first Ottoman centuries praise the pashas of Gaza for their tolerance and humanity towards non-Muslims. One such benevolent ruler was Hussein Pasha. In 1660 the Gazans owed a large sum to the governor of Sidon. The French representative in Sidon, who was the famous traveller Chevalier d'Arvieux, offered Hussein Pasha of Gaza a loan to help him pay his debt. When the Frenchman met Hussein Pasha at Ramle and handed him the agreed sum, he was invited to Gaza. The visit is described in great detail in the second tome of his monumental four-volume account of the East. D'Arvieux has nothing but praise for the magnanimity of the Pasha, his firmness with marauding Bedouin, his broadmindedness in matters of faith and his kindness to the poor. He even carried out archaeological excavations. The good ruler was removed by a plot. He was summoned to Constantinople, accused of Christian practices, and beheaded.

The French loan to the pasha casts light on a new phenomenon, which was to accompany the Ottomans all through their long decline: the ever-increasing meddling of European powers in the affairs of the Levant. In the beginning the foreign interests took discreet and consensual forms, such as the French education of Maronite priests or the construction of a

Franciscan monastery at Jaffa. But over time the Europeans began to protect local minorities and pilgrims, build schools and even, in the twilight years of the Ottoman empire, to take over transport, postal and other services. It was not only foreign rivals who took advantage of the Ottoman setbacks during the wars with Austrians and Russians. For generations local chieftains, like the Druze emir Fakhruddin in Lebanon and the Bedouin Galilean Daher al-Omar, turned Ottoman rule in Palestine into a nominal affair. The security and peace which had made the first Ottoman sultans so popular among the Gazans were gradually eroded. An ominous sign of decline was the Bedouin raid in 1754 against the yearly Meccan pilgrimage caravan from Damascus. The booty, loaded onto thirteen thousand camels, was disposed of in the souks of Gaza. The purpose of the robbery was to humiliate the Ottoman Sultan Othman III, who had deposed a Syrian governor favoured by the Bedouin.

A humiliation of a quite different magnitude befell the Ottomans in the summer of 1798, when the French general Napoleon Bonaparte landed in Alexandria with more than twenty thousand soldiers, famously including a hundred scientists. Napoleon beat the Egyptian–Ottoman forces at the Battle of the Pyramids and then turned in the direction of Palestine, styling himself as "liberator from the Ottomans and protector of Islam". The strongman of the Levant, the Bosnian Jazzar Pasha who ruled from the coastal fortress of Acre in northern Palestine, went south to confront Napoleon. In late February 1799 Jazzar's forces were thrown out of Gaza by the French, almost without a battle. In a letter to the French government Napoleon summed up: "The next morning we advanced on Gaza, and found three or four thousand cavalry marching toward us. General Murat commanded our cavalry . . . We charged the enemy, who did not even wait for our attack, but fell back." Napoleon drove Jazzar's army north, all the way to Acre, where British forces reached him and helped him survive a gruelling French siege. In August 1799 Napoleon abandoned his Oriental campaign and returned to France and greater glories.

One of the men sent out by the Ottomans to set their Egyptian house in order after the havoc wrought by Napoleon was the Albanian tax-collector and businessman Muhammad Ali. After massacring the remnants of the Mamluk ruling class of Egypt, he took over the country and began to modernise it, with a view to taking over the whole Levant. From 1831 to 1841 Muhammad Ali and his son Ibrahim, supported by the French, ruled most of Syria and Palestine and frightened its peoples by modern and efficient tax-collection. When the Ottomans, with British support, beat back the Egyptians the last, decisive battle was at Gaza, from where the embattled infantry of Muhammad Ali fled to Egypt in small fishing crafts.

Gaza City was hit hard by an outbreak of plague in 1839, but in the relative calm maintained by the reformed Ottoman state during the remainder of the century, the population kept rising, to 15,000 in 1860 and to more than 35,000 in 1910. Food was plentiful and cheaper than in northern Palestine and rents were lower than in Jerusalem and Jaffa. Most Gazans, however, lived in mud hovels. The American John Fulton reported in 1890: "At a distance [Gaza] has an imposing appearance. It is a place of considerable wealth, derived from traffic with caravans, but the inhabitants live in the meanest and most sordid way. Notwithstanding its population of fifteen to twenty thousand, Gaza is emphatically a place of ruins. The existing houses have been built of the ruins of previous structures. The roofs of squalid hovels are supported by fragments of beautifully sculptured capitals . . . " Fifteen years later, when M. Meyer visited Gaza, most families still lived in shacks or whitewashed adobe huts. The most imposing building in town was the Great Mosque, al-Jami al-Kabir, flanked in the Turkish fashion by four minarets. It occupied the site of the former Crusader church, which in turn was built on the ruins of the first mosque, which had been erected over the first Christian temple, which took over the premises from the pagan Marnas temple.

In many ways Gaza was like other Palestinian towns during the last Ottoman decades. Foreign influence and trade increased, but there was widespread anxiety over conscription, as the authorities resorted to ever more drastic measures in pressing young men into service for the wars in the Balkans and Yemen. The overwhelming majority of those mobilised never returned. Many more died from epidemics than in battle. But in one respect Gaza was far ahead of the rest of the country: it was, if only for a few months a year, part of the global economy.

Railways and steamships were continuously biting into the profits of the desert caravans, but the camel-borne desert trade survived until the Great War. Caravans still set out from Gaza on a prearranged date in order to meet the Damascus pilgrims at Ma'an in Transjordan, bringing them fresh supplies. It was the shared interest in those routes that generally kept the people of Gaza and the Bedouin on good terms, which was a condition for the remarkable export trade around Gaza during the last Ottoman decades.

At the turn of the 20th century, Gaza's yearly exports are said to have filled twenty-five large ships, bringing in a revenue of 1.5 million dollars. Meyer lists its primary export items as "barley, corn, wheat, pumpkins, sesame, dates, fruit, poultry, eggs, wool, skins and hides." Avraham Almaliach, the leader of the Sephardic community in Palestine, described the yearly barley-bonanza of the Gaza region (larger than the present Strip) with amazement: "During the barley harvest many huge ships bound for Liverpool, Hamburg and other great cities anchor outside Gaza." Great profits were made and lost during the hectic speculation surrounding the three-month harvest. The tycoons of the business were some local families – the Shawas, the Bseisos, the Suranis and the Radwans – together with Jews from Tripoli in Libya. Still not knowing the season's barley price, they leased the fields from the owners at a fixed price and paid them after they had received payment from the German breweries and the English gin-distilleries.

Another international cash-crop which turned many Gazans into rich men was one of the most vile-tasting fruits known to man: the "desert watermelon", *citrullus colocynthis*, which grows wild in the desert areas east of Gaza. The bitter fruit, although much smaller, looks deceptively like a watermelon, a fact recorded in the account of a famine in II *Kings* 4:39:

> "And one went out into the fields to gather herbs, and found a wild vine, and gathered thereof wild gourds his lap full, and came and shred them into the pot of pottage: for they knew them not. So they poured out for the men to eat. And it came to pass . . . that they cried out and said, O man of God, there is death in the pot. And they could not eat thereof."

The Bedouin, on the other hand, knew all about the plant, called *handhal* in Arabic, and made wide medicinal use of it, to stem menstrual bleeding, to abort fetuses, to de-worm children, as a laxative and even as a calmative against mental afflictions. In all those applications exact measuring was crucial, since overdoses caused internal bleeding and death. When the Western pharmaceutical industry discovered the usefulness and versatility of the plant, a veritable melon-rush broke out. Arab and Jewish traders from Gaza would scour the Negev desert for handhal, collected by the Bedouin. The nomads, who were paid in barley, soon learned to cultivate the handhal and business flourished. Ships weighed down to the water-line with handhal seeds plied the Hamburg and New York routes. It was said that the Gazan handhal merchants, although their pockets bulged with foreign gold, grew impatient, since there were not enough luxuries in the bazaars of Gaza City on which to spend their fortunes.

Much of the wealth from the barley and handhal trades seeped down to the small-time farmers, day-labourers and the city's poor. The lack of roads, of heavy loading equipment and of a modern pier meant plenty of seasonal work which supported many families. The local industry, known for its solid craftsmanship, was also stimulated by the seasonal injections of cash. It consisted of fifty potteries, some weaveries, dyeing pools, tanneries, soap-factories, flour-mills and olive presses. But the dependence on exports had its risks. During drought or locust years there was need and misery in the towns as well as among the Bedouin, and traders and craftsmen went idle.

After the British de facto takeover of Egypt in 1882 there was an increasing traffic of European travellers, pilgrims and natural scientists passing through Khan Yunes and Gaza on their way to Jerusalem. From their accounts we get the impression of Gaza as a lively, productive town with a varied population. The overwhelming majority was Muslim, but in

1904 there was also an Orthodox church, a Protestant church, a Greek Catholic chapel and a synagogue. There were Greek, English and Italian consulates; a Jewish school run by the Alliance Israelite Universelle and a British Church Missionary Society (CMS), which began limited health-care in Gaza in 1882. A decade later, writes Theodore Dowling, "a hospital adapted from a native house" was opened. "It was", according to Gerald Butt, "the only medical centre of its kind for the whole of southern Palestine and northern Sinai; and reports from the last decade of the century spoke of patients coming to the Gaza clinic from el-Arish, Beersheba and beyond – sometimes travelling by camel or donkey for up to eighteen hours to get there." In 1908 a new CMS hospital was opened in Gaza city, the first of its kind in that part of the country. Attendance soared. In 1912 the hospital treated 29,581 outpatients, 701 in-patients and carried out 411 major operations.

The driving force behind the hospital and all other British and Christian enterprises in the Gaza area was a curious figure, who rose to extreme influence in the Gaza area. His name was Eleazar Isaac Shapira and he was described in 1879 by the great traveller S. C. Bartlett as "a Jew who had lived in California, Holland and Germany". Shapira showed Bartlett around Hebron and impressed him with his good English and his intelligence. Some years later we find Shapira in Gaza, now as a devout Christian living in a stately mansion surrounded by black servants. In 1882 the Zionist pioneer Z. D. Levontin arrived in Gaza City. Like all other visitors he was struck by the contrast between the plentiful agricultural surroundings and the dismal appearance of the city. Wherever Levontin and his party inquired about lodging and guides they got but one answer: "You must speak to consul Shapira, of the English Church." The Zionists were reluctant to throw themselves at the mercy of a baptised Jew, but after they realised that their comfort and safety travelling southward depended on it, they made a call at Shapira's home, where they were received with grace and hospitality and given rooms. Shapira offered them help in acquiring land in Rafah at the southern end of the Strip. Levontin curtly rejected the offer, needing no help from "an apostate". Shapira defended himself, saying he did not preach the gospel among Jews, only among Muslims. Shapira's remarkable influence in Gaza was underscored for the Zionists when their host summoned the Ottoman governor to his house, and the ruler promptly appeared. The governor gave the Jews an escort of armed guards who took them to Rafah. In the end they decided not to buy the tracts of land up for sale, which seemed to them too far removed from civilisation. Levontin put in an offer for the Strip's highest point, the al-Muntar hill and the area around it, but it was not accepted.

In one respect, therefore, Gaza was set apart from the rest of Palestine: the absence of Zionist colonisation. Since 1882, Jews from Eastern Europe had arrived in the country and bought land in the Jezreel Valley, in the Galilee and the Saron plains, often from owners who had until then sublet the land to local, Palestinian, tenants. The authorities, in spite of the many centuries of Ottoman–Jewish trust, took a dim view of this practice. Jews had always arrived in the Holy Land, on pilgrimage, to live and worship in Jerusalem or to be buried there. But the new Jews were different. They spoke strange languages and they came not merely to live and pray, but to remake the country in their own image. The early 20th century was one long torment for Ottoman governments, with incessant assaults on imperial territory by a host of Balkan nations, and increasingly insolent demands by the great powers. Now the most trusted subjects of the Ottoman empire, the Jews, had also lost their minds to nationalism.

At first Zionism distressed the Turks more than it worried the local Arabs. But already before the outbreak of war in 1914 and the subsequent British conquest, there were Arab Palestinian protests, pamphlets and campaigns calling for a halt to Jewish colonisation efforts. In Gaza, however, Arab–Jewish tension was late in coming. This was partly because the Jews were uncertain about whether the Gaza area was at all a part of *Eretz Israel*, the Land of Israel. Another reason was that Gazan landowners were not absentee *effendis*, like the ones in the Jezreel Valley, easily tempted by sheaves of money bills. They were hands-on managers, often from the business-minded families of Abu Khadra and Shawa, who did well from their grain sales to European distilleries and Italian pasta factories. So, although the Jewish community in Gaza City slowly grew, there was no Jewish colonisation and, though this would change, little popular anti-Zionism. In the entire Gazan sub-district – an area much larger than today's Gaza Strip – there were only two Jewish settlements, Gedera and Kastina, among the ninety-one towns and villages under the jurisdiction of the Turkish district governor – the *kaymakam* – in Gaza City.

When Enver Isma'il Pasha, the Young Turk strongman and de facto ruler of the Ottoman Empire, brought his country into the Great War in late 1914, he had gambled on a quick German victory. Central to that victory was the idea of a surprise assault on the Suez Canal. The supreme Turkish commander in the Middle East, Jamal Pasha, and his German chief of staff, colonel Kress von Kressenstein, led 25,000 men across the Sinai desert towards the canal, with a terribly cumbersome supply train of 30,000 overloaded camels and horses pulling artillery pieces by ropes across trackless wastes. Water was so scarce that they had only four days to take control of the canal before they needed to rush back to water their animals. On top of this handicap, they were spotted by enemy aircraft, and instead of surprising the enemy, the Ottomans were surprised by Indian and Australian forces on February 2, 1915, and fled back to Gaza.

When the British counter-offensive got under way two years later, Khan Yunes and Gaza were key stepping-stones towards that alluring goal, Jerusalem. Without the sweet-water wells along the Gazan coast, no army could survive long in the scorching environment. In February 1917 Khan Yunes was taken by the British and a little later Deir al-Balah, where an airfield was built. The First Battle of Gaza, March 26–27, 1917, was a failure. The Second Battle of Gaza, April 17–19, 1917, was an outright disaster, with more than six thousand British casualties. In the end, Gaza fell to the British by a ruse. The new commander of the Egyptian Expeditionary Force, Edmund Allenby, convinced the Germans, by a heavy pounding of Gaza and by a field diary "dropped" by his aide Meinertzhagen in front of a Turkish unit, that he planned a third head-on assault on that city, while he really prepared for a surprise attack on Beersheba, 40 kilometres inland. The Australian cavalry dispatched towards Beersheba was not detected by the German aerial scouts, who were chased off by a new detachment of Bristol fighters. Beersheba fell on October 31 and three days later the British forces closed in on Gaza. The destruction by the British cannons was comprehensive – traces were still visible in 1975. Nowhere else in Palestine was there damage on a scale to match the havoc in Gaza. All wood, including eaves, doorhandles and verandas and most trees inside the city had been sawed up and burnt by army cooks and freezing soldiers. Long before that all Gazan civilians had been forced to leave by military decree. The rest of Palestine, already starving, was overwhelmed by thirty thousand refugees from Gaza. When they returned to Gaza, few of them found anything of value left in place.

On the night of November 6, 1917, the Germans, Austrians and Turks fled north under the cover of darkness. On December 11, after fierce fighting, Allenby led his forces into Jerusalem. The tidings had a huge impact across the Christian world. In his public declarations Allenby gave his victory bold neo-Crusading overtones and all over Europe that year's Christmas celebrations took place in a spirit of thanksgiving for the Christian return to the Holy Places.

The battles for Gaza, Beersheba and Jerusalem were breathlessly followed by newspaper readers all over the world. Today they are largely forgotten. Instead, one other event during those weeks, which received very little attention at the time, towers over all the noisy battles in our historical consciousness. It was a short letter from the British Foreign Minister Arthur James Balfour to the British zoologist and Zionist Walter Rothschild, written after the conquest of Beersheba. It contained the words, "His Majesty's Government views with favour the establishment in Palestine of a national home for the Jewish people, and will use their best endeavours to facilitate the achievement of this object." The letter ended with a request from Balfour to Rothschild to "bring this declaration to the knowledge of the Zionist Federation".

# 8

# The British Conquest and the Mandate, 1917–1948

*"Our fathers all had Muslim acquaintances and partners. There were local fanatics who glued anti-British and anti-Zionist appeals on the walls of our quarter. But I don't remember feeling unsafe, not even during the riots in 1920 and 1921."* (Muzi Levy, a Jew who grew up in Gaza)

The Balfour Declaration did not make the front pages. The fighting in the Middle East was still far from over and the British were entangled in sticky negotiations with the French and the Hashemites of Mecca over the future of the ex-Ottoman territories. But during 1918, as the contents of Balfour's letter became more widely known, the Palestinian leaders began to realise what an unkind reversal of fortunes had befallen them: instead of the Muslim Ottomans, who had done much, if not all, they could to foil Zionist designs, they were now saddled with a Christian king whose inaugural measure was a pledge to promote Jewish national revival in their country.

The first important Jewish land purchases, in the 1880s, were made along the coast and in the Esdraelon (Jezreel) valley. The acquired land usually consisted of swamps and sand dunes whose possession involved little friction with local farmers. Since the sellers were often rich Syrians residing in Beirut they could shrug off local rebuke. The agricultural heartland of Palestine was in the hilly areas, where the Jews made few inroads. Much of the fallow lowlands were owned by nomad tribes and, after the Great War, there was a steady trickle of territory from Bedouin to Zionists.

The British occupation did not bring only Zionism to the Palestinians. It also brought trade, better prices for farm produce, investment in infrastructure – and relative freedom; to confront Zionism in the press, in local councils and in regional politics; and to organise into nationalist parties. Under the Turks, any expression of separatist nationalism, Arab as well as Jewish, had been dealt with summarily. A shocking example of Ottoman justice had been the treatment of the Mufti of Gaza, who was thought to have been sympathetic to the British and to pan-Arab causes. He was hanged, together with his son, by the Jaffa Gate in Jerusalem, and a crowd was invited to watch and take heed.

The issue of Arab–Jewish land deals was, after the matter of Jewish immigration to Palestine, the central one for the Arab Nationalist parties. Almost daily the local papers – the Arabic *Filastin* and *al-Karmil*, the Hebrew *Ha'aretz* and the official *Palestine Bulletin* – carried news items about trade in land and op-ed articles debating the phenomenon. Some families in the forefront of anti-Zionist resistance also sold land on the sly to the Jews, and internal Palestinian politics was ridden with suspicions and rumours on this issue. A special appeal from the Gaza branch of the National Defence Party, *al-Hizb al-Difa' al-Watani*, called upon all political organisations to refrain from branding each other "traitors" and "sell-outs", since this would only sow discord and serve the enemy.

As far as I have been able to ascertain, there were no Arab-Jewish land transactions in the Gaza Strip area before 1930. But long before that, the spectre of such sales bedevilled Gazan politics with hatred, accusations and false alarms. In February 1925 the Muslim–Christian Association of Gaza protested against a government go-ahead for the sale of Gazan lands to non-residents: "Under present conditions, this could only mean the Jews." That autumn the Mufti of Gaza directed a passionate call to his flock not to sell land to them. The cause for his concern was a newly concluded deal in nearby Beersheba, where "certain Bedouin landowners had sold 600 Palestine dunams [around 150 acres] to Jews", giving the Zionists their first foothold ever in the deep south of the country.

By this time it was clear that the British had been overly sanguine, not to say frivolous, about their capacity to shepherd Palestine towards political maturity and self-rule – the stated purpose of the mandates awarded by the League of Nations after the Great War. The organisations, motives and dreams of Jews and Palestinian Arabs were rapidly becoming politicised and polarised. More and more British decision-makers and colonial staffers realised to their horror that they had on their hands an equation with many unknowns but no visible solution. The Balfour Declaration had papered over the abyss at the centre of the conflict with some ingenious phrasing but, in the real world, incipient Arab-Jewish dynamics were creating a zero-sum game.

Every other year there were disturbances, more or less bloody, but in Gaza there was notably less friction than in the north and centre of the country. The Jews in Gaza city were not new immigrants, they spoke Arabic and they were not buying land. Muzi Levy, who grew up in Gaza, told me in 1971: "Our fathers all had Muslim acquaintances and partners. There were local fanatics who glued anti-British and anti-Zionist appeals on the walls of our quarter. But I don't remember feeling unsafe, not even during the riots in 1920 and 1921."

The first serious Arab–Jewish incident in Gaza during the Mandate took place in 1921, during the visit of Secretary of State for the Colonies, Winston Churchill. There was stone-throwing on Main Street and a large tumult, where several Jews were attacked. But it was stopped after a courageous intervention of Musa Alami, at the time still an unknown young man. (He later became the highest placed Palestinian in the Mandate government and in later years the most distinguished of all non-exile leaders.) Due to the riots, the Jews of Gaza stayed away for half a year, but returned after local leaders and business partners had vouched for their safety. During the bloody August riots in 1929, 133 Jews, more than half of them in Hebron, were killed by Arab mobs. Over a hundred Arabs were also killed during two chaotic weeks, some of them by Jews but most of them by the security forces. The British did not have the manpower required to deal with nationwide disturbances. In Hebron, the eye of the storm, there was just one British policeman.

Some hours before dawn on Saturday August 24, 1929, the police officer on duty in Gaza City received a telephone call from Jaffa. There had been mob violence and street fighting all over the country on Friday, he was told, and rabble-rousers were believed to be on their way to Gaza to incite the locals against the Jews. The next day, some of the Jews left the city, but most of them, unwilling to violate the Sabbath, remained. Practically all of them lived along the same streets, still today called *Harat al-Yahud*, "The Jewish Quarter". At noon, crowds started to form at street-corners and merchants were ordered by activists to shut their shops. According to the *Ha'aretz* correspondent, religious and party banners were brandished, along with daggers and clubs. The police told the Jews to take shelter in a hotel near the police station. Stones started to fly in the direction of the hotel, and most of the guards placed to protect the Jews fled the scene. The assailants entered the courtyard of the hotel and when the Jews heard cries of "Itbah al-Yahud!" – slaughter the Jews – they said their last prayers. The last remaining policemen tried to smuggle the Jews out in two ambulances. They managed to press all of them into the cars, but when they tried to make their way through the hostile multitude the policemen were overpowered and driven off. "I was sure that it was the end of us", Muzi Levy remembered, "People around me started to wail *Shema' Israel*, but the Lord heard our prayers. It is a mystery how the same situation will turn some men into ferocious animals and others into heroes risking their lives." As the crowd worked itself up for the lynching, a group of Gazan Arabs turned themselves into a protective wall around the ambulances. These brave people were led on by the leading Gazan dignitary, Sheikh Sa'id Shawa, who was a member of the Supreme Muslim Council, the most important Palestinian nationalist body. His sons Izzedin and Sa'adi jumped on to the hoods of each of the ambulances to shield the passengers. They managed to get the Jews into the police station and fend off several waves of attacks until a special train arrived from Jaffa to take the Jews away, this time forever. In Hebron, too, several of the Jews who survived the massacre had been saved by local Arabs. But Gaza was the only place in Palestine where Jews were attacked without suffering a single casualty.

One year later, in 1930, the Jew Tuvia Miller bought a 60-acre citrus orchard a kilometre south of the village of Deir al-Balah, not far from the location of the ancient town of Darom. With hindsight it is difficult not to regard the transaction as a milestone – the first Zionist settlement in what would become the Gaza Strip. But at the time it seems neither Miller nor his neighbours invested the purchase with political meaning. Much later, modern Jewish settlers at the spot began to make much of the place having appeared as a Jewish village in the Babylonian Talmud, compiled around AD 500. But Miller's aims were pragmatic – to plant oranges, not to extend Zionism.

The future Gaza strip would fall, in is entirety, within the boundaries of the British Mandate, and Palestinian nationalists never disputed that the area was part of their homeland. But among Jews, from the Bible to present times, there has never been a complete consensus as to Gaza's status. Some rabbis have insisted that it lies outside Eretz Israel. That, no doubt, is part of the reason that Zionist efforts to colonise the area were late and feeble. During the Arab Rebellion in Palestine of 1936–39, Miller's business in Darom was attacked repeatedly, and in 1939 he left it, without selling the land.

Throughout the British Mandate, Gaza was a peripheral but not isolated part of the country's economy. Zionist expansion did not affect wages, land prices and labour markets the way it did in Jaffa and Haifa. But goods and passenger traffic along the Egypt–Palestine railroad and highway generated jobs and incomes which supplemented the older pillars of the local economy, agriculture, fishing and the traditional guilds. Even though local industry was modest in terms of its machinery, Gaza's cloth, soap and basket products enjoyed high repute. During the Mandate, Gaza's transformation into a fully-fledged modern city took place. The harbour was dredged and accommodated to receive larger – but still far from large – shipping, and paved streets were laid out between the traditional town centre on the hill and the harbour to the west. In order to prevent construction on fertile land, the British subsidised building on the dunes next to the ocean. A well-planned, European-style residential area of villas, the Rimal ("Sands") grew. The first residents of Rimal were British clerks, but soon enough the grand landowning families of Gaza – the Abdul-Shafis, the Shawas, the Bseisos, the Suranis and the Sha'abans – as well as the small business elite, moved into the garden suburb. The sources and basis for wealth and influence also changed with the growth of the modern city, the arrival of banks and the growing international trade in barley, citrus and dried fruit. In Turkish times, local economic power had often rested on shares in the caravan trade, tax-farming privileges and the ownership of camels and land. But with modernity the leading *hama'il* (clans) branched out and sent their sons to study law, medicine, business and other free professions – an adaptation which did not diminish their influence.

As the city grew, mainly by semi-nomad Bedouins becoming sedentary, Gaza's population almost rebounded to its pre-1917 level. In 1945 the city counted 35,000 permanent residents, making Gaza one of the large urban centres of the country. (In 2009, Greater Gaza City was as populous as Greater Tel Aviv.) The abandoned Jewish quarter and the older Ottoman quarters, Zeytun, Daraj and Tuffah, which had been partly destroyed by British artillery fire in 1917, were largely rebuilt, while new shantytowns – long since incorporated into the city landscape – sprang up south of town.

During the years of rebellion and anti-Jewish boycotts of 1936–39, the Arab economy of Palestine had suffered. The only Arab businessmen who gained anything from the boycotts were importers of goods previously acquired from Jews. On the other hand, Arab merchants who had imported coffee, rice, spices, cars and tools for the Jewish market were hit hard. Local Arab trades which catered for Jewish customers suffered, among them the Gazan tobacco growers. The most miserable stratum of Arab society during the boycotts were the agricultural workers, the *fellahin.* Many of them had lived from carrying their eggs and vegetables on donkeys to the city's Jews, and they had also found seasonal work in the Zionist citrus-growing settlements. Some 7.4 million dunams of Arab land were cultivated in 1937, only 6.4 million dunams two years later.

The world war brought better times to Palestine's Arab farmers, not least to the grain-growers around Gaza city. The influx of foreign army personnel all over the region pushed up the prices of wheat (by 20 per cent), barley (40 per cent) and corn (50 per cent). Tens of thousands of Palestinian Arabs were hired by the military, and deposits to The Arab Bank, the larger of the two Arab banks, rose by 46 per cent during the first two war years. But the bonanza ended with the war. Between January and October, 1945, the British Army discharged ten thousand Arab workers. Wages at the weaveries and textile workshops at Majdal and Gaza fell by 40 per cent. In 1946 Tuvia Miller, the orange-grower who had been forced out by the Arab rebels in 1939, sold his land near Deir al-Balah to the Jewish National Fund. In the autumn of that year, settlers from the national-religious Zionist movement Mizrahi established a new colony there, named Kfar Darom. In the beginning they were on good terms with their Palestinian neighbours, but the newcomers would soon find out that they had chosen the most inopportune spot in all of Palestine to settle. The thirty-year deadlock of the British Mandate was coming to an end and the country was about to change beyond recognition. Gaza would change even more than the rest of Palestine. In little more than a year Gaza would have a new regime, a different economy, a different population – and a different destiny.

# 9

# The *Nakba* and the First Arab–Israeli War

## *The All-Palestine Government of Gaza, 1947–1950*

> *"Gaza is a . . . town with an original population of 25,000. It now has, in addition, about 60,000 refugees. They pack sidewalks, take up vacant lots in the public market, occupy barnyards and generally seem to fill every space which the town might have had. They live in churches, mosques, schools and public buildings . . . These people receive no relief action."* (An American diplomat, 1948)

In early 1947, the British government relinquished its mandate over Palestine and made public its decision to surrender responsibility for the area to the United Nations. To examine possible solutions for a post-British Palestine, the United Nations Special Committee on Palestine (UNSCOP), was established. UNSCOP interviewed many witnesses and experts in several countries. It heard many Jews, both Holocaust survivors and Zionist leaders, but it did not get good access to the Palestinian view-point, since the official Palestinian bodies did not cooperate with the committee; they only reiterated the Arab demand for an Arab Palestinian state. Interior Palestinian politics was in turmoil at this stage, owing to a bitter dispute between the Hashemite regimes of Jordan and Iraq and the most influential Palestinian leader, Haj Amin al-Husseini, who was not even invited to the Arab emergency summit on Palestine in October 1947.

In September UNSCOP delivered its report to the UN. Its recommendation favoured partition of Palestine into six areas. Each side was awarded three of these areas. All of the future Gaza Strip, save a thin sliver of land south of Deir el-Balah, fell inside the southwestern third of the proposed Arab state. As the fateful UN vote on the partition plan drew closer, the country slid uncontrollably into a whirl of gunfights, sniping, terrorism and murder, with the vast majority of victims on both sides being civilians. The downward spiral intensified after the UN voted "yes" to partition on November 29 and several regular war-fronts opened up between Tel Aviv,

Jaffa and Ramle. From then on, both Arab and Jewish front-pages would compress bloody massacres with two-figure fatalities into one-column items, to make space for them all.

In Gaza, the first sign of serious trouble came a week after the UN ruling, when the Arab Higher Executive ordered the formation of a citizen's guard. The war was still months away from Gaza, but the fighting around Tel Aviv had already caused a southward trickle of wealthy middle-class Arabs from the flashpoints of violence in Jaffa, Salame and Abu Kabir. Some of them rented houses or moved in with relatives in Gaza, intending to return when things calmed down, just as they had done during previous surges of inter-communal terror. No one at this early stage would have thought of calling these people refugees, but that is what they were – the first, imperceptible portent of the impending Palestinian tragedy, the *Nakba*.

On March 15, 1948, two months before the partition plan would go into effect, there was an exchange of gunfire between armed Gazans and British soldiers during the evacuation of the British military hospital in the city. British reinforcements arriving at the scene found land mines by a roadside with ignition wires leading to a detonator in a nearby orange grove. Two hundred rounds of ammunition were found and confiscated. From then on the British presence in the Gaza area was sporadic at best. Outposts and peripheral bases were the first to shut down, pending the sensitive and precarious evacuation from the main bases in Jerusalem and Haifa. On March 20 there were skirmishes over the demarcation of land between villagers from Deir al-Balah and the Jewish settlers in Kfar Darom. The same night, seven Palestinian fighters, most of them Gazans, fell during an assault on Nizanim, one of the few Jewish settlements inside the coastal segment set aside by the UN for the would-be Arab state.

While Palestine was becoming a burning issue of world diplomacy, Egypt was shaken by anti-Zionist demonstrations and riots, led by the Muslim Brotherhood, which demanded access to the front in order to confront the Zionist enemy. The Egyptian government, wary that the Brotherhood would take advantage of the war to get access to arms, resisted. But the hostile attitude of Cairo, in Haim Levenberg's words, "did not deter the Muslim Brothers, who found ways to circumvent the orders. The Society formed a scientific mission claiming to carry out explorations in Sinai. Once the mission had arrived in Sinai, it threw off its scientific cover and infiltrated into Palestine, concentrating near Gaza." One of these Muslim volunteers was a twenty-year old Egyptian of Gazan origin, Yasser Arafat, who fought bravely, although he later embellished his exploits somewhat.

On March 24 several Arab papers reported that Hassan al-Banna, the founder and leader of the Brotherhood, had arrived in Gaza on a recruiting mission. He had been received with honours by the mayor Rushdi al-

Shawa and then taken to the Ummari mosque in Gaza city. There, in a fiery oration, he had called upon the faithful to join the Holy War against Zionism. As the British retreat approached, the Egyptian authorities decided to make its peace with the eager Islamist volunteers and throw them into battle. They were equipped and summarily drilled by the army, which assumed command over them. According to an Israeli military historian, the Muslim Brothers were as poorly armed and trained as the other Arab soldiers, "but they excelled in fighting spirit and tenacity". The isolated Jewish settlement of Kfar Darom, on the main road between Gaza city and Khan Yunes, was chosen as the Brotherhood's baptism of fire. This was the first real act of Arab-Jewish warfare to take place inside the future Gaza Strip. On April 10, 1948, the Brotherhood units took up positions around Kfar Darom, which was surrounded by a barbed wire fence and minefields.

The Brotherhood force was numerically superior, by far, and at first it encountered little Jewish resistance. But it was a ruse. The Jews did not start to shoot until the Egyptians were within easy range. After losing at least 14 men, the Egyptians retreated. British officers who arrived at the scene put together a temporary truce. One of the Muslim Brothers, Kamil Isma'il al-Sharif, later wrote a book about his experiences in the war. He recalled: "Arab intelligence services ridiculed the Jews and their military capacity. The Brothers cannot be blamed for the failure."

A month later, backed up by several field cannons, the volunteers attempted a second assault. A furious battle raged for hours, and again the Jews were fortunate. The Egyptian artillery set its sights incorrectly and several shells hit the Brotherhood's advance guard, leaving 70 dead and 50 wounded. The attack was called off. The Jews celebrated their victory in Gaza, and the press hailed it as an amazing feat in the David-and-Goliath genre. The Jewish central command realised that the Egyptians were not going to leave the issue at that, and fresh troops were rushed to Kfar Darom. But this time luck turned. The reinforcement column got stuck in the sands east of Kfar Darom and was discovered by the Egyptians, who ground it down with artillery fire. Eight Egyptian armoured vehicles broke through into Kfar Darom and an eight-day house-to-house battle began. In the end, the surviving Jews fled under the cover of night and the Egyptians took control of the entire area between their border and the front.

It was not a new thing in Palestine to leave home during clashes, riots and blood-feuds – and to return when things had calmed down. But as the fighting spread to include most parts of Palestine, the mounting count of displaced Palestinians was gradually recognised as a looming emergency and possibly one of the cardinal issues at stake. The country was now being partitioned, not according to the UN blueprint, but by war. The large towns in the Arab-held sectors – Hebron, Bethlehem, Nablus and Gaza –

were overwhelmed by destitute strangers. "They come in hundreds each day, and put their belongings on the sidewalks. We can't feed them all, help us!" pleaded Suleiman Tuqan, the mayor of Nablus. No one had expected or prepared for a refugee crisis and, until late 1948, when UNRWA, the UN refugee agency was established, there were no efficient coordination of relief efforts. In December 1948, an American diplomat, quoted by Benny Morris, described the situation:

> "Gaza is a . . . town with an original population of 25,000. It now has, in addition, about 60,000 refugees. They pack sidewalks, take up vacant lots in the public market, occupy barnyards and generally seem to fill every space which the town might have had. They live in churches, mosques, schools and public buildings . . . These people receive no relief action."

On May 16, 1948, the day after Israel's declaration of independence, there was a flurry of official Egyptian announcements concerning the war. Mahmud Riyad, minister of commerce, told the Associated Press that the entry of regular Egyptian troops into the south of Palestine had calmed the Arabs around Gaza, who were now free to harvest their barley crop. An army spokesman said the coast as far as Majdal (Ashkelon) was in Egyptian hands. Two days later, on May 18, King Faruk visited Gaza and the front, while triumphant bulletins were issued about the conquest of Beersheba. The Israelis protested to the British that the airfield of Gaza was being used by the Egyptians for bombing raids.

From the moment the Egyptians began to run Gaza's affairs, they were jealously eyed by King Abdullah of Transjordan, who still nursed hopes of securing a Mediterranean harbour for his kingdom in the south of Palestine. Only a week after the arrival of the Egyptians in Gaza, the media under Abdullah's control warned the Gazans not to use the new stamps issued by the Egyptians. Only mail with Transjordanian stamps would be delivered in the Bedouin kingdom.

Ever since the UN vote on partition in November 1947, the most prominent Palestinian national leader, Haj Amin al-Husseini, who was also the Mufti of Jerusalem, had pleaded with the Arab League to let him set up a Palestinian government. The League had wavered, reluctant to take sides between Egypt, which (sometimes) supported Husseini, and King Abdullah of Transjordan, who regarded the Mufti as "a devil straight from hell".

From the outset, the Arab war effort 1947–49 was aimed at blocking partition and preventing the establishment of a Jewish state. But during spring and early summer of 1948, those goals no longer appeared within reach. As time wore on, both Egypt and Transjordan concentrated on preventing the Jews from expanding into the Arab sectors of the partition plan. Neither country could afford to go public about having downgraded their war-aims, and even less could they recognise that the war for Palestine had deteriorated into an opportunistic and bitter struggle over the scraps between the two Arab monarchies.

The Mufti and most Palestinians never forgave King Abdullah for having evicted the only serious Palestinian fighting force, the *Jihad al-Muqaddas*, from Tulkarem and Nablus at an early stage of the war. The Palestinians and the Egyptians had no illusions about Abdullah's real intentions: to add any liberated land to his kingdom, including the Gazan coast and the land-bridge between the Mediterranean and the Red Sea. It was not clear how he was going to achieve this – until a well-meaning but incurably naïve Swedish count blundered into the minefield of Transjordanian–Egyptian intrigue. Folke Bernadotte presented two plans during his short spell as UN mediator. The second of those recommended the scrapping of the idea of an Arab Palestine. It also recommended giving the Negev–Arava desert – Jewish in the partition plan – to Transjordan. (For this, Bernadotte was assassinated by the Jewish Stern gang.) It also contained the following passage: "compelling reasons for merging the Arab territory of Palestine with the territory of Transjordan . . . ". If Bernadotte had had his way, Egypt, which had already conquered substantial Palestinian areas north of Gaza, would lose its foothold in Palestine *and* see Abdullah's Transjordan extend itself all the way to its own eastern border.

The fury of the Egyptians and their Arab allies over this drove them to set up, first, a Palestinian civil administration in Gaza, and then, on September 20, 1948, an All-Palestine Government in Gaza, *Huqumat Ummum Filastin.* This was one of the more bizarre episodes of the war. Anwar Nuseibe, who served as the secretary to the Gaza government, told me many years later that the project "had not been without comic features". The Egyptians, backed by the Arab League, ordered all the top Palestinian leaders to Gaza, giving them the impression that their leadership would finally get the recognition they had sought and that the new government would be accepted as an equal in the League. The Egyptians even managed to draw in Ahmad Hilmi, one of the pillars of the Transjordanian government and the only Palestinian Arab who had received the title "Pasha" from the Sublime Porte. Hilmi would serve as Palestinian Prime Minister, Jamal Husseini as Foreign Minister and Raja'i al-Husseini as Minister of Defence. A week after the Gaza government was formed, the Mufti Amin al-Husseini also arrived in Gaza and was received as a king by the local population. The Mufti was a guest of Musa Surani, one of the richest men in Gaza, who, without being a member, took part in the government meetings, and Ahmad Hilmi was put up by the aristocratic Bseiso family. But the others were given rooms at an extremely humble inn, Diya'fat al-Walid, on 'Umar al-Mukhtar (the main street of Gaza city), which did not serve meals. A cook was found, but the Egyptians did not cover expenses, and Defense Minister Husseini stepped in and footed the bill for all. The cash-crunch of the Egyptian military government in Gaza was so severe, future president Muhammad Neguib revealed in his memoirs, that he had to pay the Palestinian truck owners who drove the soldiers from Rafah to the front out of his own pocket. The Palestinian government was first assigned a classroom in a school, al-Falah al-Islamiya. The building had no electricity, but the walls had been covered by flags of the Arab League nations and of Palestine, a festive and explicit demonstration of Palestine's supposed reception as an equal partner in the all-Arab forum.

But the only seats available for the 75–80 Palestinian leaders were the classroom chairs of little children, and the pictures of the first Palestinian cabinet meeting did not make a dignified impression. The cabinet forthwith held its meetings in the lobby of the hotel. Along with the short-lived government, a Palestinian National Council was set up with the Mufti as its President. Meanwhile, in Amman, King Abdullah was furious with those of "his" Palestinians who had broken loose from his control. The Palestinian Foreign Minister Jamal al-Husseini was later arrested in Transjordan and another cabinet member, Awni Abdul Hadi, leader of the Istiqlal party, was forced to resign. The Egyptians, frightened by Abdullah's veiled threats to conclude a separate peace with the Israelis, told the Mufti to get out of Gaza. When he refused, Egyptian agents bundled him into a taxi and drove him to Cairo.

The pressure and the threats were taking their toll on the Palestinian leaders in Gaza. Prime Minister Ahmad Hilmi had been one of King Abdullah's most trusted men and had risked his position for the sake of the Palestinian government. He now sent desperate appeals to his Egyptian colleague al-Nuqrashi to speed up the formal recognition of his government and its entry into the Arab League. The Egyptians asked him to be patient, for any day now the issue would be settled. But the League members had lost interest in the Palestinian government. One after another of its members were bought off with Lebanese, Saudi and Jordanian government jobs. On February 15, 1949, the Arab League informed Ahmad Hilmi that it could no longer fund Palestinian activities in Gaza and next time the Arab League was convened, the Palestinian government was not invited. The ignoble treatment of the all-Palestine government loomed large in later Palestinian history. It helped form Yasser Arafat's obsession with the *al-qarar al-mustaqillah*, "the independent Palestinian decision" – independent from outside meddling, which was not really achieved until the 1990s and still cannot be taken for granted.

On December 22, 1948, the Israelis launched Operation *Horev*, destined to be the concluding round of fighting in the war. Israeli forces pushed into Sinai and surrounded the Gaza area from all sides, in the hope of expelling the Egyptian Expeditionary Force from all of mandatory

Palestine. Furious diplomatic reactions from the US and Britain forced the Israelis to withdraw from Egyptian territory. The Israelis then cut off the el-Arish–Rafah road near the international border, thereby trapping the Egyptian forces inside a narrow pocket along the Mediterranean. The Israeli commander Yigal Allon prepared to storm the last Egyptian defences and reach the sea. The Egyptian commanders in the field urged their government to sue for a cease-fire. Egypt agreed to armistice talks with Israel – to the dismay of the All-Palestine government and Palestinians everywhere. On January 7, 1949, the guns fell silent. The Gaza Strip had come into being. Six weeks later its existence as a distinct territorial unit was ratified at Rhodes. The Armistice agreement included an exchange of territories, with the Egyptians evacuating the Faluja pocket inside Israel, and the Israelis leaving the town of Beit Hanun in the norteastern corner of the Gaza Strip. (Territorially, the issue was settled at Rhodes, but several thousand refugees were expelled from areas inside Israel, notably Faluja, and then, in 1950, from Majdal (Ashkelon), to the Strip.)

It was not immediately clear what was going to happen to the new area, demarcated by the contingencies of war and bursting with homeless Palestinian Arabs. During the last months of the war, as the Egyptian Expeditionary Force was driven from the Isdud (Ashdod), Majdal (Ashkelon) and Beersheba areas it had conquered in the spring, and retreated southwards, many more thousands of Arab civilians were expelled or fled from their homes. Most of them followed the Egyptian forces on their trek southward. When the cease-fire went into effect the authorities in Gaza, already at their wits' end about how to feed the April–May refugees, faced the task of providing food and shelter for 200,000 destitute people. According to PLO figures, a third of all the *Nakba* refugees ended up in Gaza. The sudden population increase of the Strip was more than 300 per cent, resulting in a native/refugee ratio of 1:3, possibly a world record.

During the months following the armistice both Israel and Egypt seriously pondered an American proposal to turn the Strip, with its refugees, over to Israel. The Egyptians would be let off the responsibility of caring for the refugees, while Israel would get more territory and placate worldwide calls to let the refugees back home. David Ben-Gurion, the Israeli Prime Minister, was prepared to give the refugees Israeli citizenship, but he met with strong opposition from several colleagues, who balked at the demographic implications. The Egyptian regime saw the practical advantages of such a deal, but it was greatly weakened by the war débâcle, and feared a domestic outcry if it ceded to the enemy the only corner of Palestine it had managed to hold on to.

# 10

# Egyptian Military Rule, 1948–1967

> *"In the morning we would find the blankets of the children's communal dormitory taken off the beds and neatly folded on a shelf. They had crossed the fence, passed the guards unseen and stood next to our sleeping children without harming them – but reminding us that they could. It was the eeriest feeling. That sort of thing was thought to be the final exam for would-be fedayeen."* (A former member of a border kibbutz)

The official Egyptian rhetoric on the Gaza Strip was one of brotherhood and solidarity. Reality took a different shape. The provisions for the All-Palestine government, which languished for years in a Cairo flat, were conveniently forgotten, and it soon became clear that the Strip would not be run by civilians – and not by Palestinians.

Before the war, Gaza had been an attractive place to live, a few hours' train-ride from Jaffa and Jerusalem but with a lower cost of living than the centre of the country. Contacts with Egypt had always been more intense than in the rest of Palestine and travelling from the Gaza Strip towns to Cairo and Alexandria was frequent. Migration between Egypt and Gaza was also common, as in the case of Yasser Arafat's father Abdul Rauf, who moved with his family to Cairo in 1927. But now, in one fell swoop, Gaza had been cut off not only from Palestine but from Egypt as well. Except for a small number of Gazans from upper-class and business families, the residents of the Strip were not allowed into Egypt. Refugee camps sprawled around Beirut, Amman and Damascus, but the only Palestinians in Cairo were those with special permits, granted after string-pulling and lengthy bureaucratic ordeals. Even if they made it to Cairo, Gazans were explicitly prevented from working, "with or without pay".

The discrimination, corruption and cruelty of Egyptian rule in Gaza was sometimes exaggerated by the Jordanian and the Saudi press, but it was real enough. Permits to visit Egypt were hard to come by, and travelling to other Arab states was well-nigh impossible. There was hunger, if not outright starvation, in the Strip during the first years of Egyptian rule and Gazans would leave no stone unturned in their ingenious attempts to get out. The Meccan pilgrimage was stopped by the Egyptians when they realised that a growing number of pilgrims defected *en route*. The more fortunate exiles settled in the Gulf states, but even the West Bank was considered a substantial step up the socio-economic ladder.

However, Egyptian misrule was not the principal factor pushing Gazans abroad. From the onset of the refugee influx in early March 1948, local leaders, churchmen and visiting diplomats had bombarded the international community with SOS-calls from Gaza. The Egyptian army, whose own soldiers in Gaza often went hungry, could offer no relief. American Quakers and the Red Cross did what they could, but need vastly outstripped means and the first refugee winters in the Strip were appalling. While Gaza had previously been the urban centre for rich farmlands, many of the fields were now on the Israeli side, harvested by the victors. For years after the 1948–49 war the Gaza–Israel line was more real on maps than on the ground. The Israeli army could not patrol it effectively and there was a steady traffic of refugees crossing into Israel nightly, some to sabotage and lay mines, but most to rustle sheep, reap their own sorghum and pick their own olives. There were also more ambitious thefts, of tractors and machinery, some of which were returned by the Egyptians as stipulated by the 1949 agreement. But the sieve-like Gazan border became a huge headache for the Israeli government. The value of lost crops and irrigation pipes was considerable. The burden of constant guard-duty for the Israelis living near the border was even costlier – 3,150 annual workdays for each settlement, according to Benny Morris. The known hardships of living near Gaza also hampered Prime Minister David Ben-Gurion's pet project at the time – populating the Negev desert with North African immigrants.

Some of the Palestinian infiltrators practiced subtle forms of gentlemanly terrorism. A former member of a border kibbutz recalls:

> "In the morning we would find the blankets of the children's communal dormitory taken off the beds and neatly folded on a shelf. They had crossed the fence, passed the guards unseen and stood next to our sleeping children without harming them – but reminding us that they could. It was the eeriest feeling. That sort of thing was thought to be the final exam for would-be fedayeen."

The plight of the refugees is well-known and easy to identify with. But for many indigenous Gazans the 1947–49 war brought hardship on a comparable scale. Landowners and day-labourers alike were cut off from their fields, and merchants from most of their markets. There was suddenly much less work – and much less pay for doing it. The arrival in colossal numbers of destitute newcomers made hourly wages crash. When a special UN agency, the UNRWA, began operations among Palestinian refugees in 1950, there was a heated debate on whether aid should be extended to non-refugees. It was not. UNRWA assistance was truly modest, but once its services got organised, the poverty of many Gazan non-refugees, not least the Bedouin nomads cut off from their hinterland, surpassed that of the UNRWA beneficiaries.

After months under open skies, most refugees were accommodated under canvas in 1950–51. During the fifties, the tent-landscape gradually gave way to sprawls of mud and brick huts, growing in rings on the perimeter of the main towns. The once unmistakeable boundaries between the camps and the surrounding urban areas are much less clear today than they used to be. In the Strip, the term for refugee camps is *Mu'askar*, which means "military base", perhaps because some of the camps were set up in, or later took over, abandoned British, Egyptian, Brazilian, or Canadian bases. Extensive stretches of camp territory now consist of four-to-five floor apartment buildings. Eight refugee camps were set up by UNRWA, two of them close to Gaza City, Jebaliya to the east and al-Shaati on the beach to the northeast. Those two are the most infamous, perhaps because they have been the ones most frequented by foreign correspondents. But living conditions in the Brazil and Shabura camps near Rafah at the southern extreme of the Strip are worse. Brazil (named after the Brazilian UNEF-contingent garrisoned there until 1967) straddles the Egypt–Gaza border with its controversial transport tunnels and has been the target of thousands of Israeli bombs in recent years. Today Jebaliya, Shaati and Brazil are virtual cities of close to a hundred thousand inhabitants each. In Khan Yunes and Nuseirat there are also large camps, while the Maghazi, Bureij and Deir al-Balah camps in the centre of the Strip are much smaller.

The abrupt and brutal demographic changes which swept the Strip during the first Arab–Israeli war were bound to cut deeply into the previous social fabric. In the post-war Gaza Strip a whole new society, with new routines, rules and power-relationships was forced into existence under the control of a foreign military government. There was tension, envy and suspicion between the original Gazans and the involuntary newcomers. Today, after generations of (not frequent) intermarriage and shared destinies, the distinction between natives and refugees has become less significant, if far from blurred.

Over the years, intra-Palestinian resentment would pale next to their feelings towards their new masters. British rule had not been popular, and on official and ideological levels Egyptians sympathised fully with the Gazans. But in many ways, daily life under Egypt was an ordeal which made the locals reminisce about the Mandate with nostalgia. Permits of any kind involved excessive paperwork and bribes. The Gazans, whose level of education steadily rose under the aegis of the UNRWA school-system, were eager to trade, study, do business and innovate. Most attempts foundered on the reefs of graft and *bakshish.*

Egyptian officers lived well in Gaza. They enjoyed low living-costs and they made creative use of the separate tax and customs rates imposed on

Gaza. Gaza's lower excise duties on tobacco products provided one of many lucrative rackets for the army. There was also a flourishing contraband trade of luxury items and alcohol from Beirut to Gaza, all of it bound for Cairo and smuggled through on Egyptian army trucks. Later, when Gaza port was made a tax-free area, opportunities multiplied. But few, if any, of the profits from these schemes trickled down to ordinary Palestinians. It soon became obvious that the only way a Palestinian refugee in Gaza could improve his living conditions was to find a way out of the Strip. As more and more Gazans made their way to the Gulf states, especially to Kuwait where they became indispensable in many trades and government departments, remittances from abroad came to play an important role in many households.

The one local branch of the economy which flourished under Egypt was the export of citrus fruits, mainly oranges. In 1948, the citrus orchards covered 6,000 dunams. (1 dunam=1,000 square metres.) Now they expanded almost uncontrollably, reaching 75,000 dunams at the peak, initiating a growing pressure on the underground fresh water strata. During the peak years, citrus exports from Gaza approached 2 million crates, mostly to Eastern Bloc countries. The primitive conditions at Gaza port limited the export options, but on the other hand created work for more people. David Zohar describes the old-fashioned anchorage of Gaza, "where stevedores waded through the breakers with bales lashed to their backs to load into lighters which were poled out to the ships moored some distance from the beach . . . "

Israeli–Egyptian relations during the first post-war years were determined by events in the Strip. The diplomacy of both countries was fraught with contradictions. The Egyptians recognised the Gazans' rights to fight Israel, but they were careful not to let the fedayeen guerillas drag them into a confrontation they were not prepared for. The Israelis, while seeking and demanding tranquility along the border, at certain stages seemed eager to exploit border violations in order to confront the Egyptian army and stifle its growth, especially after Cairo's 1955 arms deal with the Soviets.

The factors leading up to the 1956 war were numerous and complex and several of them fall outside the scope of this work. To mention but a few: The Israeli retaliation strike against the Strip in February 1955, which left thirty-eight Egyptian soldiers dead; the mounting activities of Gazan fedayeen inside Israel (in which the three future pillars of al-Fatah and the PLO – Yasser Arafat, Khalil al-Wazir and Salah Khallaf – all took part); growing tension between Britain and Egypt's new leader Gamal Abdul Nasser, who intended to nationalise the Suez Canal and the capture in Cairo of Israeli *agents provocateurs*, most of them Egyptian Jews, who were caught after bombing Western targets in Cairo and Alexandria in the summer of 1954.

On July 26, 1956, the Egyptian president Gamal Abdul Nasser ordered the take-over of the Canal Zone and nationalised the Suez Canal. The waterway formally belonged to a Paris-based company, but more importantly it was one of the last solid geopolitical assets of two waning colonial powers: France, which had built it a century earlier; and Britain, which had owned it for most of the time since. There was an indignant outcry in the West, but the US distanced itself from calls to apply force against Egypt. In late October, France, Israel's only ally at the time, convinced David Ben-Gurion to join a secret Anglo-French scheme aimed at the forcible recovery of the canal. Israel's role would be to conquer the Gaza Strip and the Sinai Peninsula, while the French and the British secured the Canal Zone.

On the ground, things went according to plan. Between October 29 and November 5 the Israelis overran Egyptian defences in the Gaza Strip and in the Sinai. On November 5, when much of Egypt's strength had been sapped, French and British paratroopers landed in the Canal Zone and retook it. But the conspiring allies had completely miscalculated the international fallout. The Canal adventure, coming on the heels of Soviet intervention in Hungary, played into Russian hands and interfered with US Middle East policies. The Americans were adamant, and they applied unexpectedly rough pressure on the invaders to retreat. The Israelis evacuated Sinai, but then stubbornly refused to leave Gaza.

The occupation of the Gaza Strip was completed on November 2, 1956. A look at the proclamations issued by the Israeli Military Government in Gaza reveals one thing beyond doubt: the original Israeli intention had been to remain there. The flurry of decrees and ordinances immediately let loose upon the Gazans were not limited to military matters. Just days after conquest new routines concerning banks, mail service, currencies and food prices were announced and printed.

There had been three kinds of Arab fighters in the Strip: Egyptian regulars, Palestinian regulars fighting in their own formations but under Egyptian command, and the non-uniformed fedayeen irregulars who specialised in operations inside Israel. After Israel blocked their route of escape to the Sinai most of the regulars shed their uniforms. The Israelis immediately began intense screenings and weapons searches of suspected soldiers and militants. Military edict no. 9, issued on November 9, called upon "all Egyptian soldiers to turn themselves over". In the next paragraph, *Junud Filastiniyun*, "Palestinian soldiers", are also ordered to present themselves. The wording is a curiosity – thirty years before official Israel began to refer to Palestinians as such. Whoever provided hiding for military personnel would face ten years in prison.

As the Israelis, assisted by collaborators with the usual paper bags over their heads, combed the refugee camps of Rafah, Khan Yunes and Gaza

City for Palestinian fighters, atrocities were committed. Between 48 (the Israeli figure) and 200 suspected Palestinian militants were killed. Some died in shoot-outs, but an unknown number were murdered in cold blood. There is also reason to believe that there were fedayeen from Gaza among the Egyptian POWs murdered by Israeli units in the Sinai. The killing of Egyptian POWs was an exception, whereas the killing of fedayeen prisoners was not.

The apparent Israeli determination to stay on in Gaza misled the powerful al-Shawa clan into a fateful mistake. The Shawas, whose tribal roots allegedly lay in Arabia, were long-time Hashemite loyalists. Their allegiance to the Jordanian royal house had not made their life under the Egyptians easier. Rushdi al-Shawa, who eight years earlier had welcomed the holy warriors of the Muslim Brotherhood into Gaza, now accepted an Israeli nomination for mayor of Gaza City, a post he had already held during the last decade of British rule. When the Egyptians returned the following spring, Rushdi al-Shawa and other members of his family would suffer gruesome fates for serving under the Zionists. Rushdi's life was spared only after the intervention of the Saudi royal family and – later – his brother Sa'adi was tortured until he lost his mind.

During the brief Israeli interlude of 1956–57 Gazans were not, as they would be after the 1967 war, allowed inside Israel, but Israelis nevertheless scrambled to have a look at the Strip. "We had coffee by the beach or in the garden of the legendary Marna House Hotel, and we spent money like drunken sailors in their markets," one old-timer recalls. "This was a time of great austerity in Israel, and our jaws dropped when we saw how little they charged. We bought so much that they had to start trucking goods from Egypt to Gaza."

There were some sniping incidents, but in spite of the historical background, and the recent summary killings of suspected Palestinian fighters, the Israeli tourists were not harmed. There was surely unease and bitterness, but the hatred was cooled off by curiosity and commerce, and negligible compared to its present magnitude.

For a few short weeks both Israelis and Gazans really believed that times had changed, and that the Egyptians would not return. Zvi Elpeleg, then a young officer, today a distinguished scholar, told me about an absurd moment during Israel's first weeks in the Strip, as the new regime tried to make itself agreeable after the initial heavy-handed measures:

> "Our chief of staff Moshe Dayan, restless as always and believing he could overthrow deep-seated realities with clever stratagems, had one of his bright ideas. It made us shudder, but we had to go along with it. We were ordered to arrange an evening of classical music for the benefit of the aristocratic Gazan families. I don't remember if Dayan picked the music as well, but I remember that the programme included both Bizet and

> Offenbach. The symphony orchestra of the Army was ordered to Gaza and preparations were made. When our secret service heard about the event they naturally decided to plant microphones in the hall in order to pick up the reactions and perhaps some useful gossip from the Palestinian dignitaries. Unfortunately, we were not allocated any refreshments to match the musical display. All we could offer was grapefruit juice in paper mugs and the plain wafers of those days, called *wafla.* I tried to explain that such tawdry fare would be an affront in the eyes of our Arab guests, whose social gatherings were not complete without epic spreads of delicacies. But it was too late. The secret service microphones did not function very well in the din, and when the Shin Beth men listened to the tapes afterwards the only intelligible words were a sarcastic rhyme by Musa Surani, one of the most venerable Gazan patriarchs. It went like this: *'Azamuna li-hafla, wa-a'atuna bass wafla* – 'They invited us to a party, but all they gave us was wafers.'"

It took the Americans – at that time still a long way from becoming Israel's allies – several months to twist the arm of David Ben-Gurion and force the Israelis out of the Strip. Ben-Gurion already resented the Americans for having deprived him of Gaza in 1948 and, in late December 1956, he told the American ambassador in Tel Aviv that returning Gaza to Egypt would be a "fatal mistake". During dramatic rounds of diplomatic wrangling, the US even threatened Israel with sanctions. In the end, Israel was evicted from Gaza, but with two important concessions to show for its intransigence: Egypt was forced to stop the harassment of Israeli shipping in the Red Sea and the new UN military force, UNEF, which was set up to patrol the international border between Israel and Egypt, had its mandate expanded to include supervision of the ADL – the 1949 Armistice Demarcation Line between Israel and the Gaza Strip – a severe setback to the Palestinian fedayeen.

UNEF was the UN's first experiment with armed peacekeeping forces. For ten years its 82 (later 40) observation points along the 1949 line served as an effective buffer between Israel and Egypt. During that time, UNEF turned the 50-kilometre stretch into the most tranquil section of the whole conflict. Its success considerably boosted the UN's claims to be seen as an actor on the international stage, rather than merely as a diplomatic forum.

On the whole, Israel was happier than Egypt with the arrangement. The observation posts were all on Egyptian-held territory and, in addition, there was a 500-metre restricted zone along the Israeli border, where no movement of Gazans was permitted without prior coordination. At the rim of this zone many of the Palestinian Liberation Army's 8,000 fighters were positioned.

As the population grew, so did the pressure on each square inch of arable land inside the Strip. With time, UNEF began to look the other way when Palestinian farmers sowed and reaped in the restricted zone. The more militant Palestinians were, of course, disgusted by the new arrangements, which effectively put an end to the armed struggle against Israel. Not only did UNEF keep them away from Israel, but the regular Palestinian forces kept them away from the restricted zone – and even, it was claimed, turned infiltrators over to Egypt's secret services. To Yasser Arafat and his friends it was pointless to remain in Gaza under such conditions. In order to keep the struggle against Israel alive, they would have to devise a new strategy. They did, but it took them nearly a decade.

The Palestinians in the Strip were divided along the lines sketched above, but it is very difficult, in retrospect and without the testimony of a free press, to gauge the relative strength of public opinion. Umm Shadi from the refugee camp of Khan Yunes, born in 1938, remembers: "The main thing, then as now, was to put food on the table. There were thousands of soldiers in the PLA. Some resented them for doing Nasser's bidding and stopping the fedayeen on their way to Israel, but their families cared more about the salary they brought home. The UNEF people also brought in a lot of work. My first job was when I went with my mother to mop floors at the Colombian base here."

Many older Gazans remember the foreign soldiers with affection. They normally did not wear UN gear, but stuck to their own uniforms – and customs. The tough and hard-drinking Finns, the shy Swedes, the jolly Brazilians and the Indians in their brown turbans were visitors from that vast and varied outside world which remained out-of-bounds for Gazans. The wives of the foreign officers usually treated their Palestinian cooks, drivers, cleaning girls and gardeners with more respect than they had encountered serving Egyptian and Palestinian employers.

Materially, things improved, but not spectacularly. To an outsider, such as Canadian Army Captain J.A. Swettenham, based in Rafah 1957–58, the prevailing impression was one of poverty:

> "Driving north to Gaza, the land becomes more and more fertile, until at Gaza itself there are orange groves, cypress trees, mimosa hedges and masses of flowers. Irrigation from underground cisterns . . . is practiced. Here the nomadic tribes give way to the villagers who live in mud-walled houses and cultivate crops. It is interesting to see oxen, camels and donkeys pulling wooden ploughs which do little more than scratch the surface of the ground. Methods can have changed very little since Biblical times, and it is a common sight to see long-robed, veiled women returning from the wells with earthenware urns balanced on their heads. All this is in great contrast to the mechanised agriculture practiced by the Israelis on the other side of the Demarcation Line."

The closeness of Israel was one of the psychological factors that set the Strip apart from all other Palestinian places of refuge. Here the Israelis were more than a painful fact and source of bitter memories. They were clearly visible from countless spots inside the Strip, working the fields, patrolling the Demarcation Line and living their lives in the border settlements. Before the 1957 arrangements, a large proportion of Gazan men had been inside Israel, to test their courage, to sabotage or to steal agricultural equipment, especially irrigation pipes. To Gazans, the Israelis were not an abstraction. Their dynamism, and the visible progress they made in the shape of ever-higher yields and better machinery, was a twinge of pain added daily to the unremitting grief over the lost hearth.

One of the countless border incidents of the time puts this uncanny proximity into relief. In March 1956, Palestinians who had crossed the line in order to reap the crops of Kibbutz Nahal Oz had ambushed and killed a young security guard, Ro'i Rothberg. The deed was a planned revenge for beatings received from Rothberg on other occasions. The event was common enough, but it has become part of Israeli history because of the extraordinary eulogy pronounced by the Chief of Staff by Rothberg's open grave. Moshe Dayan's speech was broadcast the same day on Israeli radio and figured prominently in the newspaper coverage. The words were really addressed to what Dayan saw as a worrying Israeli complacency in the face of constant threats, but the tone and the underlying assumption had a striking effect on contemporary Israelis:

> "Yesterday at first light, Ro'i was murdered. The calm of the spring morning deceived him and he did not notice those lying in wait for him. Let us not, on this day, blame the murderers. What can we say about their terrible hatred of us? For eight years they have sat in the refugee camps of Gaza. They have watched as we, before their very eyes, have turned their lands and villages, where they and their forefathers used to dwell, into our home. It is not among the Arabs of Gaza, but among ourselves that we must seek Ro'i's blood. How did we come to shut our eyes, how did we come to turn away from facing our destiny and see, in all its cruelty, the destiny of our generation? Can we forget that this group of youngsters [the frontier settlers] carries on its shoulders the heavy gates of Gaza [a reference to the Biblical story of Samson]? Beyond the borderline there surges a sea of hatred and revenge against us; a revenge that is only waiting for our alertness to slacken . . ."

It was highly unusual – in the Israel of 1956 – for an official voice to pause and assume the perspective of the enemy. Even more unusual was Dayan's refusal to describe the situation in terms of the prevailing self-exculpatory categories of the type: "They rejected the partition plan, not we" and "Who started the war anyway?"

Dayan understood the geography and the psychology which made Gaza different from all other Palestinian exiles. The Palestinians outside the cities of Lebanon were proscribed and restricted by apartheid-style laws. But even so, there were plenty of escape hatches for the ingenious. Palestinians in Lebanon could rise to power, riches and influence and move away from the squalor without leaving the country. So could their brethren in Damascus and Amman. But in Gaza there was nowhere to go physically, and there was nowhere to go socially. After the UNEF-administered border controls began to function in 1957, Gaza became a restricted area in the obvious sense of the word. But it was already a banishment in terms of social mobility and opportunities. The Egyptians, sometimes in tandem with old rich Gazan families, really functioned as a superior caste, controlling and taxing every economic initiative, from prostitution – the cheap brothels of Gaza were well known in Cairo and drew many visitors – to valuable and beneficial projects. Abu Monzer, a brilliant engineer from Rafah, told me in 1982:

> "The Egyptians, with the bakshish they demanded, would bleed your project dry before you could launch it. All the sheep you would have to slaughter and all the feasts you had to arrange and all the gifts you carried to the Military Governor on his birthday were just the beginning. That's why Palestinians from Gaza made it big wherever they went. Having worked under the Egyptians, they were like long-distance runners who have trained at high altitudes. At ground-level conditions they were unstoppable."

For years, Yasser Arafat and the PLO were interlocking concepts. *Abu 'Ammar* and *al-munazzama* – "the Organisation", the colloquial shorthand for the PLO – were unthinkable without the other. But that isn't how it began. The PLO was created by the Arab leaders, led on by Egypt's Gamal Abdul Naser, in early 1964. The stated purposes were lofty, but one of the undeclared hopes of the new Palestinian umbrella organisation was to counter the growing influence of Arafat's Saudi-financed and unpredictable al-Fatah group.

Arafat wanted sponsors and donors, but he accepted no patrons. The cause of Palestine would not be administered by the foreign offices of the Arab states or by Palestinian puppets such as the PLO figurehead Ahmad Shukeiry, anointed by Nasser. At the time, when Egyptian state security agents uncovered Fatah men in Gaza they jailed them, if not for long. There was little Arafat could do about that. But he never accepted the PLO – unless it was taken over and run by himself. He would have his way, sooner than anyone expected.

The PLO made little headway in Gaza. Ahmad Shukeiry hailed from an aristocratic northern Palestine family, whose ancestors had sat in the

Ottoman parliament and owned large tracts of land between Acre and Haifa. The men around him in the first edition of the PLO leadership were mostly middle-class Hashemite or Nasserist loyalists from the West Bank or Gazan provincial elites. There was little to endear them to the impoverished Gazan refugees with their predominant fellah and southern Palestine background. The Fatah triumvirate, on the other hand, did fire the imagination of Gazans. To begin with they were known locally and all had a Gazan past: Arafat, because of his family roots, Salah Khallaf and Khalil al-Wazir, because they had fled to Gaza in 1948, lived there as refugees and infiltrated the border areas as fedayeen – until Nasser silenced the Gazan front by turning over patrolling to the UN in 1957. When the PLO was created, the regular Palestinian force in Gaza, the PLA, was formally incorporated into the new body in order to give it some substance beyond Shukeiry's grandiloquence. In reality, of course, the PLA remained under total Egyptian control. Gazan units were even sent to Yemen to fight in Egypt's proxy war against Saudi Arabia there, something which generated many bitter jokes in Gaza: "Here we are, on the doorstep of the Israelis, but prevented from fighting them by the Egyptians – who ship us across the sea in order to fight other Arabs!"

# 11

# Israeli Conquest and Occupation, 1967–1971

*Some in the defence establishment, some in academic circles, lobbied vigorously for the establishment of a Palestinian state during those "virgin weeks" of occupation (in 1967). People still argue whether that was a golden opportunity squandered, or an unrealistic pipe dream. The Defence Minister, Moshe Dayan, pleaded for the prompt establishment of Palestinian self-rule in the conquered territories, but met with little enthusiasm in the cabinet.*

Returning from work on May 16, 1967, Major General Indar Jit Rikhye, the Indian commander of the UN forces in Sinai and the Gaza Strip, was preparing for an afternoon of golf. (The game was played on the landing strips of the old airfield near Gaza city. As there was no grass, greens were made from pieces of wall-to-wall carpet, unrolled and carried by barefoot Palestinian caddies.) The general, an energetic and competent professional, took great pride in the achievements of UNEF in the Sinai and around the Strip, where an exemplary calm reigned, in stark contrast to the increasing cross-border violence along the other armistice lines.

But as Rikhye was about to leave his villa near the summit of Gaza hill, he was called back by a servant. There was an urgent phone call. On the end of the line was his Egyptian colleague Ibrahim Sharkawy, who told him to stay put, because a special courier from Cairo was on his way, by military airplane, with "a very important communication".

Some time later the messenger, another general, handed Rikhye a short note from the Egyptian Chief of Staff: "I have given instructions to all UAR armed forces to be ready for action against Israel . . . our troops are already concentrated in Sinai on our eastern border . . . I request that you issue orders to withdraw all [UN] troops immediately."

Rikhye described the note as "a shattering blow". He concluded, on the spot, that "with UNEF's withdrawal, war would be inevitable". Rikhye refused to evacuate any UN soldiers until receiving explicit orders from New York. But his estimate was correct. The die was cast. The crisis snowballed out of control so fast that Rikhye did not even manage to get his peacekeepers out of harm's way.

In retrospect, the Egyptian president's eviction of UNEF appears suicidal. But while Israel, the UN and Egypt had profited from the calm along the Israel–Egypt lines, Abdel Nasser was the only partner to the deal who had also paid a heavy price. Ever since international forces were stationed along the Egyptian–Israeli lines, Nasser had been taunted by his rivals in the Arab world for "taking shelter behind the UN"; for "emasculating the Palestinian resistance" and "guaranteeing Israel's security". Such rhetoric was not the prerogative of Yasser Arafat and the radicals. Whenever Nasser meddled in Jordanian or Saudi affairs, the media of those countries would lash out viciously on the matter of UNEF in Gaza. (UNEF's role in the Sinai was less controversial, because it did not involve the suppression of Palestinian armed struggle.) There were thousands of armed Palestinians under Egyptian command but their only conquests, according to the hecklers, were the wide boulevards of Gaza City, where the refugees were allowed to let off steam with tiresome regularity during ever-repeated manifestations. In the words of one UN officer: "Thousands of the town's citizens trod the macadamised roads on festival occasions and on days of political demonstrations; cubs, scouts, girl guides, students, auxiliary force cadets, gymnasts, industrial and agrarian workers, soldiers, dignitaries and folk in colourful uniforms and Arab dress, carrying a medley of coloured flags or with weapons slung over their shoulders. They marched in procession roaring, 'We shall return . . . '".

The most elaborate event in this vein fell every year on May 15, when PLO leader Ahmad Shukeiry arrived to give his grand speeches – scornfully dismissed by those Palestinian factions which actually fought Israel – about throwing the Jews into the sea. But when the war finally came, the reviled Palestinian Liberation Army of Gaza would acquit itself far better than any of the defamers had expected. As the Swedish UNEF guards by "King's Gate" – the check-post on the Gaza–Tel Aviv road – were withdrawn on May 19, the PLA took up positions next to the line, within speaking distance of the Israeli forces on the other side.

The Gaza Strip was the first territory conquered by Israel during its six-day blitz in June 1967. On the morning of June 5, the Strip was severed between Khan Yunes and Rafah, by tanks and armoured vehicles racing towards the Mediterranean. But the Israeli chief of staff Yizhak Rabin did not give the go-ahead for a conventional conquest of the Strip. He knew that the Palestinians and the Egyptians were well dug in and possessed impressive firepower. The Arab strongholds in Khan Yunes, Rafah and Gaza City could only be overrun at a high cost, in terms of casualties, time and equipment. "Let's leave Gaza encircled and carry on with the desert war in the Sinai," Rabin told Shayke Gavish, the head of the southern command. "Seeing the full picture, the Gazan commanders will surely surrender."

But as soon as the fighting units of Gaza got word of the Israeli air attacks against Egyptian air bases their field cannons and mortar batteries unleashed a rain of projectiles over the Israeli border settlements, causing great damage to livestock and property. Several groups of Palestinian fedayeen entered Israel and placed landmines along the main roads to Ashkelon and Netivot. There were enough Arab armoured forces in the Strip to carry out offensive operations and, rather than evacuating Israeli settlements, Rabin reluctantly gave the order to start operations against the Strip.

The battles for the three main Gazan cities were among the bloodiest of the short war. Israeli military historians agree that the Palestinian soldiers fought with great courage and tenacity. The defence of the Strip was the responsibility of several units of the 20th Palestinian division, two infantry battalions, two small armoured battalions, two field cannon battalions, two brigades of national guards, three reserve infantry battalions, a commando unit called 329, the fedayeen battalion 141 and five "popular resistance" battalions hastily trained and armed since the outbreak of the crisis.

The brevity of the war gave the impression of an Israeli walkover. Palestinian nationalist chroniclers, who usually fervently highlight instances of anti-Zionist resistance, have not done justice to the PLA's performance during the first three days of battle. On the eve of June 5, the first day of the war, Israeli forces were at the gates of Khan Yunes, Gaza City and of Rafah, the latter being the best-defended stronghold, surrounded by twelve kilometres of tank-traps, dug-down field cannons, communication trenches and mine-fields. The anti-tank batteries were efficient against the Israeli Centurions and Pattons and pillars of black smoke rose against the sky, visible from Gaza City and from deep inside Israel. Rafah was the first large battle of the June 1967 war. It was really two battles, one north and one south of the city. In Khan Yunes and near the Ali al-Muntar hill southeast of Gaza City, equally bloody battles raged. The defenders were superior in firepower, but they were cut off from reinforcements and supplies and they had no air support – the Egyptian air force having been annihilated before the ground war started. Thus the Israeli Air Force was free to play the role of flying artillery, turning all Egyptian Army vehicles into sitting ducks. Most of them were abandoned, with a crippling loss of mobility. Towards sunset on June 6, the second day of the war, Israeli forces were inside Gaza City and Rafah, although they would face snipers and fedayeen for days and weeks. But Khan Yunes beat back a third Israeli assault and was not taken until June 7. Shortly before that the Egyptian military governor surrendered and was taken prisoner.

In Gaza City, the Israelis made their provisional headquarters at the Sheherazade hotel overlooking the beach; in Khan Yunes the local girls' school Haifa was set aside for the same purpose. Later, when the British Tegart forts, damaged in the fighting, were repaired, the military government was installed there, notably in the Saraya building in Gaza City. The local and the foreign press were allowed inside the Gaza Strip almost immediately, long before it was reasonably safe. A Canadian reporter was killed by a plastic mine and for several days reporters had to keep their heads down as Israelis and Palestinians exchanged sporadic small-arms fire. White rags were hoisted from many rooftops, but Israeli spokesmen admitted "small remaining pockets of resistance". Both international and Israeli correspondents were surprised by the relative cleanliness and order in UN-run Gaza. There was poverty but little misery and, apart from recurring but infrequent assaults on the UNRWA grain depots, there was order. The freshwater and sanitary infrastructures had already began to feel the pressures of overpopulation, especially during the rainy season. But the hardships of 1967 were trifling compared to the chronic emergencies of later years, when open cesspools expanded around refugee camps and threatened to engulf them. One Israeli journalis sounded almost indignant when reporting that Gaza seems "no poorer than the poor areas of Israel, while the posh streets of the Rimal quarter, where the Egyptian generals and the Gazan business elite resided, wouldn't shame any European country".

According to the UN, on the eve of occupation there were 450,000 residents in the Gaza Strip, 315,000 of whom were refugees. (This was well below a third of the 2009 figure). When the Israelis made their first census the numbers dropped, supposedly because families living on UN rations had been reluctant to report their dead elders and face a reduction in their daily fare.

As the last guerrillas were flushed out the curfew was gradually eased and the Strip's inhabitants were allowed to resume their day-to-day affairs. The two sides warily eyed each other. As in 1956, the locals were eager to do business with the Israeli tourists. But beyond buying and selling, the Gazans treaded warily. The Israeli killings of disarmed fedayeen in 1956 and the gruesome Egyptian reckoning with all those who had accepted posts in the short Israeli administration of 1956–57, were still fresh in local memory.

Several Israeli journalists noted that, unlike in East Jerusalem, Bethlehem and Hebron, there were few smiles or attempts at fraternising. Looks were sullen, as if by decree. Few of the young Israelis patrolling the streets, still giddy with victory, would have grasped the ominous symbolism, from a Palestinian point of view, of the encounter. Eight years later, Abu Hani, a sardine fisherman from the Shaati camp, told me about the strange morning when he first found himself face to face with the Israelis:

> "I was a kid of nine when we left Salame [a village between Jaffa and Tel Aviv] in late 1947. I had no real memory of the Jews. I grew up with the

dreams and slogans about us returning home. I had the most concrete visions of returning, of shady afternoons under the old *Jumeiz* tree, of living in a big house again. I was perfectly prepared for that to happen in 1967. And then, what happened? Instead of us returning and driving them away *they* come here and start running Gaza! I recognised the smiles of triumph and relief on the faces of those young Israeli soldiers – those were *our* smiles, the smiles we had prepared for our glorious day of return, the smiles of victory we had painted on the walls of the UNRWA schools as children. I suddenly felt like a fool for all my dreaming."

On June 11, the Gaza municipal council was summoned for its first meeting under Israeli rule. The Israeli commander present, reserve lieutenant-colonel Yizhak Moda'i, later a well-known Likud politician, greeted the assembly and mayor Ragheb al-Alami expressed thanks to the Israeli authorities for "their proper conduct", i.e. for the absence of rape and looting. The two local bus companies, many of whose vehicles had been damaged in the fighting, were given permission to raise the fare from one piaster to two. All but one of the 150 native policemen in Khan Yunes were allowed by the Israelis to resume work. Seen against the background of later events, these first tentative interchanges seem almost idyllic. This was partly due to the scant damage caused by the fighting. There were power failures which went on for some weeks but, with few exceptions, schools, shops and government offices were back to their normal schedule before the end of June.

There was, we now know, a group of Israelis, some in the defence establishment, some in academic circles, who lobbied vigorously for the establishment of a Palestinian state during those "virgin weeks" of occupation. People still argue whether that was a golden opportunity squandered, or an unrealistic pipe dream. The Defence Minister, Moshe Dayan, who had been forced upon Prime Minister Levi Eshkol by a public outcry on the eve of the war, pleaded for the prompt establishment of Palestinian self-rule in the conquered territories, but met with little enthusiasm in the cabinet. The feeling in the government was that the new situation was temporary, and that there was no sense in creating facts on the ground in areas whose future was yet to be decided. In a 1969 conversation with historian Shabtai Teveth, Dayan sketched the respective positions thus: "The government majority assumed that we, because of our massive victory, would be able to dictate [both] the borders with our neighbours and the future of the Palestinians under our control." Dayan's view was that the world would never accept this, and that Israel, therefore, had to take steps to make any new order more palatable to the Arabs and the international community.

After the Arab League's famous three "No's" in early September 1967

– "no" to negotiations with Israel, to recognition of it, or peace with it – the feeling grew in Israel that time was on its side. The incipient settlement movement, which would not begin to polarise public opinion for another few years, was the main benefactor of the Arabs' blanket refusal.

We do not know if peace was a real possibility, but we do know for certain that the complications of occupation surfaced almost immediately. At the second session of the Gazan municipal council, on June 19, the temporary Military Governor Moshe Goren warned local leaders that the curfew would not be eased if they did not show more vigour in collecting hidden arms and keeping down the looting of stores. A week later, Goren complained that there were "thousands of members of Ahmed Shukeiry's PLO movement and large amounts of arms hidden by the local population".

The gentlemen of the municipal council were mostly doctors, businessmen and scions of grand old Gazan families. They had been hand-picked by the Egyptians and had little legitimacy in the eyes of the people, especially of the refugees. They were of course all *muwatinin* – from the original families of Gaza, whose daughters were rarely allowed to marry a refugee. Not all of those leaders had been happy with the way the Egyptians had armed and trained the refugees. The rise of the PLO, still an Egyptian plaything rather than the independent organisation it would become under Arafat, was viewed by dignitaries and entrenched interests as a de-stabilising factor.

But even so, any Israeli hopes of mobilising the city council aristocrats against the PLO were overly sanguine. The mayors of the Gaza Strip towns had no guns at their disposal, except for a few hundred lightly armed local policemen, and their chief ambition was certainly not to team up with the Israelis, but to avoid being branded as collaborators if the Egyptians returned. If the Israelis wanted to disarm the Palestinian fighters, they would have to do it by themselves. The Shabak, as the Shin Beth security service came to be called after 1967, spun informer networks across the taken territories. Much of the PLO and PLA organisations were destroyed and many weapons found.

But the Strip was never completely disarmed, and unannounced arms searches, with the sealing-off of entire blocks, tiresome queuing and sudden curfews, became part of daily life. Penalties for illegal possession of arms soon soared from 2 or 3 years, at the outset, to fifteen years in jail. But arms found their way into the Strip in much the same manner as they do today, via the sea and the desert. When the militants ran out of hand grenades they invented a substitute, a TNT-filled Pepsi-Cola can which seems to have been quite effective. One such attack had the potential of ruining the workdays of thousands. On January 11, 1968, 250 grams of TNT in a soft-drink can exploded near an Israeli patrol. It was hurled by someone seen escaping in the direction of Shaati, the large refugee camp on the seashore north of Gaza City. All men aged 17 to 50 in that section of the camp were rounded up, taken to a stockade and interrogated. A week earlier, houses had been blown up in the village of Beit Hanun and in the refugee camp of Jebaliya in reprisal for landmine attacks against Israeli trucks. In addition, a week-long ban on leaving the Strip was imposed.

The Israelis brought draconian, often collective, punishment and a new administrative order whose intricacies could not be negotiated with the time-honoured measures of string-pulling and graft. But they also fought polio and TB, repaired schools and hospitals, relaxed censorship and – a minor revolution – opened up the whole country, including the newly-occupied areas of Jerusalem and the West Bank, for travel. Thousands of Gazan families were only an hour's bus ride away from their former homes. Many made the trip and returned stunned, having found their houses gone or with Israeli families living in them. Travelling also brought about the partial reunification of the Palestinian people. Since 1948, contacts between Gazans, West Bankers and Israeli Arabs had been sporadic, cumbersome and indirect. Now, with the "open borders" policy proclaimed by Defence Minister Moshe Dayan, Gazans could visit Jerusalem, Nablus and Nazareth. Economic, academic, political and religious cooperation flourished – the future Hamas founder Ahmad Yassin was one of the first young Gazans to tour the northern parts of the homeland. Thousands of Gazans went to live in West Bank cities, hundreds of Gazan youths were sent to vocational schools there, and all Gazan psychiatric cases were sent to Bethlehem for treatment. In addition to the Gazans travelling to Israel and the West Bank, a growing number of visitors from Arab countries – 110,000 in 1971 – were given tourist visas each summer. The vast majority of them were Palestinians.

Many thousands of Gazan refugees were also forcibly moved from their camps to the Aqabat Ja'aber and Tel al-Sultan camps near Jericho, which had been partly abandoned during the 1967 war. Many of them refused to live in the scorching climate, with little hope of employment, and crossed the Allenby bridge into Jordan. The Jordanians accused Israel of trying to export the refugees and closed their border to Gazans.

The most comprehensive change of the Six Day War was invisible at first, but its implications would be overwhelming. In May 1967, the salary of a farmhand in Israeli agriculture was between twenty and thirty Israeli pounds a day. In August the same year, it was seven pounds, sometimes as low as three pounds for women and minors, after the job-contractor had pocketed his share. This was more than a brusque economic turn. For both Gazan and Israeli society, it would amount to a cultural revolution. In Zionist thinking, and in Israeli praxis, there had been nothing disreputable in farm labour, construction, street-sweeping or garbage collection. Ever since the second wave of Jewish immigration, which began in the early years of the 20th century, an almost Soviet-style cult of physical labour had animated the Zionist enterprise. Well into the 1950s, muscular, square-jawed labour heroes swinging pitch-forks and sledge-hammers starred on the election posters of the socialist parties and, until the 1967 war, physical labour was amply rewarded. This was not merely a matter of ideology. The powerful labour union Histadrut doubled as the country's largest employer *and* largest investor, and jealously guarded the privileges of blue-collar workers.

But now, the market refashioned the economic landscape – and defined the future framework of Israeli–Gazan coexistence. With Dayan's decision to open borders and markets, the Strip became a part, if not a partner, of the Israeli economy. In time, Gazan labour in Israel would become infamous, the mere words calling to mind the endless queues of sleepless workers lining up at dusk for the security control at the Beit Hanun (Erez) checkpoint, before being allowed to continue towards Tel Aviv. But the beginnings were less grim. Soon after the war, with several harvests approaching, the kibbutzim (collective settlements) and the moshavim (cooperative settlements) east of the Strip received offers from job contractors in Khan Yunes, Rafah and Gaza. At first the kibbutzim, in an ideological reflex, refused to take part in "unworthy forms of exploitation". But other farms began to experiment with Palestinian labour and quickly reduced their costs. A Gazan, especially if he had some skill, could also look around Tel Aviv by himself for a job and, supply and demand allowing, bargain for a decent salary. But the agro-labourers were unable to do that. A farm does not need individuals, it needs three hundred pickers for two weeks or a month. That is where the *ra'is*, or job contractor, comes in. Let it be said that the reviled ra'is-system is not an Arab invention. It appears everywhere where labour is abundant, land ownership limited and demand scarce or seasonal, such as in rural Brazil or Paraguay or in Italy before the great emigrations. In a society where influence, opportunity and every other resource are shared out via client–patron relationships, one should not expect a free labour market. A few years after the UNEF force had been installed in Rafah in 1957, its commander discovered that most of his local employees, cooks, gardeners and cleaners had been subcontracted by a local ra'is who did no work himself but lived on the commission he skimmed off their salaries. The Anglo-Saxon work-ethic of the commander rebelled against what he saw as a racket, and he put an end to it. The move was resented by many locals, who regarded the practice as part of life.

Soon the kibbutzim which had been too noble to hire Gazan labour found themselves in a quandary. Their crops competed on the market with the produce of neighbouring moshavim and other settlements which did employ Gazans, and the temptation grew to make ideological adjustments. After a few years and many stormy debates, all but the most rigorous southern kibbutzim, those of the Hashomer Ha-Tsa'ir movement, had begun to base their agrobusinesses on Gazan labour.

The rapid, almost frantic entry of Gazan labour into the Israeli economy was due to extraordinary circumstances created by the war. Normally Israel did not cry out for workers, but for technology. It was, and remained well into the 1980s, a labour-extensive economy whose main industries thrived only thanks to an extremely protectionist tariff-system. Very little of the country's industrial output could compete internationally, and it depended, for its foreign currency earnings, on a few water-wasting crops, mostly citrus and cotton. But now, in the euphoria and confidence following the 1967 war, the economy suddenly expanded on an unseen scale. Enormous public works, not least the upgrading of the Egyptian airfield at Bir Gafgafa in central Sinai, the roads and the fortifications along the Suez Canal and, a few years later, the beginning of large-scale settlement of Palestinian lands, stirred the lethargic labour market. Simultaneously, many of the kibbutzim, exposed to tougher competition from Moroccan and Egyptian orange and cotton-growers, took their first steps towards diversification and industrialisation. Particularly on collective settlements, where earnings were shared, it became an increasingly tempting proposition to let the Gazans pick the fruit and direct available hands to other pursuits.

The decision to hire Gazan farm-hands was hard to stomach for many kibbutzniks. Zvi Miller, a member of the left-wing kibbutz Urim recalls:

> "We were appalled by the low wages of the Gazans. In order to raise their consciousness we told them – they knew their deal was miserable but they did not know the figures – how the contractors fleeced them. We helped organise a strike against the ra'is. He was always around, measuring the yield of each picker. When confronted with the striking pickers the ra'is promptly paid up and we, naïvely, celebrated the triumph of universal solidarity. We never saw any of our striking companions again. They were on the blacklist of that ra'is, and probably on the blacklists of all the other contractors, too."

In the beginning the Palestinian resistance groups issued dire warnings to those working in Israel. Grenades were thrown at buses transporting labourers to Israel and at the queues of breadwinners by the Erez checkpoint. The PLO feared the vision of Moshe Dayan – a vision now being recycled by Benjamin Netanyahu – of defusing the conflict by economic means, tempting the Palestinians with material progress to forgo their national aspirations. In retrospect, Dayan's project seems sanguine, almost quixotic. But at the time, Israel's modest investments in the Strip and the scramble of Palestinians to Israeli work-places frightened the exiled leadership, with good reason. In the summer of 1971, the deputy leader of the Marxist PFLP movement, Fawzi Alwahidi, was given three life-sentences by an Israeli military tribunal for having killed three Gazans, one of them a woman, who had worked in Israel. During the trial it became known that Alwahidi had himself worked in Israel for eighteen months.

The exposure to Israeli markets raised the cost of living in the Strip, and the only way to adapt was to work in Israel, or for Israel. The PLO, gradually realising that its degree of popular support was not threatened by the new economical realities, stopped defining the workers as traitors in their leaflets and, during 1972–3, the campaign against them fizzled out. But not all work was underpaid or demeaning. The dream for a young Gazan was a steady job in an Israeli factory, which also made him eligible for the health and pension programmes of the Israeli National Insurance Institute. It reached the point where the graduates of Gaza's vocational and technical schools refused to work in the Strip, where daily pay in a workshop reached 25 Israeli Pounds in the mid-seventies. At the new Israeli industrial complex at the Erez checkpoint, built specifically to facilitate the use of Gazan labour, pay was 35–40 Israeli pounds a day. But ambitious Gazan mechanics and engineers would only work there as a last resort. I remember Bashir Abu Nahel, a young man from the Shaati Camp who started out as a complete underling at the Of-Or factory in the Israeli development town of Ofakim, taking home 20 pounds a day. Some time later, he earned 100 pounds a day, with social security and health insurance for his family laid on.

There were many such young men. The Israeli State Employment Agency had offices in the main Gazan towns. There were possibilities of real economic integration, and there was plenty of good will on both sides. But such prospects were bedevilled by the political status of Gaza. The Israeli government clearly wanted to hang on to the Strip after the 1967 war, as eagerly as they wanted to be rid of it later. Even the left-wing Mapam party at first insisted that the Strip should remain under Israeli control. The demographic implications of keeping Gaza would have been easy to calculate, but they were curiously absent from the Israeli debate.

Affairs in the Strip never came close to the degree of relative calm achieved in the West Bank. The PLA units had been defeated and many of its men killed, but they were not destroyed. In the autumn of 1968, the Israelis were shocked to discover that all the top magistrates in the Strip, approved by its military government, were actually al-Fatah agents, who fed – via runners who moved between the Strip and the West Bank – all important information to Yasser Arafat. There was never one calm week in the Strip, and during 1969 the Israelis seemed to be losing their grip. There were days when there was no bus service between Gaza City and nearby Beersheba in Israel, because the Israeli drivers from the Egged cooperative refused to enter the Strip, where their blue buses were choice grenade targets. Life in the urban centres and the refugee camps was becoming an endless run of explosions, curfews, searches, expulsions, deportations, closures and special decrees. The railway line was blown up as soon as it was put together and not even the main street of Gaza City, the 'Umar al-Mukhtar, was safe for travelling. The Red Cross had its headquarters in a villa on that street. But the surrounding gardens were ideal for lobbing grenades at Israeli patrols, which promptly responded with automatic fire. In the summer of 1970, their nerves in tatters, the Swiss clerks moved out.

At this stage, the PLO was no longer an Egyptian puppet. Yasser Arafat, the Fatah leader who took over the PLO in 1969, was one of few Arab leaders whose reputation passed untarnished through the 1967 purgatory. Slowly but surely he gained international recognition for his movement. Apart from a few pro-Jordanian upper-class families, support for the PLO in Gaza was overwhelming and growing, especially among the refugees. The Israelis were in a bind. The following casualty numbers give an idea of the trend. They include Gazan civilians, Israeli civilians and Israeli security personnel, but not armed Palestinians.

| | Dead | Wounded |
|---|---|---|
| 1967 (June–Dec.) | 0 | 54 |
| 1968 | 10 | 48 |
| 1969 | 19 | 254 |
| 1970 | 103 | 623 |

# 12

## Ariel Sharon's "Dirty War"

### The Beginning of Jewish Settlement, 1971–1972

*Apart from the depressing sight of barbed-wire mazes, the inconveniences and the road-block harassments, the Israeli colonies had deeper ideological and psychological implications. The contrast between the prospering settlements, with their lordly privileges and their hemmed-in neighbours, was too stark not to cause resentment. Clearly, the good life of the settlements was a graphic daily reminder to the Gazans of their own narrowing prospects.*

Apart from withdrawing from the Strip, which no one in Israel advocated, there seemed to be only two choices: to open up a political process in Gaza or to try to crush the resistance. The popularity of the PLO blocked the political option. The prime mover behind the decision to use force on a massive scale was general Ariel Sharon, the 1967 war hero who took over the Southern Command of the Israel Defence Force (IDF) in 1969. But he did not get the go-ahead until the summer of 1971.

Ariel Sharon's "dirty war" against PLO–Fatah would become well known, but it has not been researched in any detail, as the relevant documents remain classified. Many decisions were probably never put on paper, but settled verbally between Sharon and Defence Minister Dayan. True, Israeli politicians back then did not leak secrets the way they do today, and there were no human rights delegations, Palestinian photographers or communications networks at hand to document events. But it is still remarkable, from our vantage point, that such an ambitious and far-reaching military operation could begin, and continue for weeks, without making a blip on international news-screens.

The objective of the campaign was to put an end to the near-freedom of action enjoyed by Palestinian fighters inside the refugee camps. With time, Ariel Sharon and his ebullient approach would come to be characterised as "bulldozer-like". That metaphor originated with the real bulldozers sent in to the most combative refugee camps, Shaati, Jebaliya and Rafah. Circular patrol roads were laid around the camps, as well as a grid of them superimposed on the densely populated refugee slums; 12 kilometres for each camp. The destruction of buildings for this purpose made more than ten thousand people homeless. Most of them were resettled in the Brazil and Canada camps in Rafah, some were deported to the Sinai desert, and several thousand received new homes in El-Arish, the coastal town in northern Sinai, in the former dwellings of Egyptian officers and clerks.

The euphemism employed by the Israeli army to describe these changes was "thinning out". After some weeks, Transport Minister Shimon Peres, chairman of the ministerial committee responsible for the Gaza refugees, announced that 2,000 refugees had been relocated to El Arish, and that another 2,000 were on their way. According to Peres they had "abandoned resistance to the project, seeing that they were receiving housing far superior to their former dwellings". But in an interview with Israeli radio, one Jebaliya resident, Mustafa, denied these claims:

> "[We] received a three-room apartment with toilet facilities, running water and electricity. The building is better than the one I lived in before, but it is not my home. We were told there was plenty of work [in El Arish] in road-building and at the Municipality – at 3.10 Israeli pounds a day. In Jebaliya, I could live without working. Everything was at the expense of UNRWA, education, health . . . I could live for a whole month on a few days' earnings. Here I am isolated. My father, my brother, the rest of my family still live in the Strip . . . I don't know El Arish and its customs . . . I am cut off and without hope."

On August 14, 1971, all the Palestinian groups in Gaza sponsored a strike against the evictions. Shops were closed, taxis stopped running and most of the 15,000 Strip residents working in Israel stayed at home. But the strike quickly came to grief. The shutters of the closed shops were welded together and the owners were forced to donate large sums to a local orphanage. The cars of the striking taxi-drivers were impounded and were only returned after they had apologised to the military governor, general Yizhak Pundak.

On September 7, the "thinning out" was officially suspended, due to a "temporary shortage of alternative housing"; 1,700 families, 6 per cent of the entire refugee population, was said to have been relocated. In fact, many of the homeless had rejected the Israeli alternatives and taken loans in order to build their own homes inside the Strip and avoid ending up in El-Arish. By then, most of the new, electrically lit, patrol-road grid was already in place. On September 19, rather late in the day, Israel received a UN reaction. In a report, Secretary General U Thant called upon the General Assembly to "ensure the immediate halt of the destruction of refugee homes in the Gaza Strip".

The evictions and the patrol roads were only a prelude to the showdown against the PLO envisaged by Ariel Sharon. The grenade attacks and the firefights in the camps continued but, from the Israeli viewpoint, in a drastically improved setting. As the camps were combed by soldiers in armoured patrol carriers, Palestinian casualties soared while Israeli losses became a rare event. Sharon led the troops on in person as huge arms caches were uncovered and many of the Palestinian commanders were killed, caught or forced to flee. Militarily, these were desperate times for the PLO. A year earlier, during "Black September", Jordan's special forces had killed hundreds of armed Palestinians and driven their leaders out of the country. The following September, in 1971, was no less black for the PLO: its last pockets of resistance in Jordan were being mopped up in the northwest of the country. The Israelis made psychological use of this during the fighting in Gaza. The leaflets dropped over the camps said, "You know what happened in Jordan. Don't waste your lives in vain. Lay down your weapons, come forward and you will be fairly treated."

It appeared that armed resistance was nearly broken. Every day, Palestinian fighters were captured or killed. During October and November 1971, there were no Israeli losses at all in the Strip and one of the local commanders, Ziyad Husseini of the PLF, wrote in desperation to the PLO leadership in Beirut: "All our bases are being uncovered, we are totally paralysed . . . cannot carry out any operations." One particularly useful innovation, frequently employed in later years, was the use of Arabic-speaking Israeli soldiers, dressed as locals. Israel soon felt confident enough gradually to relax military rule. Egyptian weekly magazines were allowed in, shops in the main towns were allowed to stay open until midnight, and the nightly curfew was reduced to three hours, midnight–3a.m. Another tell-tale sign of the PLO defeat was the wealthy orange grower Rashad al-Shawa's decision, in late September 1971, to accept the Israeli offer to lead a new municipal government in Gaza City. Rashad al-Shawa was an extremely wily and prudent politician, and he only accepted the Israeli offer after months of reflection. Eighty years earlier, his legendary father Haj Sa'id had been the mayor of Ottoman Gaza. Two of his brothers had been broken, one of them had lost his mind, after being tortured by the Egyptians for collaboration with Israel and Jordan.

The possibility of an Egyptian return was never dismissed by the traditional, non-refugee Gazan leaders courted by the Israelis. During the Israeli summer offensive against the PLO in 1971, Egyptian president Anwar Sadat revived the Gaza Bureau of his Interior Ministry, a signal to both Gazans and Israelis that Egypt had not renounced its interests in the Strip. When Moshe Dayan commented on this in the Knesset, his words were meant to reassure the Gazans: "This would mean that anyone who is in line for appointment as mayor of Gaza, or any other job in the Strip, will be subjected to prior approval from Cairo. Egypt wishes to tie the Strip to her apron strings again. We have to see to it that all such strings are severed." One such string was cut with the Israeli decision to make possession of Egyptian currency a criminal offence in the Strip.

Shawa said he would only consider taking on the job as mayor if the people pleaded with him to do so. A petition with 5,000 signatures was promptly produced – no big feat considering that the Shawa family businesses fed, directly or indirectly, a large part of the population of Gaza City.

Rashad al-Shawa was often portrayed by Palestinian radicals as a relic of a benighted class-system, or as an Israeli or Jordanian puppet – a view now replaced with a more balanced assessment. Shawa faced an infernally difficult situation, as a Jordanian loyalist trying to improve living conditions in the Strip without antagonising either the PLO, Israel or Egypt. From his first day in office, al-Shawa used his good offices with Israeli leaders, especially Moshe Dayan, to press for tangible reform in Gaza, especially for the social classes furthest removed from his own. The curfew was lifted during Ramadan; 300 administrative detainees – Gazans jailed without trial – were released; a green light was given for establishing the first Gazan University and the concrete walls screening off the Umar al-Mukhtar boulevard in Gaza City from its side-streets were pulled down. (They had been erected in 1969 to protect the traffic on the main thoroughfare from grenades.) To al-Shawa's critics, such achievements were meager sops won by cringing before the enemy, but the mayor's standing among ordinary Gazans improved. It did so even more after the first serious political crisis since the 1967 war, the Husseini affair.

After midnight on November 22, 1971, the Israeli military governor of the Strip, general Yizhak Pundak, was woken up by his staff. Rashad al-Shawa needed to speak to him urgently. The mayor, visibly shaken, told Pundak that the most wanted man in Gaza, the local leader of the PLF faction Ziyad Husseini, had just committed suicide in his – al-Shawa's – basement. The Israelis were aghast. What was a person like Husseini doing in "their" mayor's basement? Al-Shawa revealed that more than a month earlier Husseini had sought shelter in his home, relying on the mayor's commitment to the time-honoured laws of hospitality. While sheltering the wanted man al-Shawa had negotiated a deal with the Israelis and the PLO, giving free passage to Lebanon for the last Palestinian fighters in the Strip.

Al-Shawa's passport was confiscated and he was, without being arrested, subjected to several months of daily interrogations. Delegations of Gaza Strip mukhtars – village elders – pleaded with the Israelis to let him continue in office, and so did the Jews who had fled Gaza in 1929 and cherished the memory of how the Shawa family saved them from being lynched. In February 1972, al-Shawa was reinstated by Dayan. In August the same year, King Hussein of Jordan decided to issue passports to all residents of the Strip, provided al-Shawa vouched for the applicant's good conduct. In October, he was deposed for having disobeyed a military decree, but he would return. With the Israeli victory against armed groups in the Strip, the military option – even to those who approved of it in principle – lost all attraction. The shrewdest strategy, when you want to tempt guerillas and terrorists to abandon violence, is to offer them a non-violent, i.e. a political option. The Israelis, however, were unable to offer anything of the kind, since the only real issues in Palestinian politics were those which collided with Israel's ambitions in the Strip. With the political and the military venues blocked, the only form of well-being the Gazans could seek from the Israelis was material: higher income, better services and decent housing. We have seen how the Israelis tried to resettle Gazan camp residents in northern Sinai and in the Judean desert. But the most ambitious project was the construction of new neighbourhoods inside the Strip, two in Khan Yunes and one each in Rafah and Gaza City. Small plots were also offered camp-dwellers for the construction of private homes.

The Israelis, or at least the more clear-sighted among them, attached great importance to these efforts, precisely because they knew that material comfort was all that the Gazans were going to be offered. The best-case scenario, from the Israeli point of view, was that possession of their own homes would dilute refugee identity. Once they had something to lose, their motives to resist and their ambitions to return would fade, it was hoped. Such a reckoning may seem vain and naïve with hindsight, but the PLO regarded the Israeli housing and resettlement efforts with dread. The PLO knew, just as the Israelis knew, that the refugees and their plight was the hub around which Palestinian national consciousness rotated. The Israelis hoped to drive a stake through the heart of that consciousness by replacing the refugees' attachment to lost homes inside Israel with a new, local, attachment.

At first the PLO came out strongly against the new neighbourhoods and branded those accepting the Israeli terms as traitors, but to no avail. Refugee families jumped at the opportunity to live in real homes with modern amenities. But on the whole, Israeli hopes were dashed. To be sure, the new neighbourhoods saw less radical resistance to the occupation than the camps. But I soon noticed during my visits to the showcase resettlement project Sheikh Radwan near Gaza city, that there was no corresponding change of attitudes. Later research by Norma Masriyeh has borne out this impression.

It is not impossible, however, that the Israelis could have lured the Gazans away from radical nationalism, had they acted with more foresight and less arrogance. One obvious strategy to win over the Gazans would have been to create real economic opportunities inside the Strip for the thousands of young Gazans returning from higher studies in Egypt and Israel. Another way would have been to abstain from colonising the overpopulated territory.

One day in late 1971 a New York-born kibbutznik on reserve duty in

Gaza was told to fence off large areas close to the beach between Rafah and Khan Yunes with barbed wire:

> "In the afternoon, Bedouin fishermen returned from their work. Their camels were loaded with fresh fish. There were forty of us soldiers, but I was the only one who spoke any Arabic. When I told the Bedouin that from now on they would have to make a detour of twelve kilometres to get where they wanted, there was a terrible scene. Ariel Sharon told us later that those Bedouin had no legal claims to the areas we had blocked off, they had only been there for thirty years and the best thing would be if they returned to the Sinai."

That was the beginning of the Israeli settlement drive in the Gaza Strip, a thirty-four year exercise in futility, waste and political folly. It was said in Israel in 2005, when Sharon evicted the Gaza settlers and razed their homes, that "the only man obstinate enough to bring about such an absurd enterprise in the first place was Sharon, just as he was the only one tough enough to uproot it once it had proven a success". (A success in terms of the settlers' export earnings from mangoes, yams and organic boutique herbs.) It is true that, in 1971, Sharon was no more than an area commander carrying out government policy and that he had no political power at the time. But he had not yet joined the anti-Labour coalition and still had plenty of influence with the Labour establishment. The settlers themselves, at least at the time of their eviction in 2005, mostly belonged to the ultra-nationalist fringe, but the decision to colonise the Strip was taken by a Labour government. In 1970, the remnants of the Jewish village Kfar Darom, conquered by the Egyptians in 1948, was turned into a "Nahal" military outpost. The historical task of Nahal units has been to prepare the ground for later civilian settlement, especially in peripheral or difficult areas. But Kfar Darom was not turned over to civilians until 1989, and there was really no sign of any settlement plans until October 19, 1971, when an official told the Israeli press that four thousand dunams, close to a thousand acres, were being fenced off for "future civilian use". All in all, according to this source, 8,400 acres in the area between Deir al-Balah and Rafah would be set aside for settlements. Most of the territory was dunes, but more than three thousand acres were farmland. The area in question was 34 square kilometres, almost 10 per cent of the Gaza Strip, and it would form the basis of the largest and most affluent Israeli settlement bloc, Gush Katif, which covered a large part of the Mawasi area, the breadbasket of the southern part of the strip.

According to official spokesmen the areas taken over were state lands, untilled and unused apart from the sporadic activities of Bedouin squatters. No more than 50 Arab families were affected by the measures, according to these sources. It is true that the Bedouin had no titles and no papers. But some of them had enjoyed the usufruct of the olive-, citrus- and date-groves from time immemorial, even though they still practiced nomadism. Most roaming Bedouin own, or control, some agricultural lands. Their wandering schedule is adapted to the growth cycles of their fruit trees, which are tended with the same care as those of the settled population. Their ownership is anchored in long-recognised tribal codes and customs. But the victims of Sharon's evictions were mostly from the Malalha tribe, which had entered the Strip recently, as squatters, during Egyptian rule, and whose claims were not backed up even locally. (Before being driven off lands by the Israelis, they had often already been pushed aside by the wealthy landowners in the area.)

A few Bedouin received a pittance of compensation, but the colonisation programme met no real obstacle. Israeli courts have rarely ruled in favour of undocumented traditional rights. The central factor here was neither rights nor titles, but the simple fact that nowhere else in the Strip, except in what became Gush Katif, could a continuous and economically viable Israeli enclave have been superimposed on the slender and problem-ridden territory.

The Israeli settlements in the Strip gave some Palestinians steady and comparatively well-paid jobs. The settlers of Gush Katif were not racists like those of Hebron and northern Samaria, to whom the humiliation of Palestinians has become part of the meaning of life. In spite of the fanaticism implicit in the whole endeavor – wedging in rural settlements between over-populated urban slums – the Gush Katif Jews were hard-working and non-violent people, who often enjoyed decent relationships with their Palestinian employees, most commonly from the Malalha Bedouin tribe which lived around the old Turkish railway station in Khan Yunes. I spent some time in the area in 1992, and noticed how the landless and often blue-eyed Malalha were at the very bottom of the local pecking order, barely respected even by the other Bedouin clans, who were mostly 1948 refugees from Beersheba. The Malalha were known for their physical beauty and for their willingness to toil. At private homes and coffee-houses, I was regaled with a reverse Cinderella-story, said to have occurred a year before. A young Malalha man had scratched his way to medical studies in Cairo. In the metropolis he had managed – an impossible feat inside the crowded Strip, where privacy is the rarest of commodities – to become friendly with a fellow student, a girl from the mighty al-Shawa family. The Shawas were naturally taken aback by the prospect of such an alliance, but the lovers held out against prejudice, married and made their lives in Cairo.

Perhaps the story was embellished, but the social circumstances that formed its backdrop were real enough. The family with whom I stayed were Beersheba Bedouins. The eldest daughter, a first-year high-school student, introduced me to the subtle distinctions of the local caste-system.

The difference between old non-refugee elite families – the Muwatinin – and the newcomers was amazing to observe. The refugee children and the "natives" attended different school systems during their elementary education and hardly met until high-school. My young informant told me: "The rich families, Aqaads, al-Astals, al-Farras and al-Aghas even speak differently. They go to Cairo for the weekend and return in European clothes while our mothers clean the floors of the Jews."

On the declarative level, the rich families, whose scions usually held important municipal posts, said all the right, pan-Palestinian things during their speeches at memorial day parades. But during private talks they would often let hear a nostalgic sigh when reminiscing about the good old days before their high-yield district had been overrun with landless and penniless countrymen.

These rich families were rich not only by Gazan standards. Next to the Jewish fields in the Mawasi, huge Palestinian cucumber, date, and banana plantations were spread out. Several of them had standing delivery contracts with the main Israeli juice-makers.

To those Palestinians who did not work at the Israeli colonies and enjoyed no spill-over effects from the new Israeli businesses, the settlements were constant thorns in the flesh. To protect the settlers from attacks at home or while driving, a new traffic and security zoning system was gerrymandered. The overriding motive of this system was the safety and convenience of the settlers, almost always at the expense of the convenience of the Palestinians living nearby. Suddenly the scenic route between Deir al-Balah and the Mawasi area was closed off for security reasons. These arrangements around the Katif Bloc disrupted life on all levels. During summer, the people of Khan Yunes, the second largest city in the Strip, were used to picnic in the "shalitat", the tourist bungalows built by the Egyptians in the 1950s. There was a kiosk, a coffee-house and a restaurant – specialising in the *Sreda*, the fat sardines from the Nile delta sizzling on the coals in clouds of smoke. Urchins with raspy town-crier voices offered soft-drinks and refreshments loaded onto donkeys. Young and old would gather under improvised sun-tents to listen to jokes and joha-stories from the old homes. But under the new regulations, Palestinians could not move along the beach, they could only spend time in certain specified areas. After a few hundred meters of jogging or walking they were forced to turn around by concertinas of barbed wire. Even the short trip to the beach became an ordeal, with tiresome road-block searches and ID-checks. The number of watchful Israeli border police on the assigned tourist stretches was another challenge to the holiday spirit.

Apart from the depressing sight of barbed-wire mazes, the inconveniences and the road-block harassments, the Israeli colonies had deeper ideological and psychological implications. The contrast between the prospering settlements, with their lordly privileges and their hemmed-in

# 13

# The Quiet Years, 1972–1986

*A week before the Israeli withdrawal: on April 12, 1982 youths in the refugee camp of Nuseirat carrying copies of the Qur'an and shouting "Allahu Akbar" clashed with Israeli security forces. The soldiers complained that they were unable to disperse the young firebrands, not even by tear-gas and shots in the air. It was a portent.*

The military option, after the 1971–72 Israeli campaign inside the refugee camps, was not viable for the decimated and disarmed Gazan groups. Neither were there any political options – other than hustling for patronage via the elite Gazan families, the military governor or the ever-present Shabak security service.

After the 1973 October war, Egyptian president Anwar Sadat began to put pressure on PLO leader Yasser Arafat to join him in a peace offensive against Israel. Sadat even threatened to cut off relations with the PLO unless Arafat supported him in his efforts. Similar pressure was also brought to bear on Arafat from Jordan. Arafat was not unwilling, though his inner circle recoiled in horror at the idea of a public recognition of Israel's right to exist. Arafat's prolonged foot-dragging on the peace issue was mainly tactical. He refused to be a secondary partner to negotiations masterminded by Sadat or King Hussein. (His refusal paid off in 1993, when Israel finally gave up its hopes of settling the Palestinian issue via non-Palestinian actors.)

In November 1977, stunning the region and the world, Sadat decided to go it alone. After his visit to Jerusalem and during the ensuing peace negotiations, Sadat tried to force the Israelis to settle the Palestinian problem along with the other issues on the table. The peace treaty between Israel and Egypt was concluded in late March 1979. Up until the last moment, Egypt fought hard to link its treaty obligations to Israel's implementation of the Palestinian autonomy plan.

The later famous "Gaza First" formula was first suggested by Egyptian negotiators at the Camp David talks in 1978. Palestinian self-rule would be tested in the Strip, and then extended to the West Bank, based on the lessons learned in Gaza. When Sadat hosted Prime Minister Menachem Begin in Aswan in January 1980, he repeated the proposal. Both Israelis and Palestinians were quick to suspect an Egyptian plot to reaffirm its former control of the Strip. The Israelis tenaciously resisted an Egyptian demand to establish a military liaison bureau in Gaza as part of the peace settlement, and the PLO weekly, *Filastin al-Thawra*, published in Beirut, denounced the "Gaza First" idea:

> "Why is Sadat reviving the idea now? . . . [he] believes that if he succeeds in applying self-rule in Gaza . . . he will be in a position to create a Palestinian alternative [to the PLO] that he and Begin could employ to provide cover for . . . fragmenting the Palestinian people's right to self-determination . . . "

The suspicions were not baseless. Today, in 2009, Egypt's government is insisting that the Strip is part of Palestine and thus by definition Israel's problem, to be sorted out with the Palestinians. Not so at the time of the first peace negotiations. Several Egyptian policy makers regarded the Strip as part of classical Egypt, basing the claim on the many pharaonic remnants on Gazan soil. During the 1970s, the Israeli archeaologist Trude Dotan dug up an impressive collection of human-face sarcophagi out of the dunes of Deir al-Balah, some with the royal scarab of Ramses II. These finds were given widespread publicity in Egypt, with an emphasis that was not exclusively archaeological.

Arafat was the only Arab leader who did not take part in the Arab world's boycott of Egypt after the peace with Israel. Undoubtedly he saw the opportunity which arose during the peace talks. Egypt could apply more pressure on Israel than the PLO could ever have mustered on its own. But Arafat was too isolated among his colleagues and in the region to have dared to break ranks and go along with Sadat. The first Palestinians who came out openly in favour of Sadat's initiative were branded traitors by the PLO. Some were hurt or killed, and all internal Palestinian debate on this important issue was silenced.

The only Palestinian leaders who insisted that the Egypt-Israel peace and the autonomy proposals were good things were the mayors of the main Gazan towns. They dared to do so because they possessed a real power-base of their own – and because they had Arafat's discreet permission. I spoke with Rashad Shawa, the mayor of Gaza City, soon after the March 1979 peace treaty. Naturally, his support for the peace process was qualified with the obligatory caveat of those days: "all moves must be coordinated with the PLO, the sole legitimate respresentative of the Palestinian people".

So, I asked Shawa, if such steps "must be coordinated", did that mean that he was in fact coordinating them with the PLO? Shawa, by necessity prevented from answering the question, smiled a sphinx-like smile. The issue was delicate, for just a stone's throw further down the Umar al-Mukhtar boulevard from Shawa's imposing office was the home of Dr Haidar Abdul Shafi, the head of the Red Crescent in the Strip and the most prominent PLO voice. He was set hard against the autonomy proposals and would settle for nothing less than a removal of the settlements and the establishment of a Palestinian state.

But in a typical example of open-ended Arafat diplomacy, both Shawa and Abdel Shafi were allowed to explore possibilities. Shawa was threatened but, like the other mayors, not harmed, most probably due to Arafat's protection. Both Suleiman al-Azaze in Deir al-Balah and Zarwal al-Astal in Khan Yunes were leaders of powerful landowning families, and both were outspoken champions of the "Gaza First" option. Al-Azaze even had a portrait of Sadat in his home, and when asked about the PLO threats he shrugged: "They can't just take over my town."

Zarwal al-Astal of Khan Yunes was just as defiant. He told me that it would have been madness to turn away and sulk when suddenly an opportunity presented itself to get rid of the hated Israeli colonies around Khan Yunes. The Israeli plantations brought jobs to lesser Gazans, but to the al-Astal clan, which owned much of the adjacent land and competed with the privileged Israeli settlers for water and markets, business and politics were thoroughly blended.

There was plenty of support for, or at least expectant curiosity about, Sadat's diplomatic manoeuvres and the "Gaza First" plan. Especially the 10,000 or so young Gazans who had lived in Cairo and had Egyptian degrees spoke warmly, but off the record, about it. The West Bank was ablaze with protests against the peace treaty, but there were no riots, and very little serious protest, in the Strip. On the other hand, most of those who had good jobs in Israel – many of the 40,000 migrant labourers did – prayed discreetly for the status quo.

In the end, after several years of sterile negotiations between Israel and Egypt, the autonomy schemes – and with them the "Gaza First" option – came to nothing. Perhaps this was inevitable, since Prime Minister Menachem Begin was intent on not ceding an inch. His conception of Palestinian autonomy was tailored to fit his own conviction that Eretz Israel was non-negotiable. Begin's autonomy pertained only to individuals, not to territory. It would forever remain "administrative", and never become "legislative". All control of state land would be Israeli.

Naturally, the PLO could never have accepted any of this. But the PLO's blanket refusal to take any part in the negotiations played into the hands of the Israeli maximalists. When a united Arab world, supported by the PLO, denounced the autonomy talks between Israel and Egypt as a sham or a sell-out, it was a simple thing for the Israelis to let an endless series of meetings get bogged down – and to let colonisation continue. After Israel returned all Egyptian land in April 1982, Egypt's cards were no longer strong enough to force Israel to negotiate in good faith on the Palestinian issue.

As the map departments in the respective foreign offices prepared for the Israeli hand-over of Sinai, an unforeseen problem surfaced. The delineation made between the Ottoman Empire and Egypt in 1906 had been forced upon the Turks by the British, who wanted them as far from the Suez Canal as possible. The line between the Mediterranean and the Red Sea was drawn straight across the town of Rafah, which constitutes the southwestern extreme of the Strip. In those times, border arrangements were mostly informal and, in practice, the border did not hamper any activities in Rafah, not even after the Egyptian conquest of the Strip in 1948. The Israelis also accepted the status quo and even merged "Ghazza Sina" – the Sinai Gaza – and "Ghazza Filastin" into one administrative unit after their 1967 conquest of both Sinai and the Strip. But after the rough Israeli security measures in the summer of 1971, 600 refugee families whose homes were levelled by bulldozers to make room for the Israeli patrol roads were moved to houses in Camp Canada and Camp Brazil – refugee areas utilising the barracks of the defunct UNEF force – on the Egyptian side. They, and many others who had not counted on a peace deal, now faced separation from jobs and families.

Israel asked the Egyptians to concede citizenship to the refugees on their side, but Cairo refused. Egypt then asked Israel to be given control of the Palestinian part of Rafah, but Israel refused. In the end, nearly a hundred homes were razed to make way for the new 1982 border and 20,000 people found themselves on the "wrong" side of the fence, bitterly lamenting their separation from a richer economy. The main loss, for the inhabitants of Egyptian Rafah, was the evacuation of the Israeli settlement Yamit on Sinai's Mediterranean coast, which had provided them with much business. After the new border was created, travel between the two Rafahs became a bureaucratic nuisance. The cost of the permit charged by the Israelis – fifty dollars – was prohibitive, and only eighty people crossed the line on a daily basis. (Today those same residents of Egyptian Rafah and their descendants thank their lucky star for not being residents of the Strip.)

In 1982, a real, separating, modern border was unavoidable. In the weeks running up to the final Israeli withdrawal, Defence Minister Ariel Sharon fumed at what he described as slack Egyptian control of Palestinian arms-smuggling efforts from the Sinai via Rafah into the Strip. These deliveries spurred the first serious PLO activities in the Strip for years. In the weeks before the Israeli retreat from the Sinai, there were grenade attacks against Israeli troop-carriers in the Strip. Another first, barely noticed in the din of big-power politics created by the Israel–Lebanon tension and the Falklands War, occurred just a week before the Israeli withdrawal: on April 12, youths in the refugee camp of Nuseirat carrying copies of the Qur'an and shouting "Allahu Akbar" clashed with Israeli security forces. The soldiers complained that they were unable to disperse the young firebrands, not even by tear-gas and shots in the air. It was a portent.

Soon afterwards, the leading Gazan politician in the Strip, the mayor of Gaza City, Rashad al-Shawa, was deposed for refusing to provide the refugee camp Shaati, next to Gaza City, with municipal services. He was not going to help Israel, he said, to make the camps disappear by merging them with the towns of the Strip. Shawa's exit marked the beginning of the end for the landowning, non-refugee elite; a power vacuum which would soon be filled by other actors. Shawa was resented both by leftist radicals and islamists, but widely respected by most ordinary Gazans. His ties to Israeli and Jordanian power centres meant that he was one of very few Gazans who were capable of influencing things on the ground. He was also, with all his prudence, a leader who would speak his mind even when silence would have served his interests better. His constant scolding of the PLO, its detachment from the Palestinian masses, and its corrupt habits was courageous under the circumstances. His conviction, often and eagerly voiced, that the future of the Strip lay with the kingdom of Jordan, was no less controversial.

The peace between Egypt and Israel, the inability of the Palestinian fighting organisations to challenge Israel on the ground, and the absence of any channel for political activity – even non-violent parties were forbidden – were important factors leading up to the first Palestinian uprising in December 1987. Material factors will not explain that unexpected eruption. Work, in most human societies, functions as a non-radicaliser, while joblessness tends to radicalise. Israel put all its faith in this formula. When the occupied Palestinians began to work inside Israel after the 1967 war, Defence Minister Moshe Dayan insisted that they would enjoy the same wages and conditions as Israeli employees, including annual holidays, sick leave, child allowances and – added some years later – health insurance. The edge of Palestinian resentment would continually be blunted by economic opportunity. There was misery in Gaza, but most measurable indices of poverty showed steady improvements in employment, buying power and hourly pay. The situation of the Gazan labourer in Israel was often summarily described as exploitation and even bondage. There was plenty of abuse, to be sure, with illegal Gazans sleeping on the floors of Tel Aviv restaurant kitchens and under-aged Gazans working long days in the fields for pitiless wages. But the general picture was complex, with at least three different groups of Gazan labourers, some of whom enjoyed labour-union wages and full social benefits. In 1986, with a year to go before the breakdown of the 1967 occupation model, 86.1 per cent of households in the Strip had an electric or gas stove inside their kitchens (12.7 per cent in 1974); 38.9 per cent had washing machines (3 per cent in 1974); 92.8 per cent had electricity (34.5 per cent in 1974) and 75.1 per cent (13.9 per cent in 1974) had running water.

In the mid-80s, real unemployment in the Strip was negligible. There were between 35,000 and 40,000 Gazans working in Israel. Of these, around 13,000 were entirely legal, which meant that they had been hired through one of the nine Israeli employment bureaux in the Strip. Any Israeli who wanted to hire Gazans legally had to do it through one of those outlets.

After the "dirty war" against the armed resistance in the Gazan refugee camps, the Israeli government felt secure enough, in May 1972, to open the Erez crossing into Israel for all Gazans, with or without jobs. This was the beginning of non-legal employment of Gazans in Israel. Of the close-to 24,000 non-legal Gazans making their living in Israel, 14,000 were semi-legal, meaning that they lacked work-permits issued by the relevant Israeli authorities, but still received their salary in the prescribed way – via the Ministry of Labour – and were protected by the Histadrut labour federation. Part of their income was set aside for social and health benefits and they were never prosecuted.

The real illegals were the 8,000–9,000 Gazans who received their salary in cash at the end of each work-day and who arrived in Israel most mornings without knowing if and where they would work. These workers, who had to rise before sunrise to have a chance, arrived at the infamous "slave-markets", 10 to 15 open areas, most of them near principal road-crossings around Tel Aviv, to bargain for work. The largest and best-known was the one in Yehuda Ha-Yamit street in Jaffa.

For years, the "slave-markets" and of poor Gazans were part of the early morning Israeli landscape. The sight of shivering and badly-clad Gazans squeezing together around an improvised camp-fire with a coffee-pot meant that labour was to be had cheaply for those who needed a sewer cleaned up, pianos moved or building-blocks hauled. The atmosphere around those fires always appeared cheerful and friendly, but the moment a possible employer appeared all companionship was shelved. If someone called out "Ten needed for 450 a day!" a huge scramble would break out, with pushing and shoving in order to squeeze in before the others into the van of the Israeli road-builder or contractor. On rare days, it was not a buyer's market and daily rates would soar to almost a 1,000 shekels.

But even the illegals were not treated as the Palestinian illegals of later times. Gazans were used to having their papers checked at all times by border policemen or girl soldiers. It was humiliating, and it was a nuisance, but only the very few Gazans banned from entry were prosecuted or fined. The ones without permits were not. (In 2009, a Palestinian from Ramallah who sneaks past the Israeli separation fence can earn fifty dollars a day at a building site around Tel Aviv, but he must spend all his spare time hidden. If discovered he is slapped a prohibitive fine, if not jailed.)

The daily exodus of Gazan workers into Israel had several important secondary effects. It pushed up wages inside the Strip by making labour scarce in a place where it had always been abundant. And it caused resentment at the bottom of the social ladder in Israel's southern towns, where under-employment and scant wages were routinely blamed on the government "opening up the country" to the Gazans.

By the mid-80s, there were tens of thousands of Gazans working in the Arab oil states in the Gulf, many of them highly successful and most of them a reliable source of Gaza-bound remittances. All in all, material standards were steadily on the rise, and each visit to a Gazan home, especially the kitchen, was a graphic index of the upward trend. When I first visited the Strip in the mid-seventies, Gazans scarcely lived better than Cubans or Paraguayans. A decade later, on the eve of the first Palestinian uprising, any Cuban would have eyed a Gazan home with undisguised envy. It is important to bear this in mind as we strain to make sense of the Intifada, Gaza's most famous contribution to modern Palestinian history. There was nothing inexorable, in terms of basic economic measurables, about the outbreak of hostilities in early December 1987. Moshe Dayan, the architect of the open border policy which let even Gazans without permits work in Israel, firmly believed in the pacifying effect of work. There was nothing outlandish in this belief, which was borne out by the situation on the ground after the defeat of the Gazan resistance in 1971–72. In many global trouble spots, access to work and rising material standards have made unruly minorities or marginalised groups back away from rebellion.

But the long years of apparent compliance and relative calm in the Strip lulled Israeli decision-makers into committing, as so often before and after, several conceptual mistakes concerning the Palestinians. The most fatal fallacy was that the Palestinians had tacitly accepted the status quo imposed by Israel, including the settlements all over Gaza, the total ban on political activity and the all-pervading presence of the Shabak security service. Gazans with innocent requests or applying for trivial permits often found themselves facing a Shabak operative, whose task it was to find out if the applicant could be coaxed to offer anything in return for the concession.

But, in addition to Israeli mistakes and shortsightedness, there was something more deeply wrong with the Israel–Gazan symbiosis, something structural. There was mutual dependence, to be sure. Israel depended on Gazan work and Gazans depended on Israeli jobs, but there was no equal sharing of benefits. On the eve of the 1987 Intifada, income per capita in the Strip, in spite of the steep rise during the 60s and 70s, was not more than a sixth of Israel's. Household appliances had multiplied in Gazan homes – but living space had shrunk. Institutes of higher learning had been established in the Strip under Israeli rule, but on the eve of the 1987 cataclysm, while 3,000 Gazans per year received BAs or comparable diplomas, the proportion who found work in their fields of study was negligible, which added in predictable ways to the general mood.

According to classical economic theory, the following is supposed to happen when two economies merge under free market conditions: a flow of cheap labour from the poorer economy into the richer one; and a flow of investments from the richer one into the poorer one. In the case of Israel and the occupied territories, only the first development – the movement of cheap labour into Israel – took place. Under natural conditions, the Gazans would have spent their rising incomes on high-tech Israeli products, while Israeli capital would have moved into Gaza, aiming at low-tech production there for the Israeli market. This happened to some extent, in spite of bureaucratic harassment and other obstacles, but not to any extent sufficient for genuine economic integration.

Why? One reason was that the Israeli government never formulated any explicit long-term development plans for the territories. Israeli capitalists feared that the areas, like the Sinai in 1982, would suddenly be swapped in a peace deal and were reluctant to invest. More importantly, Israel protected its own markets ruthlessly from all Gazan competition, agricultural or otherwise. (The West Bankers, who were able to sell part of their harvests to Jordan, were better off. Egypt, Gaza's only alternative market, had tariffs as draconian as Israel's.) Often government initiatives to improve Gazan infrastructure were stifled by Israeli interest groups; as when the labour union Histadrut torpedoed plans to modernise Gaza's harbour for fear it would compete with the Israeli port Ashdod, whose dockers constituted a powerful block of Labour Party voters.

# 14

# The Outbreak of the First Palestinian Uprising, December 1987

*It is often stated that the all-seeing, omnipresent Israeli security service, Shabak, knew nothing in advance (of the Intifada). The Gazans used to joke that the Shabak, served by thousands of collaborating ears and eyes, used to "know about a Palestinian's plans before they had taken shape in his head". But this time, even after all hell had broken loose and raged for days on end, the Shabak was bamboozled. The reason for this cluelessness did not occur to anyone: no plan existed.*

I visited Gaza at least once a month in the years prior to the December 1987 rising. Of all the Gazan and Israeli administrators I used to consult, few if any regarded themselves as sitting on the edge of a volcano. Of course, people would often sigh and say "This can't go on forever", but nobody was gearing up for an emergency. The only ones who did were the members of the Muslim Brotherhood, and neither of the main players – Israel and the PLO – took them seriously.

At the beginning of the occupation, and for more than a decade, work, increasing incomes and new levels of consumption did temper the Gazan spirit of resistance. But with each additional year of occupation, the returns of incorporation into Israel's economy diminished – from the Gazan point of view. There were two sides to this; one economic and one psychological. Israeli producers, and Israeli labour unions, jealously guarded their privileges vis-à-vis Gazan competitors. Citrus fruit produced in Gaza was often shipped out from the Israeli harbour of Ashdod, not from Gaza. Enterprises relying on Gazan labour were not encouraged to establish production in the Strip. The exemplary labour conditions imposed by Moshe Dayan at the beginning of Israeli rule, with unionised Gazans integrated into the Israeli social security system, were undermined and hollowed out. There were countless instances of money being deducted from paychecks to pension and unemployment funds which later failed to honour their obligations to the Gazans.

It did not take much pressure, from the Histadrut labour union or from the protectionist lobby, to subordinate the economy of the Strip to the perceived needs of Israeli markets. The prevailing Israeli view of production and trade was a Zionist version of Peronism: keeping out all competition with sky-high tariffs, and securing a minimum of foreign currency by exporting a few favoured products such as cotton and citrus, which could only be sold with profit if the irrigation water was given away for free by a political party with a monopoly on power. In the 1980s, when Israel began to abandon its antiquated zero-sum view of global trade and invest in technology, there was a golden opportunity to co-opt the Gaza Strip. With its low wages and idle surplus of engineers and professionals, the Strip would have been a natural field of investment, since tens of thousands of Israeli experts, scientists and engineers had fled the rigid, politically controlled Israeli economy. Quite a few Israeli entrepreneurs understood that Israel stood to gain much more, politically and economically, by moving electronic plants to Gaza than it did from letting the Gazans haul garbage in Tel Aviv – and formed partnerships with Gazans.

Some, often successful, joint ventures came about, but the overwhelming number of initiatives were torn to shreds or wrapped in the red tape of the Israeli bureaucrats who ran the Strip. In 1982, all non-martial aspects of the occupation had been lumped together and labeled "the civil administration". The only civil thing about it was that its clerks wore civilian clothes instead of uniforms. I have accompanied Gazan acquaintances inside the maze of the Israeli administration buildings. Instead of greasing the path for non-violent people willing to risk their money – *and* willing to help the civil administration create jobs in the Strip – it appeared that the standing orders were to shoot down any reasonable, creative initiative on sight.

Incomes rose, but the hourly pay did not include any compensation for the gruelling commute between the Strip and the workplaces in Israel. (Only a handful of Gazan workers were allowed to spend the night in Israel.) I knew a man from Rafah who worked as a gardener in Jerusalem. He rose before daybreak and spent at least two hours going to work. When a security incident provoked stricter controls at Erez, the northern Gaza-Tel Aviv portal, his travelling time became three and a half hours. When darkness fell, he would turn back home, lucky if he could find a seat to crash on during the long ride. Of course, many employers arranged for their Gazan builders or cooks to spend the night illegally, sleeping on kitchen floors or in building sites.

The Israeli writer Avram Hasson, who worked with Palestinians from day one of the occupation, told me:

> "One striking thing about the Palestinians we first saw in the summer of 1967 was their neatness. They were poor, but clean. Their clothes were patched, but ironed. They had no jobs, and few job prospects, but they went to school and studied hard, dreaming about making it in the Gulf.

> Then, almost overnight, the big scramble for Israeli jobs began, and their young men left school in droves. Who was going to study English when he could earn enough in a year to buy a used car washing dishes in Tel Aviv! Before we arrived, whoever had a car in Khan Yunes – any old wreck – was a dignitary."

After a few years, the cost of living in the territories had risen and "working for the Jews" went from being a dream to becoming a necessity. Those who slept over in Israel did it on factory floors or in sheds without showers. They wore Israeli hand-me-downs and, by the time of the Intifada, the average Gazan in a Tel Aviv street looked like he had spent the night in the gutter. Their disheveled appearance did nothing to combat the negative stereotypes among those many Israelis who, as the years went by, got used to viewing the Gazans as nothing but hewers of wood, drawers of water and placers of explosive devices. This was a long way from Moshe Dayan's vision of the occupation in 1967, according to which the Palestinians would forsake their national ambitions in exchange for a decent, if not fair, share of economic growth. It had worked for quite a while but, during the 1980s, the improvements in total income were eroded by the population explosion in the camps. The Palestinian share became a mess of pottage in the eyes of those Gazans who witnessed the wealth and the much higher growth across the border.

A month after the outbreak of the Intifada the Palestinian writer and lawyer Rajah Shehade said:

> "The policy of Moshe Dayan, to stay out of people's lives as much as possible, to retain some level of politeness and consideration . . . is all gone. [Now] the administration has been taken over by Gush Emunim [the Jewish settlement movement]. Ephraim Sneh [the former head of the Civil Administration on the West Bank and later a Labour politician] was the last decent man. He could not take it any longer. Since he left there is no one, no one, to turn to in times of crisis."

The lack of urgency on the Israeli side was not universal. On November 2, five weeks before the Intifada, the Israeli press found out about an ambitious report called "Gaza 2000", prepared by civilian experts and handed to a few decision-makers. It was a painstaking investigation into several fields, including water resource depletion, housing, population growth, refugee resettlement and labour markets, aiming at a precise prediction of conditions in the Strip at the time of the turn of the century, twelve years away at the time. The results, which would prove remarkably accurate, sketched a bleak picture: the Strip population in the year 2000 would have passed the million mark, negatively affecting access to fresh water and living space. The program to resettle refugees – less than 700 families a year – was already far behind natural growth in the camps and would not make a dent in the reality Israel had hoped to turn around. On one score, the report made a prediction which would be borne out in a matter of weeks: the refugees would take over local leadership from the traditional, non-refugee landowning clans.

It is often stated, correctly but with exaggerated amazement, that the all-seeing, omnipresent Israeli security service, Shabak, knew nothing in advance. The Gazans used to joke that the Shabak, served by thousands of collaborating ears and eyes, used to "know about a Palestinian's plans before they had taken shape in his head". But this time, even after all hell had broken loose and raged for days on end, the Shabak was bamboozled. The reason for this cluelessness did not occur to anyone: no plan existed. The Israeli prime minister, Yizhak Shamir, clearly in earnest, kept repeating for weeks that this was a conspiracy of a few terrorists, a gang of hooligans imposing their violent ways on a community.

The first Palestinian rising against the Israeli occupation began on December 9, 1987, in the refugee camp of Jebaliya, south of Gaza City, during and after the burial of four Palestinians killed by an Israeli truck as they returned from their work in Israel. During the clashes, a youngster was shot dead by Israeli soldiers and the confrontations, which normally would have ebbed out towards evening, intensified and spread to Khan Yunes and to the Shaati Camp – and, after a day or two, to Nablus, East Jerusalem and all of the occupied territories.

At the outset, the first Intifada was an unarmed, spontaneous mass movement. It remained so for a remarkably long time. For a few days it looked like no more than another Gazan riot, bound to rage and then pass away, like a rainstorm. But it soon became clear that the shock-waves from the tremor at the Jebaliya refugee camp were vibrating through Palestinian politics, Israeli attitudes and the rules and the whole choreography of international press coverage. It even changed teenage and student fashion all over the world, as the black-and-white checkered keffiyeh, hitherto a symbol of rural tradition, became the banner of popular urban resistance. After a few months of conflict, I visited the famous Hirbawi keffiyeh mill in Hebron, and its obsolete machinery screeched and squeaked as it tried to keep up with soaring international demand. By March 1988, the keffiyeh was worn *en masse* by students in Los Angeles demonstrating against US policy . . . in Nicaragua!

The causal links in the run-up to the eruption have been traced backwards in different ways by different observers, and any attempt to quantify and order the relative importance of such nebulous factors as outrage, humiliation, fear and hatred is bound to be arbitrary. In early November, there were several petrol-bomb attacks against Israeli patrols, and severe clashes between soldiers and students at the al-Azhar Institute in Gaza City, with heavy doses of tear-gas and plastic bullets. Perhaps the real countdown began on November 11, when high-school girls in Deir al-Balah stoned a passing carload of Israeli settlers. The settlers fired back live rounds at the girls and killed 17-year old Intisar al-Attar. The next day, two girls from the al-Zahra school in Gaza City were wounded by automatic fire, possibly by settlers, and there was a noticeable rise in the overall temperature, with stone-throwing, student protests and the blocking of roads by both the army and locals. A fantastic rumour, planted by Islamists, circulated all over the Strip, saying that the wounded class-mates of Intisar al-Attar had been taken to Israeli hospitals and murdered there.

An index of the seriousness of the situation was the decision of the coordinator of Israeli policy in the territories, Shmuel Goren, to visit the wounded Palestinian girls at the Shifa hospital in Gaza City. Such gestures were highly uncommon, and even rarer was Goren's warning that the trigger-happiness of the settlers played into the hands of the PLO. The head of Southern command, general Yizhak Mordechai, was equally put out by the settlers' tendency to take the law into their own hands. Mordechai's opinion, voiced in an interview with the newspaper *Ma'ariv*, that the settlers behaviour was unjustified, infuriated the colonists.

Unrest, sporadic but persistent, continued all through November. Then, on the afternoon of December 6, near Palestine Square in downtown Gaza City, Shlomo Takal, an Israeli merchant, was knifed to death. A curfew was declared and the usual dragnet was hauled through the refugee camps. Two days later, an Israeli truck crashed into two Palestinian collective taxis with workers returning from work in Israel. Four were killed and seven wounded.

Next day, December 9, the world's front pages were all spotlighting a momentous event: the decision by Ronald Reagan and Mikhail Gorbachev to abolish short- and middle-range ballistic missiles. In Israel, the travails of the brittle coalition government was at the centre of attention: Foreign Minister Shimon Peres' hint that the Gaza settlements were a burden made Prime Minister Yizhak Shamir boil over: "Israel", he swore, "would never hand over Gaza to the terrorists." But in the Jebaliya refugee camp south of Gaza city, where the four dead workers were about to be buried, no one paid any attention to global or Israeli politics. Shortly before the funerals, a fresh rumour, probably again spread by the Islamists, made the rounds of Jebaliya's alleys. The previous day's car-crash, it was said, had not been an accident, but a deliberate act of vengeance, staged by the Israelis to avenge the killing of Shlomo Takal three days earlier. The indignation caused by this belief was the first spark of the great conflagration. Refugees clashed with Israeli soldiers on reserve duty, who were stunned by the unexpected assault from young men, women and even children. The

Israelis, understaffed and unprepared, fired into the crowds. The result – the death of 17-year old Hatem Sisi and scores of injured – added more volatile fuel to the nascent rebellion.

To the shorthanded Israeli units, and to the foreign correspondents who hurried to Gaza, all this appeared as bolts of lightning from a clear sky. And so it did to many Gazans. When I first arrived in Gaza city, before anyone had named the uprising, there was one novelty, apart from the violence and high tempers. Normally my contacts among the Gazans and among Israeli officers posted in Gaza were eager to explain and analyze all that went on, often in the cocksure and emphatic manner particular to Israeli and Palestinian pundits, as if the hundred-year old tangle were really quite a straightforward affair. But now they offered few coherent explanations. They all appeared dazed and frustrated, even indignant, as if the rules of their game had suddenly been changed without their being informed.

The conditions had indeed changed, seemingly overnight. But what had really changed was not the quantifiable indices of analysts and sociologists, but the psychology of the Israel–Gaza conflict. In private life, we see it happen all the time – something snaps inside a battered woman or a repressed underling, and the system of deterrence used until then collapses. The established threshold value of force required to keep Palestinians docile was explosively breached, collectively, overnight. Plastic bullets, rubber bullets, tear gas, even live fire, had become like gnats to them.

The initial inability, on the part of the Israelis, to realise this and see the riots for what they were – a spontaneous and genuine popular revolt against the occupation – gave the Gazans several valuable weeks. When reinforcements were sent to the main flashpoints around Gaza City or curfew orders were slammed on the refugee camps of Shaati and Jebaliya, the Intifada – as in the story of the wolf and the prairie dogs – reared its head in the southern Gazan village of Bani Suheila or in the small and normally peaceful camp of Mugazi. The Israelis, accustomed to regarding the maintenance of public order as nothing but a security problem, cranked up the dose of military violence as they usually did when faced with disturbances. But in doing so now, they unwittingly sustained the uprising and promoted its international breakthrough. After three days of clashes, the Gaza riots spread to Nablus in the West Bank and then, like a bushfire, to every village in the land. After the clamour around the Reagan–Gorbachev nuclear deal had subsided, the story began to make its way onto the front pages of all the world's papers.

Israel's bicephalous, not to say schizophrenic, government, was a brittle power-sharing agreement between Prime Minister Yizhak Shamir of the Likud, the most doctrinaire ultranationalist ever to lead the country, and Labour's foreign minister, Shimon Peres, the least dogmatic of contemporary Israeli leaders. Peres knew already, in his heart of hearts, that no peace worth its name could be achieved without engaging with the PLO. But any contact with the PLO was still a criminal offence, and Peres had to tread warily. The militant settlers' movement Gush Emunim tried its best to blame everything on him: "There is no doubt that Peres' declaration (mentioned on p. 101) was the spark that set Gaza aflame", the settler's mouthpiece *Nekuda* maintained.

Peres was the first Israeli decision-maker who understood the international implications of the rioting. After a few days he told his staff at the foreign ministry that this was the worst public relations fall-out since the bombing of Beirut in 1982. On December 12, prevented by political realities to recommend talks with the Palestinians, Peres spoke of "demilitarising" the Strip – a code-word denoting the unmentionable concept of withdrawal. Today, one or two dead Palestinians or Israelis barely make it into the summing-up columns at the margins of Western papers, but at the time one dead civilian Palestinian a day – on March 19, 1988, the hundredth Palestinian died – had severe diplomatic repercussions. It should be remembered that it took several months before the Israelis began to keep the press out of the hot zones, and the startling sequences of women and children facing armed soldiers in riot helmets proliferated on TV screens.

Peres' party colleague and political rival, Defence Minister Yizhak Rabin, was as uncompromising as Shamir on essentials, but he was aware of the ongoing erosion of Israel's image. The world's cartoonists had field days casting the Palestinians as nimble Davids next to the slow-moving Israeli Goliath, who showered his surroundings with blind and brute force, while getting more and more entangled in a stubbornly denied reality. Rabin's remedy, however, brought Israel's image from the frying pan into the fire. To bring down the tally of fatalities and put fear back into the rioters' hearts, Rabin ordered the soldiers to confront the Palestinians with batons instead of bullets. Two days of this produced 197 Gazans with broken bones and their limbs in casts, a sight that brought the Palestinians ever more publicity and sympathy – and fuelled the ongoing polarization of Israeli society.

The Palestinian side was also bursting with contradictions. Those denounced by Yizhak Shamir as the fomentors of trouble, the "terrorist PLO leaders", were at a complete loss regarding what was taking place and what to do. Soon enough bulletins and decrees issued by underground guidance committees and a "Unified National Leadership", the UNL, began to crop up. They were composed by locals, not by the PLO in Tunis. There was a bewildering downpour of leaflets as all the political groups in Gaza – the Fatah, the Popular Fronts and the pro-Syrian and pro-Iraqi factions – scrambled to climb the bandwagon. The quickest to react was the Muslim Brotherhood, the "Ikhwan". On December 14, 1987, the most prominent Ikhwan leader in the Gaza City area, the wheelchair-bound Sheikh Ahmad Yassin, gave the go-ahead for the first underground communiqué. The message on the flyer was not signed "Ikhwan", but bore a mysterious and unknown acronym, HMS, pronounced "Hamas" which stood for *Hariqat al-Muqawma al-Islamiya*, the Muslim Resistance Movement.

Yasser Arafat would, in due course, reap rich fruits from the Intifada, but at the outset he greeted it with more apprehension than delight. The lively turmoil on the ground exposed the fiction that he and the exiled Tunis leadership planned and ran resistance in the territories. The proliferation of self-styled or, even worse, authentic leaders issuing orders and appeals on his turf was deeply worrying to him. It took, in the words of Said Aburish, a month for Arafat to adopt the Intifada: "The PLO was stunned . . . but remained afraid to commit itself . . . Although [Arafat] instructed the PLO radio in Baghdad . . . to exhort the people . . . it was Arafat who during the early days of the Intifada manifested the most reluctance to provide the rebellion with support . . . Abu Jihad [Arafat's deputy, Khalil Wazir], the man responsible for the occupied territories . . . had an impressive knowledge of local conditions and pleaded for an immediate PLO response. When the Intifada would not die and Arafat finally bowed to the inevitable, Abu Jihad ran after it with remarkable speed. Because he knew every village, school and large family in Gaza and the West Bank, he "adopted" the Intifada and provided it with the necessary financial backing and logistical support to keep it alive."

It is true that, with time, Abu Jihad's ability and hard work gave the PLO some influence over events, but for several months the Intifada belonged to no one. It expanded and contracted according to its own laws, like a flow of molten rock or a tidal wave, often in direct contradiction of Palestinian interests and the analysis of responsible local leaders. Thus the UN undersecretary Marrack Goulding, a dignitary highly sympathetic to the plight of the Gazans, was stoned by refugees in Rafah. The *New York Times* reporter John Kifner was attacked and wounded near Shifa hospital in Gaza City and Dr Ahmad al-Sha'ab, one of the most selfless Palestinians, was lynched and almost killed by rioters in Khan Yunes. Al-Sha'ab was in charge of liaison with Israeli medical authorities and worked around the clock to get the severely wounded to hospitals in Israel. The rumour referred to above, about the wounded being murdered in Israeli hospitals, was still believed by many, and as Dr al-Sha'ab was dispatching ambulances to the Soroka hospital in the Israeli city of Beersheba, a crowd set upon him, chanting: "He hands over our people the Jews".

Such events underlined the chaotic, unplanned and volatile character of the Intifada. I had been in the Strip many times during periods of unrest, in a car with yellow Israeli number plates – Gazan cars had silver-coloured ones – but I had never feared for my safety. If the Israelis received the foreign press in a reserved manner, the Palestinians usually did it keenly, knowing we were the only corrective to the press releases of *Dover Zahal*, the Israeli Military spokesman (more reliable then than now, to be sure.) But with the advent of the Intifada rules and rationale were swept away. Reporters, diplomats, the UN, aid workers, even Palestinian dignitaries of the old cut who pleaded with the rebels not to damage property – all appeared part of the same odious establishment which had collaborated in their exile and humiliation.

Appeals and flyers and instructions were endlessly megaphoned from mosques and rooftops. And in time a new leadership crystallised, which did get a handle on developments. But it took a long time. In the beginning, the Intifada was a like a runaway horse. The Israelis and the PLO insisted that the PLO was its actual rider, but it was not. "We have detained hundreds of organisers", Defence Minister Yizhak Rabin declared on December 24, with no results to show for it in the field. After a few months, the Israelis really had rounded up most of those who issued revolutionary leaflets and spurred the crowds on. They were locked up in makeshift prisons and then in the new, huge prison camp built in the Negev desert – Ketziot. In late summer 1988, thousands of Palestinians were brought there, after conveyor-belt convictions by military courts applying the infamous article 119 of the Emergency Regulations of 1945, an item passed by the British to deal more swiftly with Jewish nationalists. But the Intifada rolled on, with or without "organisers". It was the horse, not the rider, and that was a hard fact to digest – for the Israelis and for the press corps. The world is full of "spontaneous" and "popular" rebellions and movements which are really very well organised, funded, armed and controlled. No one had ever seen a thing like this carrying on for months on end.

The 1948–49 Palestinian refugees were often received appallingly in the Arab capitals around which they flocked. According to local, government-directed media, eager to absolve the national Arab armies from the débâcle which led to the creation of Israel, the Palestinians had not stood their ground but abandoned their homeland to the Jews, sold it, betrayed it. Now, forty years later, the refugees and their struggle were glorified in the Arab world. What politicians and armies had shied away from, namely confronting Israel, these unarmed heroes were doing with their bare hands. The heroism of the Gazans, and later of the West Bankers, responded to a pent-up need in the Arab world. Youngsters from Morocco to Baghdad were making the confident V-signs of the Gaza urchins. The TV footage stirred the public, and the spontaneous outpourings of sympathy obliged state media to surf the wave, even though the implied purpose of much of the coverage was to contrast the valour of the Gazans with the self-seeking prudence of the Arab governments. After a week of unrest the Kuwaiti newspaper *al-Qabas* published a poem by the Syrian author Nizar Qabbani, called *Awlad al-Hajar*, "Children of the Stones". It was reproduced and quoted thousand-fold, memorised in classrooms and set to music, elevating the Intifada in Arab minds to levels far above the immediate issues at stake in the back-alleys of Jebaliya. The Palestinian rising was, in fact, the first affirmative, emblematic pan-Arab event in a long time. For years, leaders and generals had baffled the hopes they had fanned – and here, suddenly, the lowly and downtrodden were salvaging Arab honour without guns, without any speechmaking. The central theme of Qabbani's verses was that the Palestinians facing the occupation army were fighting for all Arabs, that their blood was washing away the sins of "the comfortable ones":

*They dazzled the world*
*With nothing in their hands but stones*
. . .
*They fought for us until they died*
*While we sat in our coffee-houses,*
*One of us looking for an apartment,*
*Another one amassing a fortune,*
*Or planning a fourth marriage . . .*

Qabbani denounced "generations of treachery, hustling and prostitution". In his view, the Arab elites were now being awakened from their cowardice and their materialism, and redeemed by the stone-throwing children. It was powerful imagery, especially in societies where social critique is usually condemned to express itself in roundabout ways. Since then, and to this day, Palestinian suffering and resistance has taken on an iconic and cathartic role in Arab debate and identity. TV channels, especially during Israeli–Palestinian tension, broadcast bloody riot and bombing scenes for hours, to a backdrop of suggestive music. Far from belittling Palestinian suffering, as after the 1948 *Nakba*, state-run Arab media now highlight it – partly out of genuine compassion, partly as an escape valve for the release of domestic anger and frustration.

# 15

# Economic Warfare and the Rise of Islamism, 1987–1991

*"Gaza . . . became the first city in the history of the Mediterranean where swimming was formally banned. A number of flyers were distributed warning people about the moral dangers inherent in indulging in the pleasures of the sea. Toward the third year of the uprising, even an innocent stroll on the seashore – by then the only social outlet for a community confined by . . . curfews . . . was viewed as sacrilegious."* (Salim Tamari)

The Intifada made for powerful poetry, but for those inside the vortex it meant the total disruption of normal life. Schools and universities closed down – sometimes by military decree, sometimes by order from the rioters. The curfews, especially in the camps, became longer and more rigorously enforced. Homes were turned upside down during aggressive searches and people would be dragged out of bed by Israeli soldiers in the middle of the night and told to paint over rebel slogans sprayed on their walls, pull down a Palestinian flag from a pylon or remove boulders strewn across a patrol road. In time, the tax authorities were also mobilised in the harassment campaign. Fewer and fewer Strip residents made it to their jobs in Israel and strikes were proclaimed with ever-increasing frequency. Sometimes the Israelis closed the border to show the Gazans that working across the line was a privilege, not a right. Already on January 11, 1988, Prime Minister Yitzhak Shamir made his first threat to keep Palestinians out of their jobs if the riots continued. Palestinian businesses suffered greatly, but their owners mostly complied willingly with the strikes or wisely kept their mouths shut.

The Gazans suffered, but they kept a close watch on the Israelis and they saw them suffering as well. In addition to the international outcry, there were two smarting setbacks in the UN Security Council and, above all, huge disruptions in the economy. Many Israeli employers, factories, restaurants, builders and even municipalities and government agencies, were unable to replace their Palestinian workers. After a few months of confrontation, the Bank of Israel estimated that the country had lost $650 million in exports, through Palestinian boycotts of Israeli goods and the creation of local micro-industries in the territories. The televised riots made tourists cancel their trips to the region and most Israeli hotels stood empty. As the field-hands of Gaza went on strike or found themselves under curfew, oranges and grapefruits bound for Europe rotted on the trees.

It was natural that the Palestinians, militarily inferior, should seek to hurt Israel where she was most vulnerable. Until the Intifada, the occupation, although endlessly discussed in op-ed pages and routinely condemned by the UN, had cost Israel little in terms of diplomatic relations and trade opportunities. The Arab boycott of companies trading with Israel drove some multinationals – Pepsi Cola and Scania trucks were the most notable examples – to wind up their operations in Israel, but on the whole the occupation had been a free ride.

In the first stage of the uprising, the rioters in the Strip had no detailed plan of how to bring the Israeli economy to its knees. But quite soon a very definite idea crystallised out of the smoke and mayhem: a total break with everything Israeli. All contacts, relationships or dependencies; jobs, loans, trade, tax-paying; even applications for building permits were defined as collaboration, and thus taboo. Since the Palestinians, and especially the Gazans, had been reduced to almost complete dependence, this idea took some arm-twisting to enforce. In February 1988, I took my car to a trusted mechanic in Khan Yunes. He shook his head. It was forbidden. When I tried to convince him just to have a look under the bonnet, he pointed to a couple of charred wrecks next to us. Those, he explained, were the remains of cars belonging to Israeli Bedouin from Rahat, some of his oldest customers. He had tried to argue with the rebels who set them alight that they belonged to Arabs, not to Jews: "They knew I was telling the truth, but they did not care. The cars had yellow, Israeli licence plates, that was all they needed to know. I am all for fighting the occupation, but I am not sure, if we succeed, what we are going to get in its place."

The garage owner who uttered those words was a peaceful man. His business barely recovered. Many years later, the Gaza Strip was fenced off from Israel and he lost his Jewish customers for a second time. By then, few Israelis dared to enter Gaza, so he used to cross into Israel, tow the ailing car to Gaza, and return it. He and his sons were born mechanics. The words "I'm sorry, it can't be fixed" never crossed their lips. When Hamas and its satellite groups began to develop mortars, and later rockets, to be fired at civilian Israeli targets across the border, they were pressed into service. The work was odious to them, but it was paid.

Shopkeepers were pressured by the activists not to keep Israeli goods – not a simple order to carry out, since very few of the Israeli items had Palestinian alternatives. Sometimes the radicals would raid all shops in a camp or a village, collect enemy products in sacks, and burn them in the public square.

Hostility to the Jews as the people which had dispossessed them ran deep with Gazans, but it was always tempered by the courtesy shown to individual guests, regardless of race or creed. In spite of everything, many Gazans had formed bonds of friendship with Israelis. But during the Intifada, and later during the Islamicisation of politics and mores, Gazans were admonished from above to exclude Jews and *franji*s – whites, Westeners, non-believers – from the almost instinctive hospitality which is a defining characteristic of traditional Palestinian life. Individual Israelis, the staff of water or electrical companies, were attacked and sometimes killed in the Strip during the Intifada but then invariably helped by bystanders after the attacks. Palestinian hospitality is at the core of their identity, and old habits tenaciously resisted the dictates of fanaticism. Once, during the first months of the Intifada, I visited friends in the Khan Yunes refugee camp. When I arrived, I found the patriarch Abu Salim having coffee with a Druze Israeli soldier. Abu Salim's daughter, a high-school girl, was crying and scolding her father. She explained to me that the Druze had greeted her father and asked for directions. The older man, as custom bid him, had asked the stranger to sit down and share a pot of coffee. The local young rebels had repeatedly warned Abu Salim that any hobnobbing with Israelis would be seen as collaboration and punished hard. Abu Salim, who had fled from his home in Faluja in 1948, was adamant. His principles would not be the subject of any political dictates. A guest was a guest, even if he wore the green uniform of the Israeli border police. The soldier soon realised that he had put his host in a delicate position, downed his coffee and took leave, but the scene was typical during the Intifada years where the values of tradition collided daily with the ideals of the moment.

Cutting all moorings to the Israeli economy was a giant enterprise. As fewer Gazans worked in Israel and less Gazan goods found their way to Israeli and foreign markets, average income plummeted. Most items in most stores, especially food products, were Israeli. In order to survive without them, the Gazans reverted, or tried their best to revert, to the village life of their fathers. The whole economy was redirected to serve the one aim of subsistence, which was seen as the only way out of the occupation – political and military paths being blocked. Carrots were grown in flower pots, fish were kept in tanks and rabbits in back-yards, cows were bought clandestinely from Israelis and smuggled in, and fields with export crops such as strawberries and cucumbers were plowed up and sowed with barley and lupin – the yellow turmuz bean sold by Gazan children at street corners and red lights. Israeli Arabs and peace activists smuggled in seedlings, seeds and money.

There was great hardship, but also euphoria. It was not yet freedom, but a palpable and intoxicating air of freedom. Having lived as minors under guardianship, they now followed only their own rules. In March

1988, when Gazan policemen, tax collectors and other clerks resigned from the Israeli civil administration, the entire Israeli system began to quaver. Many of those workers had held their posts since Egyptian times, and very few of them would have resigned if they hadn't been forced to by the rebels. The Israelis hit back. On March 13, 1988, the first total curfew of the Strip was declared. All traffic between Gaza and the West Bank was banned and international telephone lines to the Strip were cut off. Hereafter, large areas were declared off-limits to the international press corps.

There were fire-bombs thrown at Israeli patrols, but they were rare and ineffective. The Israelis were fought with sticks and stones. After four months of daily clashes, there were still no Israeli fatalities in Gaza. There were firebrands among the rioters who preached armed resistance, but they were kept at bay. Most activists agreed that live fire against the Israelis would give the enemy a pretext for fielding tanks and artillery against them (a common sight during future clashes).

The Intifada retained the attention of media and diplomats long after the world had gotten used to the stone-throwing, tear-gassing scenarios repeated daily in different locations. The reason for this was that the failure of the Israelis to enforce the previous status quo began to change the bigger picture. First of all, it clouded Israeli relations with the US. Apart from its votes on UN resolutions, the Reagan administration launched a full-fledged peace plan, built around an International Peace Conference. After Prime Minister Yitzhak Shamir flatly refused to play along, the Americans dropped him as serious interlocutor and worked through Foreign Minister Shimon Peres. While Shamir continued to regard the PLO as taboo, the director of the foreign ministry, Peres' man Avraham Tamir, declared that peace negotiations without the PLO would be meaningless. The Palestinians marvelled and took heart as the glaring fissure they had opened up in the enemy camp widened. There was bad blood, verging on hatred, between Shamir and Peres before the Intifada. When Reagan invited Peres to Washington as if he, not Shamir, were Israel's leader, the Labour–Likud coalition hung by a thread.

Those complications now belong to history, but the apple of contention thrown by the Palestinians into the court of Israeli politics is still there. Since December 1987, the abrasive issues of territories, settlements and occupation are at the centre of Israeli life, monopolising its politics, dividing its people, devouring its resources, eroding its international reputation, and sapping its strength. All elections since then have pivoted around this only. In addition, the need to turn soldiers trained to handle field-guns and tanks into baton-wielding riot police facing civilians became, and remains, a huge drag on long-term military planning. After half a year of the Intifada, general staff member Menachem Einan revealed that the new duties forced upon the army had severely disrupted its preparations for its original task, the defence of the country's borders. This observation, which infuriated Shamir, has been echoed countless times by military planners since. In short, Gaza might have appeared a small stone under Israel's cartwheel at the time, but twenty-two years later the country has not recovered its balance. Its fighting units still waste their most valuable time at dreary checkposts, rifling through the shopping bags of Palestinian villagers.

To Yasser Arafat the Intifada became a blessing in disguise. After sitting on the fence for weeks, the PLO joined the fray. Arafat's fears of being upstaged by the new spokesmen and leaders in the field did not go away, and there were cruel and cynical attempts by him to sabotage some of the most creative and popular initiatives at grass-root level. The real spadework which allowed Arafat to force his authority upon the direction of the dangerously independent Intifada, the United National Leadership, was done by Abu Jihad, alias Khalil al-Wazir, the PLO's most capable organiser. From the beginning, the selfless Abu Jihad had criticised Arafat's hesitant attitude. Grudgingly, Arafat let him get to work with funds and instructions to local leaders. The Israelis were obsessed with their wish to regard all trouble as fomented from abroad. (The security services knew this to be untrue, but there were limits to what they were able to convince wilful politicians.) When threads leading back to PLO headquarters in Tunis began to appear, they were eagerly picked up and displayed. In early April 1988, the Israeli cabinet decided to assassinate Abu Jihad. The decision passed after fierce opposition from Shimon Peres and from the cabinet's most prominent dove, Ezer Weizman, who even denounced the deed publicly. If any further proof were needed that the Intifada was of their own making, not Arafat's, the Israeli leaders got it now. After Israeli commandos sprayed Abu Jihad full of bullets in Tunis on April 16, there was no lull at all in the field. In Gaza, where Abu Jihad grew up and made his reputation during the border wars of the 1950s, resistance surged.

Over time, the Israelis helped create the reality they had dreamed up at the outset of the Intifada. The more neighbourhood leaders and university intellectuals Israel carted off to the new makeshift prison camps, the more control Yasser Arafat gained over events. Israel's knee-jerk accusations of Arafat also did his bidding. The American and European leaders who were told by the Israelis that the violence and the turmoil were really remote-controlled by the PLO, could only reach one conclusion: neither negotiations nor peace were conceivable without Arafat and the PLO.

A few months before the outbreak of the Intifada, Arafat had been humiliated by Arab leaders, treated like an undesirable gate-crasher at an important summit in Amman. Now he was edging closer to his goal: pan-Arab and global recognition of his exclusive right to represent his people. Local Palestinians leaders, even those who deeply resented Arafat's vengefulness and posturing, realised the huge importance of this achievement and played along. One could not interview a Palestinian leader in the territories without first being treated to the obligatory litany of the PLO being "the sole legitimate representative of the Palestine people". Even the upright Feisal Husseini, the undisputed first spokesman of Jerusalem's Arabs, who was shabbily treated by Arafat, insisted on this, as did the new young leaders of Gaza. Privately, young Gazan leaders like Muhammad Dahlan and Sufyan Abu Zaide had plenty to say about the corrupt ways of the PLO and its leader, but there was never a hint of criticism in their communiqués or interviews. They were all keenly aware that Israel was standing poised to drive a wedge between Arafat and the local leadership.

It was a busy Gazan autumn day in 1988, close to a year after the outbreak of the Intifada. I needed some relief from the effort of trying to turn the dizzying whirl of politics, violence and misery into structured news analysis. I found an Israeli public phone – many of them had been uprooted by then – and called in my piece. Naim, the Gazan driver – it had become too risky to use my own Israel-plated car – read my thoughts and asked if he should head for "the shed". The shed was a jumble of driftwood and corrugated iron sheets roughly nailed together at the southern end of the Shaati refugee camp on the Mediterranean shore. Its owner, Marwan, was a genial man in his 50s, a camp resident for 40 years, but with vivid memories of his childhood in Abu Kabir, a neighbourhood south of Tel Aviv. On a smoky charcoal grill he barbequed fish and squid, which were served with an elementary salad of tomato and parsley – and beer. For those who could afford it – and few locals could after months of strife – Marwan's shed was an oasis.

But when we arrived, the shed was gone. Nothing remained of it but some scattered planks and a heap of broken beer-bottles. Had Israeli collective punishment been extended to such a degree? "Look," said Naim, "the bottles still have their caps." They had been broken while full. *Ya harbethum*, "a plague on their houses," he mumbled, fear in his voice.

There was no doubt in his mind what had happened. This, he said, was the work of the Ikhwan, the Muslim Brothers. Many people, indeed most, in the Shaati camp were abstemious. Those who consume *Khamr* – the collective term denoting all alcoholic beverages – were almost all young and middle-aged males. Formally, Islam is uncompromising with regard to alcohol, but much less so than it is with regard to pork, and until the rise of Islamism there were plenty of Gazans who prayed often but sometimes took a drink. Prior to the Intifada, the issue was not an infected one. I have been at wedding parties in Gazan refugee camps where sheikhs, veiled matrons and religious dignitaries sat at one table sipping tea and lemonade, without taking offence at the whisky and wine flowing freely at the next table. That was but one example of the rather relaxed cohabitation between tradition and secular life which characterised Gaza before the rise of Islamism.

Such live-and-let-live attitudes were cemented during the years of Egyptian occupation, when the Nasserist taboo against mixing Islam with politics was enforced in Gaza. Islamism, the view that faith and observance are not personal choices but the primary building blocks of politics and society, was a half-clandestine ideology during Egyptian rule. The Muslim Brothers, the Ikhwan, surely resented beer-drinking and all the other abominations of modernity, but it was only during the first Intifada that they felt strong enough to challenge the existing modus vivendi between modernity and tradition.

It was natural that the Islamic revolution should begin in Gaza. The Gazans had always been more traditional. Clans, families and village ties had partly survived the exodus and the transformation of farmers into urbanised refugees. The proportion of refugees was higher than on the West Bank. The Marxist fronts were strong in the Gazan camps, but few elders regarded their radical sons and daughters as an insult to tradition, and few of the PFLP and DFLP firebrands failed to respect their elders. The young and their militancy enjoyed prestige, for they were carrying on the struggle, the struggle that had failed during the *Nakba* and in 1967. The terror attacks and airplane hijackings of the late 1960s had, for the first time, brought the refugee plight worldwide publicity. There was not a hint, at least no hint visible to the casual observer, of the abysmal rancour which bedevils secular-Islamist relations today.

But long before the Intifada, those facts had begun to change. Modernity, Marxism, international politics, education and other darlings of the secularists had not brought the expected blessings. Had they paved the way towards a Marxist utopia, or towards anything worth having, the eruption of December 1987 would never have taken place. The disappointment with the PLO and the traditional leadership, not least Arafat's desperate attempts to exploit the Intifada in order to secure US recognition, created an opening for another kind of radicalism, one that relished not a distant future, but the past.

The first sign that the Ikhwan were out to challenge the political monopoly of secular movements came shortly after the establishment, in 1978, of Gaza's first institution of higher learning, the Islamic University of Gaza. Israel's defence minister, Ezer Weizman, who gave it the go ahead, was aware that the moving spirit behind the project was Ahmad Yassin, a wheelchair-bound Muslim Brother who ran what had been the embryo of the university, the study circle al-Mujamma' al-Islami. "The Israelis are fools," said one of my Gazan Fatah contacts, "this school is going to be a factory turning out fanatics."

The university was barely inaugurated before intense rivalry broke out between Islamists and secularists. The Islamists felt, understandably, that they, who had planned the university and secured the funding from Arab oil-sheikhs, should have the run of the place. Arafat, true to his instincts, felt that nothing at all should be beyond his control. The bitterness around this issue led to the first instance of physical fighting between the secular camp and the religious one. The Israelis, misjudging the growth potential of the new, alternative ideology, were not unhappy to see Arafat and the PLO taught a lesson on their home turf. Since Israel had no long-term plan for the Strip, politicians left the daily politics of Gaza to the security services, whose only guiding light was the principle of divide-and-rule. In that petty game, the Islamists were a handy stick to wield against the PLO.

Today the extreme cruelty of the Hamas government in Gaza, both against unbelievers and political opponents, has become its trademark. But its founder and leader, Ahmad Yassin, was not a preacher of violence. On the contrary, his reluctance to use violence became the PLO's primary propaganda tool against him. Yassin believed in patience. Years of preparation and motivation were necessary, he told his disciples, before their Islamic society could hope to challenge secular organisations. When it came to confronting Israel, the sheikh was even more prudent. Yassin cared little for the facile, Guevara-influenced sanguinity of Fatah and the popular fronts, according to which a dedicated guerilla movement could get an oppressor off balance by a few cleverly applied *focos,* incendiary strikes. Yassin believed that the endgame against Israel would be a matter for the regular Arab armies, not for the Palestinians alone. There was something Leninist in Yassin's patience. No romanticism, neither of violence nor of revolution, distracted him from his laborious setting up and tying together of organisations, networks, bases and local hierarchies. He had understood the Israeli obsession with the PLO and he exploited it masterfully to lay the groundwork for the future. "We are not in a hurry, like modern people. We do what we have to do, in order to be ready when the Creator sounds the bell", he once told me.

It mattered little to Yassin that the Islamists were taunted as ninnies and shirkers by the militants. But it mattered very much to his young followers, many of whom were as impatient and hungry for action as their secular rivals. During the 1980s, pressure mounted on Yassin to allow, if not to organise, armed resistance. The appearance of a new, competing Islamist movement, *al-Jihad al-Islami*, whose attacks against Israeli patrols brought it local glory in the years prior to the Intifada, contributed much to the jumpiness of Yassin's followers. In 1991, a group of Hamas activists in Gaza founded *Izz al-Din al-Qasam*, the movement's armed branch and the embryo of Hamas' regular forces.

When the word "Hamas" appeared for the first time, on a flyer addressed to the protesters in Gaza City a week after the outbreak of the Intifada, it was not immediately clear that Sheikh Yassin and the

**1** Prime Minister Yizhak Shamir visiting the Nuseirat refugee camp in early February 1988, during the first Palestinian rising against the Israeli occupation. Photo: Maggy Ayalon.

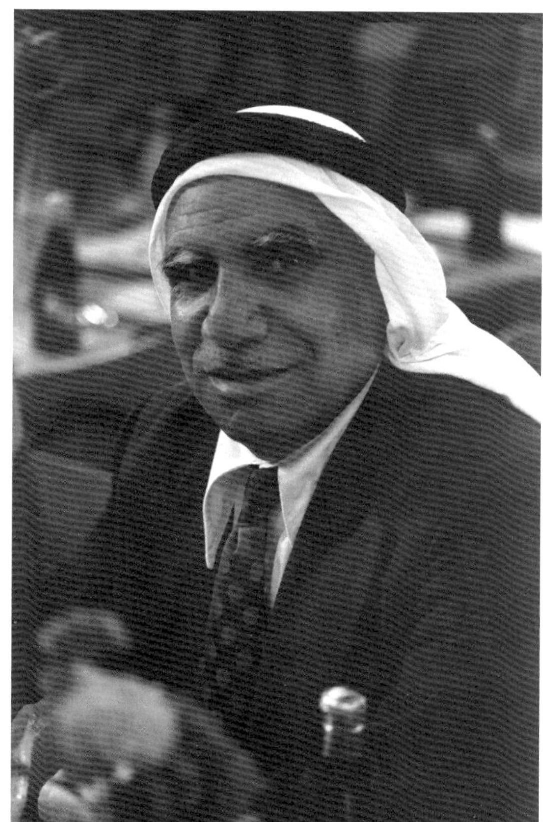

**2**
Suleiman al-Astal, mayor of Khan Yunes. One of the few Palestinians who dared to openly welcome Egyptian President Anwar Sadat's peace initiative in 1977. Photo: Sa'ar Ya'cov, 1978.

**3** Ten days after having signed the Rhodes armistice agreement, which created the Gaza Strip, Egyptian and Israeli officers work out the details of a prisoner exchange with a UN official. Photo: Hugo Mendelsohn, early March 1949.

**4** Peasant women near Beit Hanun in the northern Gaza Strip bringing back the flocks at dusk. Note the wide spaces and the unbroken horizon, long since built-up and densely populated. Photo: Fritz Cohen, December 1956.

**5** Gazan (non refugee) *fellaheen* plowing barley fields northwest of Gaza City. Photo: Fritz Cohen, December 1956.

**6** Market street near Medina Square in Gaza City. Shopkeepers dare not observe the strike called by PLO to protest Israel's "dirty war" against Palestinian fighters. Photo: Moshe Milner, August 1971.

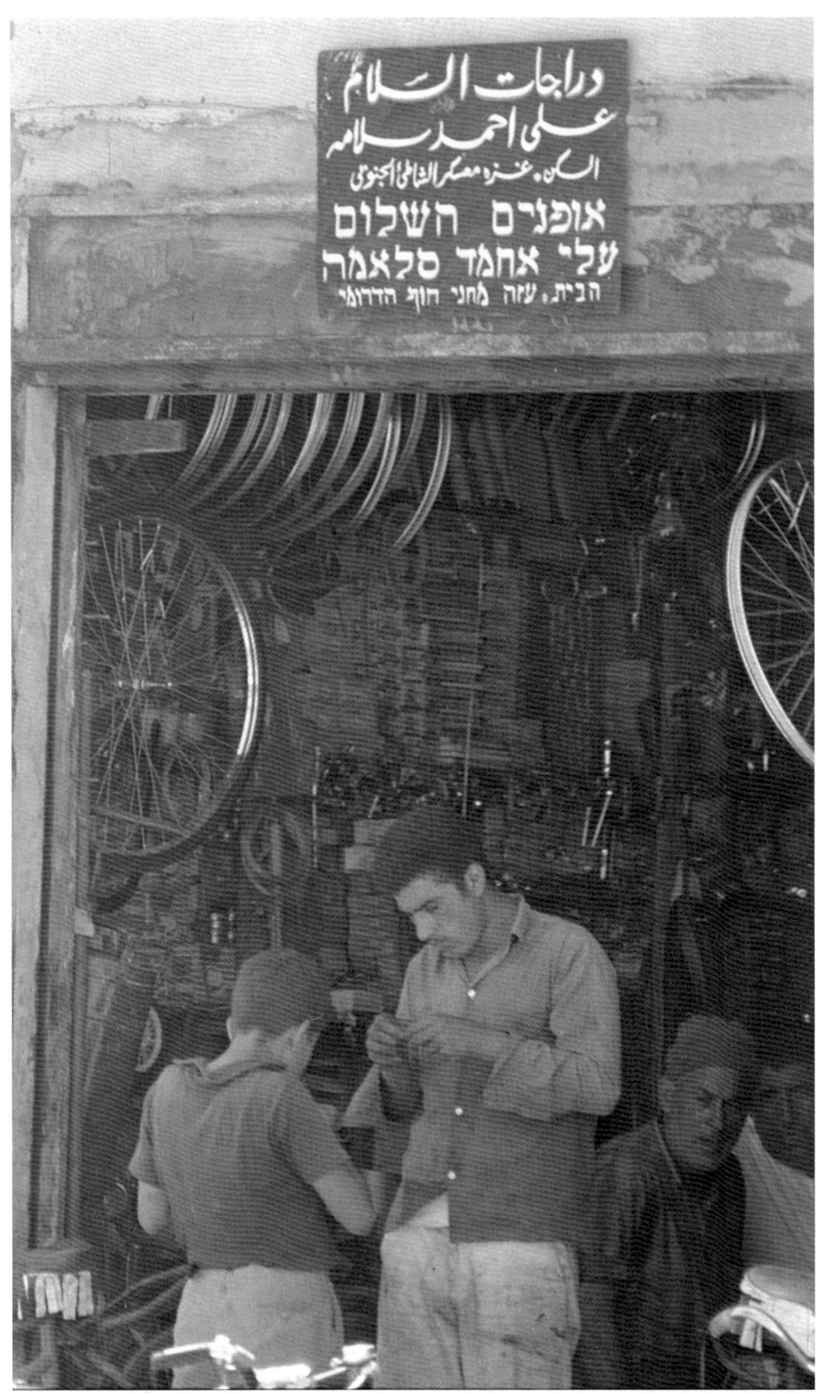


**7**
Bicycle repair man Ali Ahmad Salame calls his shop in Gaza City "Bicycles for Peace", the words written in Arabic next to Hebrew – a gesture unthinkable in later years. Photo: Moshe Milner, August 1971.

**8** Less than two months after Israel's conquest of Gaza, local policemen patrol Umar al-Mukhtar street of Gaza City. Photo: Moshe Milner, August 1967.

**9** The Israel-sponsored building project at Sheikh Radwan outside Gaza City, begun in 1973. In spite of PLO warnings, refugees rushed to sign up for the project. Photo: Moshe Milner, June 1976.

**10** The newly appointed mayor of Gaza City, Rushi al-Shawa, with an Israeli officer – the future historian Zvi Elpeleg – after the election of a new city council. When the Egyptians returned to Gaza four months later, Shawa was brutally punished for having served under the Israelis. Photo: Moshe Pridan, November 1956.

**11** The Mamluk citadel in Khan Yunes, the most distinguished historical building in the Strip. April 1973, Government Press Office, Jerusalem.

**12** Outdoor barber in the Khan Yunes refugee camp. December 1956, Government Press Office, Jerusalem.

**13** The new border fence erected through the city of Rafah when Israel withdrew from the Sinai peninsula in 1982 cut through families and neighbourhoods. Those on the Egyptian side, bitter at the time, would later bless their luck for living outside the Strip. Photo: Yosi Roth, May 1982.

**14** Women in the Nuseirat refugee camp rush out in search of medicine during a break in the curfew imposed on the Strip during the first Gulf War. Photo: Zvika Israeli, February 1991.

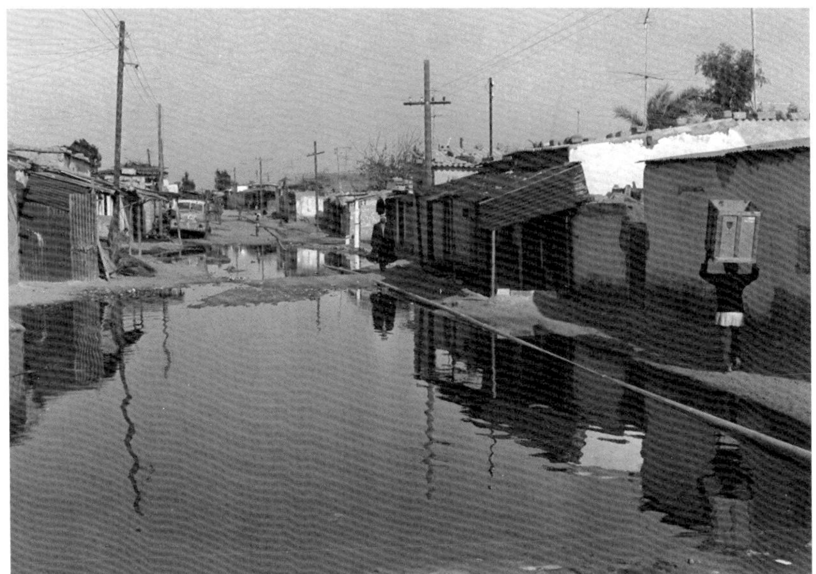

**15** A recurrent scourge: streets flooded with sewage in the Canada refugee camp, Rafah. During the peace years 1993–2000 sanitary infrastructure was much improved. But recently fighting, lack of fuel and aid-cuts to the Hamas government have put the clock back decades. Many camps dwellers live next to permanent cesspools. Photo: Moshe Milner, January 1975.

**16** Rafah refugees in discussion with Israeli Defense Minister Moshe Dayan. Photo: Nissim Gabay, December 1972.

**17** Refugee children waiting for milk distribution by American aid organization C.A.R.E. Photo: Moshe Milner, January 1957.

**18** The primitive and time-consuming conditions at Gaza harbour have always provided wages to many day-labourers and their families, but have also been a drag on economic development. Here, unbagged cement is brought ashore from a Greek freighter by shuttling lighters. Photo: January 1972.

**19** Freshly netted sardines south of Gaza City. Once an important item on the Gazan menu, but nowadays fishing is in the doldrums thanks to pollution, the Aswan dam and the exclusion zones maintained by the Israeli navy. Photo: Moshe Milner, August 1967.

**20** Boys at Gaza City orphanage inspected for lice. Photo: Moshe Pridan, February 1957.

**21** One of the first Jewish settlements in the Strip, Netzer Sireni, welcomes Prime Minister Yizhak Rabin. Photo: Moshe Milner, February 1977.

**22** Smiles and high hopes: Ehud Barak and Yasser Arafat brought the world to a high pitch of expectation, but failed to deliver at Camp David 2000. Photo: Avi Ohayon, July 1999.

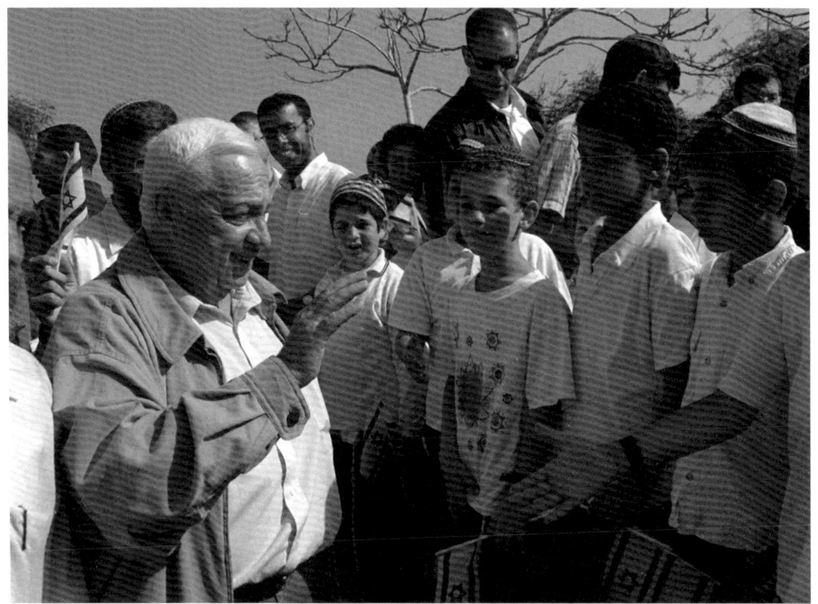

**23** Newly elected Prime Minister Ariel Sharon with Jewish settler children in the Atzmona colony. Four years later Sharon, the great champion of the Gazan settlements, would forcibly evict his one-time protégées. Photo: Amos Ben Gershom, May 2001.

**24** Israeli armoured corps lining up to enter the Strip after the abduction of Israeli soldier Gil'ad Shalit. Nearly four hundred Palestinians died during that round of fighting, but Shalit was not located. Photo: Avi Ohayon, June 2006.

**25** Dignitaries in Gaza City offering condolence to the family of a high Fatah official killed in Lebanon, January 2009. Photo: Paul Hansen.

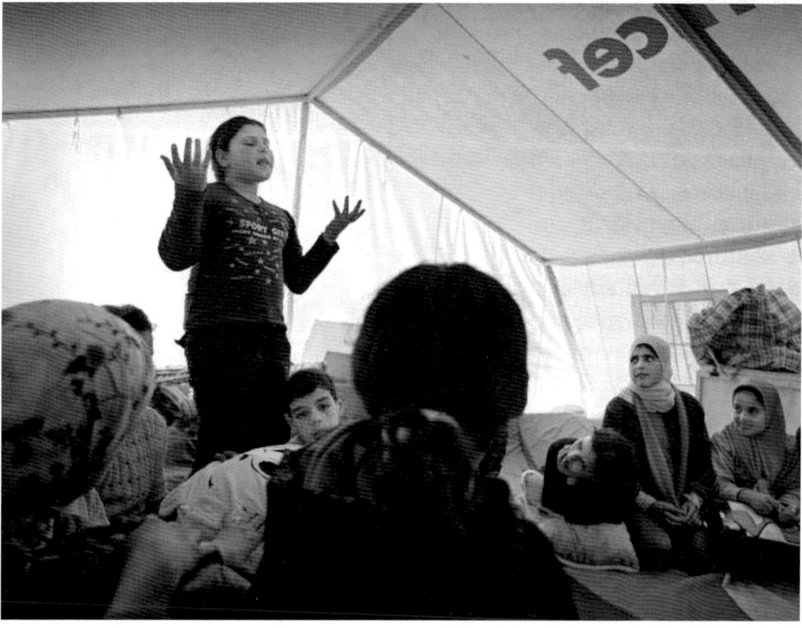

**26** A girl from the Jebalya refugee camp sings during group therapy. Psychological treatment, long frowned upon by Gazans, is no longer regarded as a sign of mental illness. January 2009. Photo: Paul Hansen.

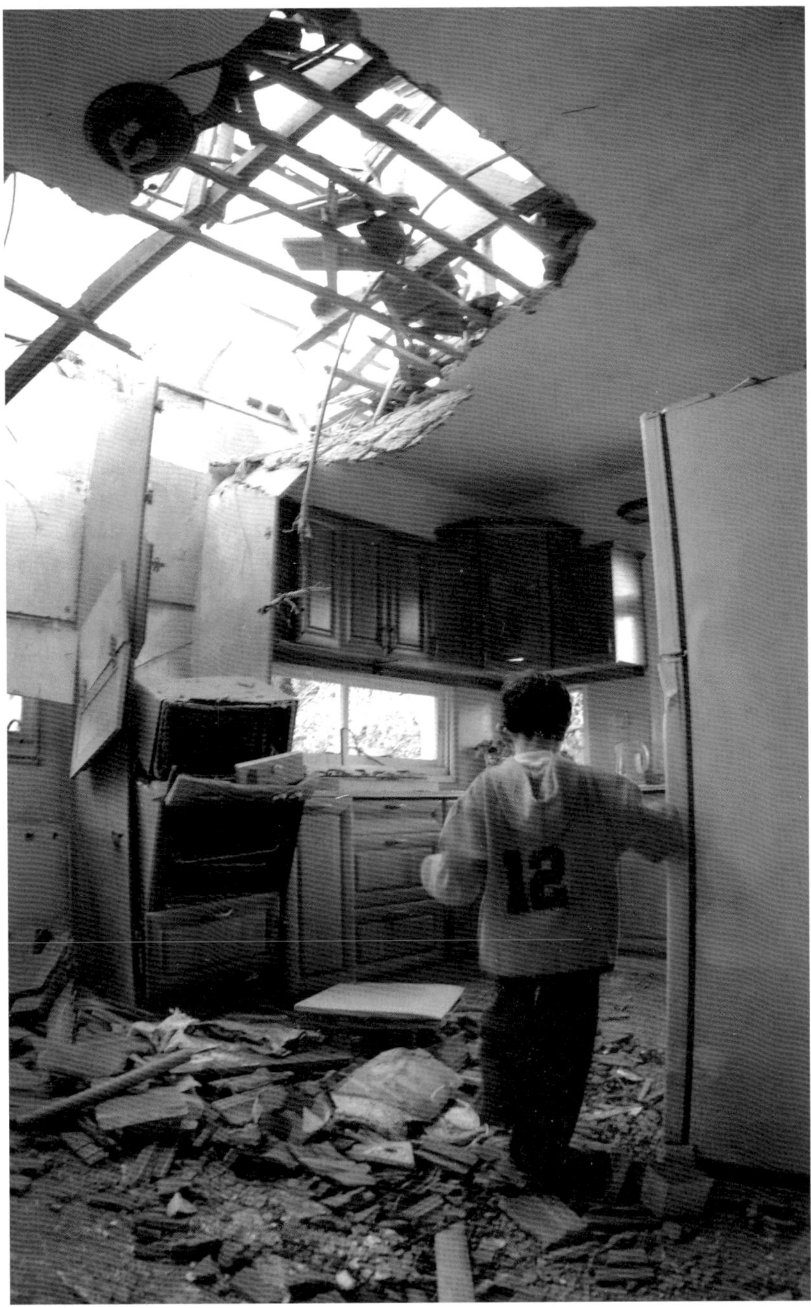

**27** Sderot (near Gaza), Israel, 25 November 2006. This is a typical picture of the damage that Qassam rockets caused. The continued rocket attacks throughout 2006–2008 caused a surge of public indignation in Israel and pushed the coalition government to scrap its tit-for-tat strategy – shelling and targeted killings from the air after Palestinian rocket attacks – and go to war (Operation Cast Lead). During the war Hamas and Jihad units intensified attacks on civilian targets in Israel, but after the war such attacks became very rare. Photo: Amir Cohen.

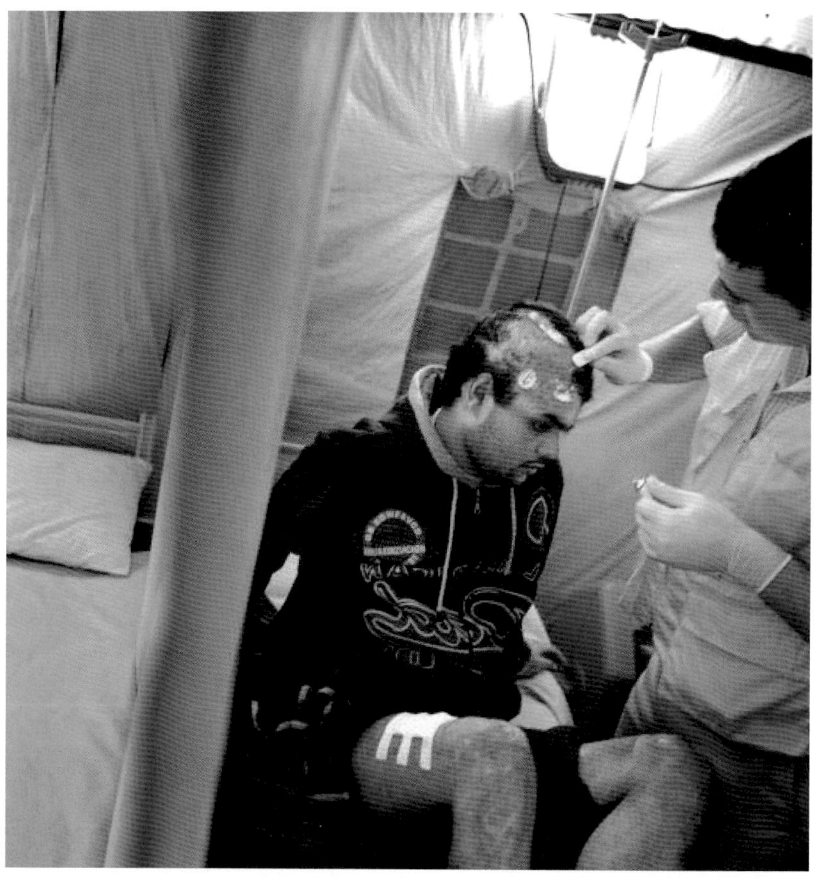

**28** The use, by Israel, of phosphorous shells in order to create smokescreen cover for its infantry units became a focus of the many Human Rights' reports which followed the 2008–9 war. Here, a man from the Jebaliya refugee camp is treated for extensive phosphorous burns. Photo: Paul Hansen.

Brotherhood was behind it. But it did not take the Israelis long to figure it out, and that was the end of their ten-year honeymoon with the Islamists. Hamas was really nothing more than a label used by the Gazan Muslim Brotherhood to help it come out of the closet. It was not convenient to do so under the name of a movement feared and persecuted by the Egyptian, Jordanian and Syrian regimes – as well as by Arafat and a large segment of the Strip's population.

Hamas did not only come out of the closet to fight the Israelis. It went on the offensive inside its own society as well. A few weeks after the Islamists put Marwan's beer-drinking operation out of business, leaflets appeared which branded swimming and swimsuits as stains on faith and tradition. Later on, more extreme appeals would rave against walking, picnicking and even being on the beach. The Gazans began to realise that Islamism was not only about religion or observance, but about everything. Since the 1947–49 tragedy, the seashore had been an oasis of relief and solace for people who shared bedrooms with seven other family members and whose household budgeting was an acrobatic feat. The beach, before boating and fishing became circumscribed, was one of the few places where a person could be alone, where lovers could find shelter from prying eyes, where children could run freely. In the words of Salim Tamari:

> "Gaza . . . became the first city in the history of the Mediterranean where swimming was formally banned. A number of flyers were distributed warning people about the moral dangers inherent in indulging in the pleasures of the sea. Toward the third year of the uprising, even an innocent stroll on the seashore – by then the only social outlet for a community confined by . . . curfews . . . was viewed as sacrilegious."

The beach was but one front-line in the Palestinian *Kulturkampf* raging behind the scenes during the struggle against occupation. Dress-codes were enforced among women, at first verbally, then comprehensively. At institutions of higher learning, girls were offered a narrowing choice of careers. The study of Islamic law was considered the most wholesome spiritual fare for girls, while history or foreign literature were regarded as unsuitable for pure hearts. For all their resentment at Islamist competition, the PLO–Fatah camp presented little organised resistance to defend their own, secular – or more secular – view of women's rights. Hamas had conquered the moral high ground in this struggle, making the defence of modernity seem unpalatable even to the secularists themselves. As the Israeli countermeasures took ever more drastic expressions, fewer and fewer secularists felt comfortable arguing against tradition and against Islam.

In the spring of 1989 Hamas operatives from Gaza were sent into Israel, dressed up as religious Jews, Their brief was to pick up hitchhiking Israeli soldiers. After two soldiers had disappeared the Israelis finally woke up to the challenge represented by Hamas, and the movement became the object of the most draconian measures ever applied against anyone, before or after, during the long occupation. In the coming months, hundreds of Hamas members were jailed, deported and tortured, and during the next few years Hamas would replace the PLO as Israel's principal enemy. Between the arrest of Hamas leader Ahmad Yassin in May 1989, until the Oslo agreements four years later, many thousand suspected Hamas sympathisers and operatives were rounded up and mercilessly interrogated. Leaders were exiled or isolated from their colleagues in prison camps, and the funds arriving from Gulf sheikhdoms and Palestinian supporters abroad were intercepted. Several times, the Israelis, and probably quite a few Hamas leaders, believed that the game was up and that Hamas was crushed. But by moving the upper strata of its organisation abroad, Hamas managed to stage a comeback after each crushing blow. The supply of eager volunteers appeared inexhaustible, and the rise of global wireless communications reduced the need for decision-makers to get together in person.

# 16

# Hardship, Delusion and Desperation

## The First Gulf War, 1990–1991

*Another collective blow was dispensed at the Erez checkpoint, where thousands of Gazans queued at dawn to get to their workplaces in Tel Aviv on time. About a year after the outbreak of hostilities, the rules at Erez were changed. The opening hours at the crossing were shortened and Israeli tax-men were posted at the gate, equipped with new, powerful computers. No Gazan could enter Israel without a thorough examination of his affairs.*

There is little doubt that the spectacular rise of Hamas contributed to Yasser Arafat's decision to enter peace negotiations with Israel. It was clear to him that with Hamas encroaching upon PLO domains, economically and in terms of public opinion, the only way to reassert his authority was to be physically present in the territories. But before discussing the Oslo peace process we must touch upon one more fateful transformation experienced by the Gazans during the Intifada years – the gradual disappearance of Gazan labour in Israel.

In December 1987, the inhabitants in the Strip were totally dependent on Israeli markets for jobs, raw materials and processed goods. This went for everybody, no less for shopkeepers and taxi drivers than for those who actually crossed the "green line" to work. One of the powerful motives of the Intifada was the urge among Palestinians to obliterate all ties with Israel – work, business, permits, applications – and begin to piece together something of their own. This was a romantic project, but it had some success, as with the setting up of pirate dairies whose aim was to cut loose from Israeli ones. Grotesque scenes were enacted as Israeli soldiers tracked down and led away cows hidden in caves by revolutionary milk-men.

The Palestinians knew that Israeli industry, agriculture, waste-disposal, dish-washing and car-fixing could not go on for a single day without Palestinian labour. But some Palestinian ideologues made an unwarranted inference from this fact. They convinced themselves that the Israeli economy was not only dependent on, but at the mercy of, Arab work. They believed that by striking and staying away from work in Israel they could wring real concessions from its government. To be sure, countless Israeli restaurant and orchard owners would have been quite ready to grant Gaza independence if its people would only show up for work. But not Prime Minister Yitzhak Shamir. The reality which would shake his convictions was yet to be invented. The idea that the Israeli economy stood and fell with Arab labour was widespread also among Israelis and foreign newspaper pundits. It appealed to the schematic, colonialist, third-world interpretation of the occupation.

Apart from clashing with the soldiers, the Gazans of the pre-rocket and pre-suicide bomb era had few sticks to shake at Israel. It is easy to understand the temptation which made them overreach in their use of the perceived economic weapon. Barely a couple of weeks into the Intifada, Danny Gillerman of the Israeli Manufacturer's Association asked the government for permission to bring foreign workers to Israel "in order to reduce our dependence on the territories". There was a sharp reaction from the leftist parties in the Knesset, and from the Labour unions. Foreign workers, it was claimed, would be exploited and push down salaries. They would also send their earnings in remittances abroad, while the Palestinian wages were re-injected into the economy. For a while the matter rested.

At the time, Israel was being overwhelmed by a sudden and unexpected side-effect of the Reagan-Gorbachev détente: the arrival of hundreds of thousands of immigrants from the Soviet Union. Israel needed housing, and urgently. The vast majority of skilled builders were Palestinian. Time and again the plans and timetables of the construction sector were wrecked by the strikes, closures and curfews of the Intifada. All through 1989–90, the uprising ground on and the Russians kept arriving in Israel. The demands from the business sector to bring in foreign labour became more insistent. But it was not until the "Knife War" that the government took steps to reduce dependence of Palestinian labour. The Intifada had shocked Israel deeply, emotionally and politically. But almost all of its dramatic events took place out of sight, far from the daily lives of most Israelis. The knife-attacks, when they began, were carried out by Palestinians against Israeli civilians and soldiers in the middle of busy streets and sidewalks. The attackers acted on their own, without any coordination with armed movements, and thus did not make a blip on the early-warning screens of the secret services. The knifings, although much less bloody in terms of fatalities than explosive devices left on buses, unnerved the Israelis. Most of the knife-men were Gazans who arrived in Israel to work. After the bloody killings at the Temple Mount in Jerusalem on October 9, 1990, when Israeli border policemen fired into a rioting crowd and killed 21 Palestinians, the knifings became an almost daily occurrence. Populist Israeli politicians and rabble-rousers now demanded the exclusion of Palestinians, a call which found wide resonance and prodded the government towards its decision on January 21, 1991, to allow the recruitment of foreign construction workers to replace Palestinians at building sites. By the end of 1991, there were 8,000 Romanian and Turkish builders on Israeli building sites, and the numbers grew exponentially over the coming years. Before long there were also thousands of Thai farmhands in the Negev desert, picking strawberries and green herbs.

Those jobs weren't all that were lost. As the Russian immigrants learned the language, they began to replace Gazans at petrol pumps, in restaurant kitchens and garbage trucks. The Israelis were liberating their economy from Palestinian labour, but the Palestinians had not found an alternative to their dependence on Israeli wages and markets. There were bitter debates about this in Gaza. Some Gazans, especially those who did good business with Israel, resented the way the strike weapon was used. The moderates felt that the strikes and boycotts had not only deprived multitudes of their livelihood, but also deprived the Gazans of their only leverage against the Israelis. The delusion that Israel could be brought to its knees by strikes backfired badly. The Israeli dependence on Arab labour was a tactical asset for the Palestinians, and they gambled it away playing for unrealistic stakes. Because of the ideological gridlock, Israeli governments rarely set a course and act upon it consistently. They only act when raging fires must be extinguished. Therefore, reasoned the critics in Gaza, there was no way Israel would have taken such fateful steps without having been provoked.

The standard of living in Gaza, which took a nosedive in December, 1987, went on spiralling downwards. In the summer of 1988, we saw hungry Gazans at the Erez checkpost begging Israeli soldiers and journalists for food. In February 1989, the lack of income, coupled with a drastic devaluation of the Jordanian dinar, the preferred savings currency of the Gazans, had halved disposable income for the average family. There were also complaints in Gaza that the Bank of Israel sold off its dinar reserves in order to push the exchange rate down. Israeli exports to the occupied territories slid from $928 million in 1987 to $650 in 1988. Another burden was the economic reforms of the new Israeli finance minister, Shimon Peres, which removed subsidies on a series of basic foodstuffs. The slowdown of the crisis-ridden Israeli economy spilled over and hit Palestinian subcontractors. There were still tens of thousands of Gazans working in Israel, but the number was going down, as Israeli employers became chastened by strikes and military closures. A Bank of Israel study, published after the year of the first Intifada, predicted that "the economic relationship can never be reconstructed. Employers are investing in automation and foreign labour in order to shield themselves from the effects of the Intifada." As the Intifada began to peter out in 1992, a few thousand Gazans regained their jobs in Israel, but there was no substantial overall recovery for Gazans until the autonomy accords, Yasser Arafat's return to Gaza in July 1994 and the arrival of massive foreign aid.

For several years prior to the Intifada, Yasser Arafat had been angling for a political opening. He knew that the diplomatic way would remain closed until the PLO publicly recognised Israel, something that was unacceptable to both Hamas and the radical PLO factions. Arafat had to tread warily, and to rely on go-betweens in this ideological mine-field. Soon after the outbreak of the Intifada, the Israeli daily *Ha'aretz* began to publish a series of articles by Basam Abu Sharif, hinting at PLO acceptance of the relevant UN resolutions, recognition of Israel and direct negotiations. Abu Sharif, disfigured and maimed after an Israeli assassination attempt, was a former member of the radical PFLP and had been deeply involved in the spectacular airline hijackings at Dawson's Field in the Jordanian desert in September, 1970. But during the 1980s, he had abandoned his extreme stance, become a member of Arafat's inner circle and also, along with Issam Sartawi and Sa'id Hammami, one of the first Palestinians who found the courage to speak openly in favour of a non-violent solution.

The Israeli foreign minister, Labour leader Shimon Peres, was itching to respond to Abu Sharif's overtures, which obviously had Arafat's blessing. But he dared not, facing an election campaign and knowing how happy the nationalists would be to shower him with familiar gibes of "Arab lover" and "traitor". Even had he dared, any attempt to explore new territory would have been intercepted immediately by Prime Minister Shamir.

As Israel's image deteriorated and its prime minister stonewalled any diplomatic initiatives, Arafat moved to consolidate his image as the level-headed leader of an unarmed popular revolt. By now he had fully adopted and identified with the uprising he first regarded with such mistrust. When some well-meaning local leaders suggested that the resistance be called off in return for a UN administration of the territories, he thundered: "Anyone who tries to haggle over the glorious Intifada will get ten bullets in the chest!" – words which sent Bethlehem mayor Elias Freij into hiding.

The American philosophy professor Jerome Segal helped Arafat prepare a blueprint for diplomatic action, including the unilateral declaration of Palestinian statehood, which attracted enormous attention without having any practical consequences. During months of hectic activity, the PLO leader edged closer and closer to US conditions for letting him into the living room of international diplomacy: full recognition of Israel and renunciation of terrorism.

In the Israeli elections on November 1, 1988, the nationalist Likud defeated Shimon Peres' Labour by a hairsbreadth. The two parties kept governing together but, in the new coalition, Likud's hand was strengthened. Shamir remained premier and Yitzhak Rabin kept the defence ministry. But Peres was forced from the foreign ministry by Shamir, who had lost patience with the conciliatory statements emanating from Peres and his circle of young, peace-minded intellectuals.

On December 15, Washington agreed to low-level consultations between US and PLO representatives. The news infuriated Shamir, who regarded it as little less than betrayal. In its leaflets, the United National

Leadership of the Intifada in Gaza celebrated Arafat's diplomatic feat as a great advance for the Palestinians. There were joyous "independence" celebrations in Gaza, but there was no consensus. Hamas and the radicals scorned Arafat's peace manoeuvres, and there was an unlikely rapprochement between the Islamists and the Syrian-backed revolutionary groups. Hamas leaflets in Gaza expressed horror at the "recognition of Israel" and the "grovelling before the enemy".

The rift between the PLO and the Muslim Brotherhood, now called Hamas, was already well on the way towards becoming the central factor of Gazan politics. Quite apart from the struggle for power, and for local hearts and minds, it was becoming obvious that the two movements were becoming two cultures, two antagonistic ways of life whose blueprints for the future, for daily life and for the resolution of the conflict could not be reconciled. Fatah families and clans began to object to one of theirs marrying "Hamsawi" people, and vice versa. There was no common ground, no basis for unified action, between Hamas' Sheikh Ahmad Yassin and Yasser Arafat. The international recognition and support Arafat had gained during the Intifada were mere vanities in the eyes of Hamas, especially since Arafat's aim was so plainly negotiations with Israel – which would require further concessions from him, first among them the recognition of the 1949 cease-fire lines as Israel's borders. When Arafat declared, in May 1989, that the Palestinian National Covenant, which had called for the end of the Jewish State, was null and void, there was much indignation, not only in the Islamist camp, but also among the refugees in Lebanon and Jordan.

But there was no denying the diplomatic and public relations coups achieved by Arafat during the Intifada. The crowning achievement was the passing – with US assent – of UN resolution 672, the first one explicitly to mention "the legitimate political rights of the Palestinian people". The PLO delegate at the UN was allowed to address the Security Council as the representative of Palestine. Prominent American Jews ignored the Israelis and held talks with Arafat; he was given red-carpet treatment in European capitals and his strategy kept polarising Israeli society. More and more Israelis denounced the absurdity of the country's official line, based on the pretence that the Palestinians and the PLO did not exist. The chief of staff, Dan Shomron, who had promised to put down the uprising in the Strip "in a few days", now told the Knesset foreign affairs and defence committee that the Intifada "cannot be eradicated, because it is an expression of nationalist feeling" – which earned him a sharp rebuke from Shamir. Shomron, if anyone, should have known. In February 1989, Israel had three times the number of soldiers in the West Bank and the Gaza Strip as it had needed to conquer those areas in 1967. Several thousand Palestinians were in administrative detention – jailed without trial – and more than ten thousand were in prison camps, most of them at "Ansar III", a huge new structure near Ketziot in the western Negev Desert. Thousands of infantry, artillery and armoured force soldiers spent their reserve duty chasing children in Gazan refugee camps instead of training.

And while the world watched, the disjointed Israeli government kept pulling in opposite directions. While Prime Minister Shamir promised to jail Yasser Arafat if he arrived in Israel offering peace, senior figures in the Labour party openly recommended talks with the PLO. Some held talks with the leaders of the UNL, the Intifada leadership. Shamir's science minister, Ezer Weizman, asked by a reporter if Arafat could really be trusted, replied, "How the hell should I know, if I am forbidden to speak to him". After the security services discovered that Weizman, former war hero and future president, had met a PLO representative in Geneva, there was a huge political row. But the man who would ultimately put an end to Israel's schizophrenic attitude and recognise the PLO, Defence Minister Yitzhak Rabin, was still closer to Shamir's hidebound stance than to the peaceniks in his own Labour Party. "The Intifada", he declared after more than a year of clashes, "is not a struggle for human rights or freedom. It is part of the general Arab effort to destroy Israel."

In Gaza the leaders of the different Palestinian groups followed these diplomatic developments closely, analysing them to the tenth degree in smoky cafés and in a never-ending battle of leaflets. But to those who kept the cauldron boiling – the masked activists, the stone-throwers and their parents – the subtleties of UN resolutions or the various Geneva initiatives mattered little. As the Intifada entered its third year, many families in the Strip's refugee camps survived on bread and olives. The famous gold bazaar of Gaza City had become a buyers-only market as women sold their pendants, bracelets and even wedding rings to scrape some cash together. By that time, most of the stone-throwers and protesters were children. The older ones had been detained or deterred by ever-tougher Israeli collective punishments.

Perhaps the most painful change came with the new regulations on the hospitalisation of Gazans in Israel. Before the Intifada, Strip residents who needed care unavailable at local hospitals were treated in Israel, with little or no paperwork and with most expenses covered. The rumours broadcast by leaflets in Gaza, about wounded Palestinians being murdered at Israeli hospitals, caused indignation in Israel. Should Israel treat Palestinians who had been injured during attacks against Israeli soldiers – only to get blood-libelled in return?, asked the nationalists. Defence Minister Rabin cancelled the budget for out-treatment of Gazans. There was a public outcry, following an appeal to world opinion by Israeli physicians at a London conference. In the end, Rabin reversed his decision, but with 40 per cent of the budget slashed. Around 90 Gazan children were constantly in need of treatment in Israel, mainly kidney, heart and cancer patients – and a growing number of Intifada casualties. The mounting difficulties in getting proper treatment for the children were real and urgent, but they seem almost trivial compared to the situation twenty years later, when only a few Gazans a year are accepted for treatment in Israel. (Those who can afford it leave the Strip via the underground tunnels and pay for treatment in Cairo.)

Another collective blow was dispensed at the Erez checkpoint, where thousands of Gazans queued at dawn to get to their workplaces in Tel Aviv on time. About a year after the outbreak of hostilities, the rules at Erez were changed. The opening hours at the crossing were shortened and Israeli tax-men were posted at the gate, equipped with new, powerful computers. No Gazan could enter Israel without a thorough examination of his affairs. Cars belonging to Gazans with unpaid debts were confiscated and the owners charged with a storage fee until the state had collected its due. In the past, taxmen had accepted the balance-sheets of Gazan workers and businessmen at face value; from now on they would gauge the taxable income unilaterally and arbitrarily. Interest on unpaid debts grew at an appalling rate. Such fierce measures did little to deter the rebels, who owned no cars and had no income, but brought all available pressure down upon those Gazans who refrained from violence and wanted only to work. This, it was vainly hoped, would pit the working people against the rebels and provide the deterrence the soldiers had been unable to produce.

This was also the beginning of the severe regulations which would cripple the Gazan fishing industry. The primitive facilities at Gaza City harbour had been upgraded. A new dock for the fishermen was constructed, with locker rooms, showers and deep-freeze storage laid on by the UN. Most of the fishermen lived in the nearby refugee camp of Shaati, northeast of Gaza City, which was the main entry point for smuggled drugs (for the Israeli market) and of cash from Gulf state donors bound for the rebels. The new installations, it was decreed, could only be used by those fishermen who abided by the new regulations: a limit on engine size, fishing only during "office hours" and registration of all vessels leaving or entering port. In their campaign against smuggling, the Israeli Army was assisted by Hamas, who fought vigorously against rising drug abuse. Many of their new recruits were born-again ex-addicts, who led Hamas' anti-drug squads to their old suppliers. Confiscated drug shipments were burned in Palestine Square with pomp and ceremony.

With the fishing industry languishing and work-opportunities in Israel dwindling, much depended on citrus exports, the old mainstay of the Gazan economy. The 1990–91 harvest was impressive, and a record 174,000 tons were exported, a 55 per cent rise. But the citrus producers' union – synonymous with the old landed aristocracy – complained that Israel manipulated prices in order to elbow them out of the expanding post-communist markets of Eastern Europe.

Life was unbearably hard in Gaza, and not all of its hard-pressed bread-winners found much consolation in the internal strife in Israel, the media coverage of the Intifada, the world-wide sympathy for the Palestinians and Yasser Arafat's diplomatic successes. But the leaders of the underground leadership did, and so did the PLO. There were unmistakable signs of light at the end of the tunnel.

And then, as everything seemed to be going his way, Yasser Arafat gambled away most of his hard-earned winnings in one foolish bet. In August 1990, after the Iraqi dictator Saddam Hussein invaded Kuwait, he was roundly denounced by the Arab world. But Arafat offered Saddam his wholehearted support, and he refused to withdraw it during the seven-month long crisis. Remarkably, the UNL Intifada leadership took the same line. In the first of its communiqués on the issue, "capitalist, reactionary Kuwait" was denounced. Saddam had shrewdly tied the Kuwait issue to the Palestinian one. He was ready to discuss an Iraqi pull-back from Kuwait, he said, if the Israelis withdrew from the territories they had occupied. If the US and its allies dared to attack him, Saddam vowed, he would launch ballistic missiles at Tel Aviv. The occupied Gazans, not used to Arab leaders risking anything at all for their sake, were enchanted. Israeli soldiers were constantly busy pulling down banned Palestinian flags from lamp-posts and rooftops. Now Iraqi flags, not officially banned, became as numerous.

Many sensible Palestinians tried their best to point out the great risks inherent in Arafat's policy, which Edward Said called "a terrible blunder". But it took guts to challenge the massive pro-Saddam consensus among ordinary Palestinians. Of local Palestinian leaders, the only one to denounce Saddam as the aggressor was Bethlehem's mayor, Elias Freij. Level-headed and peaceful members of the UNL, like the soft-spoken philosophy teacher Sari Nuseibeh, lost all better judgement and branded the efforts to liberate Kuwait a "treacherous, criminal aggression". He even insisted, after a week of devastating allied air attacks, that Iraq's army "was stronger than ever". (In an absurd sequel, Nusseibeh was then arrested by the Israelis as an Iraqi spy, a baseless charge.)

But to Saddam's – and Arafat's – arch-enemy, Syrian President Hafez Assad, the real traitor was the PLO. Assad had never cherished Arafat's dream of total independence from other Arab actors, and his press habitually dragged the PLO and its leader through the gutter. The Egyptian government which, like Assad, joined the huge alliance against Iraq issued a sinister threat against the PLO. Egypt, it was made known in Cairo, was reassessing its view of the PLO as the sole legitimate representative of the Palestinians. The only Arab leader who joined Arafat in siding with Saddam was Jordan's King Hussein. But everybody knew that he had sound pragmatic reasons for going against the current. Arafat had no compelling reasons for remaining at Saddam's side.

In fact, he had compelling reasons not to, because his support of the Iraqi annexation of Kuwait, one of the PLO's most generous sponsors, brought about the first humanitarian catastrophe of the war – the eviction of tens of thousands of Palestinian families from the sheikhdoms of the Gulf. At the end of the new year, 1990–91, many of those families had arrived in Gaza. They constituted living proof of the cost of Arafat's policies. Before long, several hundred thousand Palestinians, most of them wealthy middle-class residents in the Gulf, were refugees in Jordan and the occupied territories. For decades their remittances had alleviated the hardships of their Gazan relatives, now suddenly they became a burden on them. Kuwaiti money, which had kept many schools and charities in the Strip running, dried up.

I had several Gazan friends who understood that Iraq was bound to be thrown out of Kuwait, and trashed militarily. But their caution and foresight were not appreciated. In the end-of-days euphoria that swept refugee camps and activists along, there was a tangible feeling that liberation was near. These emotions fanned the Intifada, which flared up with unseen intensity, created new top scores in terms of numbers arrested and wounded – almost a thousand Gazans were injured by tear-gas and plastic bullets during October 1990. In late October, Israeli soldiers were physically driven from their posts at the Shabura camp in Rafah by unarmed crowds. The smoke, the fire and the impressive heroics seemed to reinforce apocalyptic hopes of imminent liberation.

The occupied Palestinians' departure from reality most probably contributed to Arafat's disastrous decisions. Never one to confront public opinion, Arafat realised that both Israel and several key Arab states were eager to get rid of him and cultivate a new Palestinian leadership. His only asset in blocking such schemes was his support in the territories.

And, until reality struck on January 16, 1991, Arafat did ride a wave of popularity which managed to confuse even Hamas. The islamists had kept up their war of words against the PLO establishment all through the Intifada. On Hamas leaflets, Arafat's people in the Strip were accused of pilfering Intifada funds, of supporting the "Zionist" Lebanese Shi'ite militia *Amal* and many other sins, real or imaginary. Hamas had not rallied to Saddam's side the way Arafat had. The Iraqi despot seemed to stand for everything Hamas was against; he was a ruthless secularist and nationalist and, more importantly, he had gobbled up Kuwait, the generous and hospitable base of Hamas' leadership in-exile.

But Hamas soon realised that it was not expedient to stand in the way of the popular, pro-Saddam tide. Its leaders in Gaza wavered, perhaps worrying that there was really something in the wild expectations let loose in the alleys. Saddam was aware of the deep scepticism of all Islamists, and made a great effort to reach out to them by donning traditional gear, praying with the common crowd in mosques and even adding the *takbir* – the words "God is Great" – to the Iraqi flag.

When the war broke out, the Strip was sealed off from Israel. Curfew decrees kept large parts of the Gazan population indoors, eagerly awaiting developments in the Gulf. When the first Iraqi Scud missiles hit Israel on January 22, 1991, there was much rejoicing in Gaza, and anti-Palestinian feeling in Israel reached an all-time high.

When it was all over, Iraq driven from Kuwait, and the mighty Saddam fighting for dear life against internal uprisings, there was a bitter hangover. The dreams of a magical deliverance had gone up in smoke and the prospects were even bleaker than they had been before. Israel was importing foreign workers in large numbers and public pressure mounted on Israeli politicians to keep Gazans out. Arafat's position was no more enviable. He had made such significant diplomatic headway during the Intifada years because the West had come to share the Palestinian view of Israeli occupation as illegal and immoral. How was he going to pursue that line, after having applauded the destruction, by brute force, of an independent state?

The only consolation for the Gazans and for Arafat was that the Israelis did not wake up to a new dawn either. The nationalist Israeli government expected VIP treatment from the international community in return for having turned the other cheek and refrained from responding to 39 Iraqi missile attacks. But instead of getting a blank check to continue expansion in the occupied territories, they got a brusque message from US Secretary of State James Baker: "Abandon your delusions."

# 17

# Failure at Madrid and Success at Oslo, 1991–1993

*When the contents of the Oslo talks became public, there was justifiable euphoria in the Strip. Going by the press reports, the Gaza Strip was going to become the showcase for the whole peace process. By fighting poverty and unemployment there, the Palestinian public would be won over and extremism would lose its fertile ground. The progress in Gaza would also, it was hoped, soothe Israeli fears ahead of more painful pullbacks in the West Bank. There was much talk of the Strip becoming "a new Singapore", an island of dynamism and creativity.*

Baker's attempt to break the Israeli-Palestinian stalemate was the Madrid Conference in the autumn of 1991. It terms of results and openings towards a negotiated settlement, it was a resounding letdown. Its importance lay elsewhere. Israeli Prime Minister Yitzhak Shamir was brought kicking and screaming to Madrid and forced to act out his part at the conference table. Of course he conceded nothing, but he was forced to face PLO loyalists like Faisal Husseini from Jerusalem and Dr Haidar Abdul Shafi from Gaza, both of them people Shamir would rather have exiled or put in jail.

Yasser Arafat was also brought to Madrid by the scruff of the neck. His position after Iraq's collapse was wretched. The Gulf states had cut off all funding to the PLO and the Syrians and the Jordanians were openly working towards replacing Arafat. Desperate for aid, he begged for audiences with Arab rulers, but no one would receive him. It was in that condition, battered and bruised, that Arafat accepted the Russian–American formula for the Madrid talks: no PLO delegation at the table, but Gazans and West Bankers incorporated into the Jordanian delegation.

The George Bush–James Baker administration twisted Shamir's arm in order to secure a follow-up to the Madrid talks, but he did not buckle. Negotiations went on according to the Madrid format, between an Israeli delegation and a Jordanian–Palestinian delegation, for almost two more years. But the chief negotiator on the Palestinian side, Haidar Abdul Shafi, an old Arafat critic, knew that the talks were barren. He stayed on, he told me, because it was "his duty". Even though nothing took place at the negotiating table, the indirect PLO-presence there was the only remaining Arafat asset.

Both Bush and Baker detested the Israeli settlement policy, which had accelerated by 60 per cent during 1991, after Ariel Sharon became minister of housing. But there was nothing they could do to pressure Shamir into bona fide negotiations. Shamir positively seemed to enjoy rejecting pressure. "Forget it", he replied when the White House demanded a settlement freeze.

But Bush did put an end to Shamir's career. In January 1992, the US voted with the rest of the UN Security Council in condemning Israeli deportations of Palestinians. Only days later, Washington announced the first drastic measure against Israel since relations became close under Richard Nixon. Israel was overwhelmed by Russian immigrants and urgently sought funds on international financial markets: two billion dollars during 1992 and another ten billion during the next couple of years. The only way Israel could hope to muster such amounts was if the US Treasury underwrote the transaction. If Israel carried on building on Palestinian land, Bush now announced, Israel could not count on loan guarantees for more than one billion dollars.

In Gaza, the popular Intifada had turned into armed resistance. The attacks on Israeli soldiers became more frequent and more bloody. Hamas, now awash with Gulf state contributions, became more insolent and openly challenged the cash-strapped and dejected PLO–Fatah. Sellers of liquor and pornographic movies were often found beaten to death, even if they had solid PLO connections. It was becoming clearer that Hamas had finished laying the groundwork and was now aiming for control. A measure of Arafat's fear was his active joining in the campaign for the internal elections of the Engineers' Union of Gaza in January, 1992. He personally took time off to canvass voters and record pro-Fatah videotaped appeals. The Islamists were only just beaten by a coalition of all other forces, but won four out of nine seats in the assembly.

Former Defence Minister Yitzhak Rabin, whose uncompromising attitude during the Intifada had showed little imagination and less foresight, had, like Arafat, begun to move away from old certainties. A few days after the US threats to deny Israel credit, Rabin attacked Shamir and accused him of miring down the peace talks on purpose. "Only I can make peace", he promised. The Israeli voters, not least the multitude of ex-Soviets demanding housing and work, realised that another Shamir government would cloud US–Israeli relations and usher in a long period of austerity.

On June 23, 1992, Rabin won the elections and formed a government which contained several of the most dedicated Israeli proponents of peace. On December 2, 1992, Rabin's government presented new legislation in the Knesset aimed at legalising contacts with the PLO. Government spokesmen stressed that this was merely a matter of principles. No dealings with the PLO were underway. Two days later, Yasser Arafat received a top-secret message from his economic adviser Ahmad Qurei'a – "Abu 'Ala" – with a memorandum on a meeting between Qurei'a and Ya'ir Hirschfeld, a professor at the University of Haifa. Hirschfeld, Qurei'a reported, "is regarded as a member of the Shimon Peres–Yossi Beilin group, but is also on good terms with Rabin". That meeting was the beginning of the "Oslo process", the secret talks with the PLO which culminated in the mutual recognition of Israel and the PLO and the declaration of principles signed on the White House lawn on September 13, 1993.

From the beginning, the idea of "Gaza First" played an important part in the secret talks in Norway. The idea had first been proposed in 1978, and then again by Shimon Peres at the beginning of the 1987 Palestinian rising. The Gaza first idea included massive doses of development aid, a UN trusteeship, 10,000–15,000 Palestinian security officials to take over after an Israeli withdrawal, a land bridge between the Strip and the West Bank, a new port in Gaza and a new airport near Rafah. In the end, the parties settled for a modified formula, "Gaza and Jericho First", as the first step of the peace process to be implemented.

The UN was kept out of the deal and the corridor between Gaza and the West Bank was never opened, but when the bombshell burst and the contents of the Oslo talks became public, there was justifiable euphoria in the Strip. Going by the press reports, the Gaza Strip was going to become the showcase for the whole peace process. By fighting poverty and unemployment there, the Palestinian public would be won over and extremism would lose its fertile ground. The progress in Gaza would also, it was hoped, soothe Israeli fears ahead of more painful pullbacks in the West Bank. There was much talk of the Strip becoming "a new Singapore", an island of dynamism and creativity. Sometimes the schemes sounded wildly utopian, but they were not baseless: the Gazan workforce was skilled in comparison with other Arab societies, and Gazan exiles were keen to contribute their money, know-how and leadership. Never in the history of international conflict has there been a donor scramble like the one heading for Gaza after the Rabin–Arafat deal. The international community pledged huge sums and engineering capacity to redeem Gaza's slums and provide sewage treatment, drinking water and modern housing. There were not enough Palestinian dignitaries available to receive the steady stream of ministers and director-generals arriving from Japan, Sweden, Italy, Spain, Holland and Germany. There were cases of bidding for projects where donors would try to sweeten the deal with extra perks, just to clinch a particularly prestigious drain, road or school undertaking.

Gaza never became another Singapore, but it was not for lack of funding. From the start of the peace process, the optimism of mainstream PLO and the Israeli peace camp collided with the misgivings and the grim forecasts of the Islamists and other Palestinian dissidents, and of the Israeli nationalists, led on by the settlers. As soon as the "Gaza First" ideas were first aired during the secret talks, the Palestinian negotiators insisted that the settlements in the Strip be removed soon after the Israeli retreat. But Rabin was adamant that the settlement issue be left for the final status discussions, scheduled to culminate in a peace deal no later than 1999.

The Clinton–Arafat–Rabin performance in Washington, watched live by a good part of the earth's population, was the object of some surreal haggling in Gaza. Hamas was pushing for a commercial strike of protest against the "shameful surrender" of the PLO; while the PLO was planning a classic Beirut-style fantasia, with fireworks, marches and a bounty of sweets and confetti. Hamas and the PLO agreed to close shops in "mourning" until three o'clock in the afternoon, when celebrations would commence; 76 per cent of the Strip's inhabitants supported the Oslo deal, a figure which frightened Hamas.

But in the weeks following the PLO–Israel recognition, five well-known Gazans from the PLO camp were murdered. The Israelis mounted a huge offensive against Hamas, with curfews and restrictions which marred the mood of liberation. Arafat condemned the measures, but to no avail. For the first time of many, the Islamists now branded him collaborator, puppet and handyman of Israel.

It took almost a year of tenacious bargaining until Arafat could stage his *grande entrée*, the symbol-laden return to Gaza of its most famous son. Strictly speaking, Arafat's parents moved to Cairo some years before he was born, and the leader himself always propagated the fiction of a Jerusalem birth, but he had been a Gazan feda'i fighting the Israelis in the 1950s, and his supporters in the Strip always claimed him as one of their own. On May 4, 1994, the Gaza–Jericho agreement was finally hammered out in Cairo after much confusion and drama – at the last moment, Arafat pretended to refuse to sign it, embarrassing and infuriating the host, President Hosni Mubarak. The Israeli conditions for leaving Gaza were hard and went far beyond reasonable security concerns. Article 4 read:

*When Chairman Arafat enters the Gaza Strip and the Jericho Area, he will use the title "Chairman (Ra'is in Arabic) of the Palestinian Authority" or "Chairman of the PLO", and will not use the title "President of Palestine".*

There was something messianic and, to the sceptic, ominous in the air on that unforgettable Friday, the first of July, 1994, when Arafat's armoured black Mercedes, surrounded by Palestinian Liberation Army bodyguards, reached the crossing between Egypt and Gaza. For days, the local dignitaries in Rafah, the first Palestinian town to receive the leader, had argued over seating arrangements for the gala reception they had planned for Arafat. They sweated miserably for hours in their black suits, but when the ra'is finally appeared, his security people took one look at the scene and shook their heads. It was too dangerous. Arafat stepped out of the limousine, waved, and when the crowd began running towards him he got inside again. The car disappeared in a cloud of dust, accompanied by wails of disappointment. Thousands of school-children had been busy for days whitewashing away the grafitti of strife and division from the walls along the motorcade itinerary. The ubiquitous garbage had been bagged by volunteers and tasselled strings in the national colours were tied aloft all the way towards Paraliament Square in Gaza City where he delivered his address. The procession made a detour around the Gush Katif settlement area, where "Arafat = Hitler" posters flanked the planned course.

Two issues which would cloud the remaining decade of Arafat's life were already very much in evidence: the deadly feud with Hamas, and the endless quarrels with the donor nations over transparency and monitoring of the aid flow. During the year since the deal with Israel, Gaza – more than the West Bank – had received large amounts of economic assistance, mainly from the EU nations, who were eager to buy into the – still – prestigious peace process after being worsted, indeed kept in the dark, by the Norwegians during the secret Oslo talks. $2.8 billion were pledged by the donors during 1994, but only part of it was delivered. The PLO in Gaza, claimed the donors and Palestinian critics, had no mechanisms and no institutions suitable for processing the incoming money.

In a certain sense, the only financial institution of the fledgling Palestinian state was Arafat himself and his money handler, the mysterious Kurd Muhammad Rashid, rumoured to be the only mortal who possessed the numbers to all the Swiss bank accounts of Fatah, the PLO and the autonomous government. This was already an infected issue before Arafat arrived in Gaza. He was fed up with Northern European accountants and comptrollers badgering him about the paper trails of funds he had distributed at his own discretion. Norway claimed that $100,000 bound for an irrigation project could not be tracked down. The British government complained that the Palestinian official entrusted with a $5 million contribution to the salaries of the new police force could not account for the money. Millions of Swedish crowns were pilfered by a Palestinian human rights organisation. The guests, representing donor nations, were appalled when Arafat, during one of his speeches on that historical first day, thundered against the foreigners who tried to bleed his government dry by manipulating the contributions. The ideas of accountability, he complained, were part of a hostile conspiracy to fetter his government as it struggled to take hold. "We bow down only to Allah", he declared theatrically. In reality, only a tenth of the $2.8 billion pledged by the donor nations had been received, because Arafat delayed setting up proper tax-collection and budgetary systems.

Economic policy and planning under Arafat resembled that of a medieval fiefdom. He would sit in his office at the old sports club near Gaza Beach, while lines of hopefuls formed outside. Arafat had a generous nature and he disliked turning down those beseeching him for favours, contracts, recommendations and protection. But his hand-outs and promises were an affliction for the professionals trying to put the house in order. Soon his trusted Economics minister, Ahmad Qurei'a, threatened to resign if Arafat refused to let experts take part in budgetary work and planning. Arafat had no choice but to concede some ground, for a stark chasm was opening up between the rosy horizons painted by him in his speeches and the facts on the ground. Arafat had promised 30,000 new apartments and 25,000 new jobs. There were plenty of buildings now rising in Gaza City, but even after the severe restrictions imposed during the first Palestinian uprising, work inside Israel remained the main source of income in Gaza. After Israeli settler Baruch Goldstein massacred 30 Muslim worshippers in Hebron in February 1994, Hamas swore to retaliate with five attacks against targets in Israel. The Israeli security services, who knew that Hamas usually delivered on such promises, cut down the number of permits for Palestinians working in Israel to 18,000, the lowest ever. After Arafat's return to Gaza in July, Washington and the EU pressured Israel to raise the number to 63,000, but soon afterwards an intense wave of Hamas suicide bombings commenced, and work opportunities dwindled. Fear of Hamas was also behind the first Israeli fencing in of the Strip (and a simultaneous fencing-in of the Katif settler enclave inside the Strip), which began in 1994. This fence was soon destroyed by the Palestinians. The present fence was built after the 2000 uprising and beefed up in 2005.

# 18

# High Hopes and New Dangers, 1994–1995

*In a pattern that would repeat itself countless times in the years to come, frantic mediation efforts, led by Israeli Arabs, followed the Fatah–Hamas violence. The rift was patched up for a while, but there was no true reconciliation. To the Islamists, as their leaflets proclaimed, the "Sulta" – PLO rule – was "worse than the Jews". To Arafat and his supporters, the Islamists were foreign agents in the pay of reactionary oil sheikhs and Iranian mullahs. In other words, the first condition for a civil war was taking shape: the antagonists' mutual view of each other not merely as wicked, but as traitors.*

Arafat understood only one form of administration, the one he had practiced during his tumultuous years in exile, on the road and on the run. He had no idea how much the ideas of clean government and democracy mattered to the local leaders of his own movement in the Strip. Men like Sufyan Abu Zaide, Hisham Abdul Razek and their peers had spent long years in Israeli jails meticulously organising and developing their own democratic routines. Among them, votes were taken on all issues of importance, in an atmosphere of "all-for-one" which enjoyed huge respect among Gazans in general. The idea that the Palestinian state they had fought for would be run along the lines of a robber band, its leader dishing out gold from a war-chest to current favourites, would have abhorred them, and soon did. As in the more obscure Latin American republics, all enterprises, schools, clinics, fruit-packing storehouses and parks bore brass plaques crediting not the donors but the all-encompassing benevolence of the ruler.

Arafat wanted to co-opt the local Fatah idealists. On his very first day in Gaza, he met with their most important leader, Sami Abu Samhadana from Rafah. Some weeks earlier Abu Samhadana had been rounded up by one of the new security branches – some of which had arrived well ahead of Arafat himself. The order for his arrest certainly came from Arafat himself, after Abu Samhadana had disobeyed his orders not to confront the Jewish settlers in the Strip. It was a typical impasse of those years. Arafat was negotiating constantly with the Israelis. He could strike a hard bargain but he would also make concessions. His Israeli partners were as sorely pressed by hostile opinions at home as was Arafat. But his critics, not to speak of his enemies, made the most of any issue where Arafat gave way in order to propagate the view of him as a compliant dishrag, eager to do Israel's bidding. During their meeting, the two were reconciled, but Abu Samhadana made a point of releasing his demands to the press: "al-Fatah must be reformed through open democratic procedures." Arafat, as he always did, smiled and nodded, giving a general impression of agreement. For once there was a good excuse for his autocracy. During the infernally complicated empowerment talks which preceded Palestinian self-rule on the West Bank, each paragraph stirred up a hornet's nest of conflicting Palestinian and Israeli opinion. To subject the whole process to votes and referenda would have scuttled it.

Quite apart from such pragmatic considerations, Arafat shunned checks and balances or financial audits. The primary beneficiaries of his style of government arrived together with him: nearly ten thousand policemen (with no local knowledge and no awareness of local sensibilities), several hundred PLO bureaucrats, and a handful of close advisers. In their high-handed manner, they made it clear that no power-sharing was in the offing. The avalanche of aid during the coming years trickled down – or rather sideways – through client–patron networks imported from Beirut and Tunis. No funds were distributed without Arafat's name-tag on it; bidding for public works or construction was conducted in secret. Had contracts been awarded in a transparent procedure, the lucky winners would have been able to wriggle out of the loyalty racket that was at the centre of all PLO money handling. The lack of transparency and democracy alienated those Gazans Arafat would need most in the years to come, men animated by ideals, such as Abu Zaide, Abdul Razek and Abu Samhadana – men who also had with a wide following in the refugee camps. Several of them were given impressive-sounding government jobs, but scant influence. They were shrewdly granted responsibilities during the peace negotiations, which tarred them with the brush of compromise and made them appreciate his pragmatism.

But Arafat's real nemesis were not the critics within his own movement. With the most popular Fatah leaders temporarily neutralised, Hamas' aim of discrediting Arafat's government was greatly facilitated. A few months after his triumphant return, when the fractious grafitti on Gaza's walls had been painted over by decree, as if to usher in a new era, those same walls were sprayed full once more. But now their venom was directed less against the Israelis or against rival groups, but against the new government, which was denounced as a grafting, baksheesh-taking puppet of Israel.

Soon after the Israel–PLO breakthrough in September, 1993, the Israeli chief of staff Ehud Barak was called to a government meeting and asked to gauge the capacity of the PLO to keep Hamas in check. Barak said he was not sure about that, but indicated there was evidence that Hamas would go all the way to disrupt the process. In his speeches during his day of return to Gaza, Arafat had held out an olive branch to Hamas leader Ahmad Yassin, then jailed in Israel. Had he thought it possible, Arafat would probably have tried to crush Hamas. But the slow and delicate nature of the peace process gave his Islamist rivals a structural advantage over him. While Arafat needed thousands of policemen to maintain public order, the Islamists could reap huge dividends from one- or two-man attacks. A Hamas attack on Israeli soldiers or a suicide bomb in Tel Aviv would rock the whole project, while Arafat, in order to steady it, would need a hundred peaceful days. Just two weeks after Arafat's return, the Islamists managed to turn a demonstration of angry Gazan workers by the Erez crossing into a full-scale riot; 152 new buses were burned and the gunfire exchange – the first of its kind – between Israeli soldiers and Palestinian policemen was a welcome boost for the nationalist Israeli campaign: "Don't give them [the Palestinians] guns!"

A few days after Arafat's noisy return to Gaza, another Gazan arrived back home, in a shroud of secrecy. Islamic Jihad member Adnan al-Ghoul, originally from the refugee camp of Shaati near Gaza City, was a leading Palestinian explosives expert and bomb-maker. He was deported by Israel in 1988, but now he returned via one of the underground tunnels linking Egyptian Rafah to Gazan Rafah. His mission was to produce bombs and charges for attacks against Israeli civilians, potent enough to derail the peace process.

The suicide bomb on a Tel Aviv bus on October 19, 1994, killed 22 people, wounded 56 and diminished further the domestic manoeuvring space of Yitzhak Rabin and Shimon Peres. And it put Arafat firmly where he was to remain for the rest of his life; between the hammer of Israeli security demands and the anvil of Palestinian public opinion. After the attack, the PLO was forced to round up suspects, but the Israelis were not satisfied. On November 2, an Islamic Jihad leader in Khan Yunes, Hani Abed, was blown to pieces when his car exploded, in what looked like a Shabak – the general security service of Israel – operation. There was fury in the Strip, and great embarrassment to Arafat. If the Israelis did not baulk at cloak-and-dagger operations inside the autonomous area, what kind of authority did Arafat really represent? As so often during his career Arafat, abroad at the time, made an abrupt turn from confrontation to appeasement. He rushed back to Gaza in order to put in a demonstrative appearance at the funeral of Abed. But instead of restoring his honour, he saw it dragged through the gutter in a real humiliation. Outside the Umari mosque in Gaza City, Arafat became the focus for the rage of the Jihadi multitude, which menacingly closed in on him. In an insulting speech, Dr Mahmud al-Zahar of Hamas called all those working with Arafat *jawasis*, collaborators. For once Arafat's famous bodyguard, constantly working from worst-case scenarios, was overwhelmed. In the bedlam, the leader was shoved, pushed and cursed by his own people. With pointed symbolism, his keffiyeh headgear, folded to resemble the map of Palestine, was torn from his bald head. Arafat did not appear for some days after his narrow escape, and his bodyguards looked pale and shaken.

The indignity suffered by Arafat struck fear into his circle. Few of those closest to him had any natural constituencies in Palestine. If the Arafat magic were eroded, they would be the first to pay the price. Frekh Abu Medein, the Gazan lawyer who would become Arafat's minister of justice, told him that people were getting the impression that there were two authorities in Gaza, the PLO and the Islamists, and that if the PLO did not manage to restore respect, all was lost.

On November 18, Arafat removed his mittens. The loudspeakers of the Filastin mosque in Gaza City had been blasting denunciations of Arafat and ignoring police orders to stop. During the scuffle, PLO policemen suddenly directed automatic fire straight at their adversaries. According to official statements, the police were first fired upon by Islamists. But the Islamist version, that the police deliberately fired into the crowd of demonstrators, fit the evidence better.

In a pattern that would repeat itself countless times in the years to come, frantic mediation efforts, led by Israeli Arabs, followed the Fatah–Hamas violence. The rift was patched up for a while, but there was no true reconciliation. To the Islamists, as their leaflets proclaimed, the "Sulta" – PLO rule – was "worse than the Jews". To Arafat and his supporters, the Islamists were foreign agents in the pay of reactionary oil sheikhs and Iranian mullahs. In other words, the first condition for a civil war was taking shape: the antagonists' mutual view of each other not merely as wicked, but as traitors.

The Saraya building in Gaza City, until recently the grim and visible logo of Israeli rule, now filled up again with Palestinian prisoners. Many of the wardens were the prison's former inmates from the PLO, while the new customers were the Jihadi and Hamsawi men who were busy dynamiting the peace process. The symbolism was powerful and jarring to all involved. In order to express their contempt for their jailers, the Islamists made a point of never addressing them in Arabic, only in Hebrew.

The much touted Palestinian democracy – a prominent feature of the prevailing peace rhetoric – found it hard to flourish in this fratricidal climate. There was more democracy and more press freedom in Arafat's demi-state than under most other contemporary Arab rulers but, for people eager for freedom, the net result was still a bitter comedown after the grand expectations bandied about during the opening scenes of the peace process. The first intervention against the local press came less than a month after Arafat's arrival. Distribution of the pro-Jordanian Jerusalem paper *al-Nahar* was halted in Gaza. According to Arafat, "it had violated the law and avoided contact with the Palestinian government". Jonathan Kuttab, a columnist for the leading East Jersualem daily *al-Quds*, was suspended after he protested against this. Until the appearance of Palestinian self-rule, *al-Quds* had been a reasonably independent news medium, if generally close to the PLO line. But now its editor was pressured to discipline Kuttab. Nasser Nashashibi's *Akhbar al-Balad* was also suspended after siding with *al-Nahar*. During the dramatic November of 1994, *al-Quds* itself was temporarily banned in Gaza after reporting that 70,000 people participated in a Hamas rally which government sources had estimated at 8,000. In time, the Palestinian Authority, the PA, would establish two new papers, *al-Ayam* and *al-Hayat al-Jadida*, to endorse its positions. They were heavily subsidised and spread widely, but they never achieved the credibility the PA had wished. As many Palestinians – 28 per cent – in the territories depended on Israeli state radio for its news as on the new *Saut Filastin*, the Voice of Palestine station in Ramallah.

Many were astonished that Arafat was so harsh when it came to irreverent reporting, and so meek when it came to handling those Islamists who openly defied him and risked his entire project. At each new turn he refused to confront the Islamists until every effort to co-opt them had been made. He knew that whatever fateful decisions lay ahead during the final status negotiations, he would need a popular majority, or near-majority, to carry them out. Confrontation would serve the rejectionists.

There were some within the Islamist camp who – without declaring it openly – were inclined to give the Rabin–Arafat programme a chance. Those realists were mainly local Hamas men who were appalled at what looked more and more like a downward slope towards a future civil war in the Strip. But after the crippling blows dealt to Hamas by Israel during the first Intifada, organisation and high-level decision-making had been moved abroad, and the leadership in exile, more and more aligned with Syrian and Iranian interests, was eager to see Arafat fail.

A key asset for Gazan militants out to torpedo the Oslo process was the map of the Strip after Israel's pull-back in May 1994. The main settlement area, the Katif block in the southwestern corner of the Strip, with its generous expanses of excellent soil, was a source of indignation and resentment. When first established, this strip-within-the-strip had disrupted the life and income of Palestinian fishermen, shepherds and many others. But until 1994, the block caused less direct interference in the daily life of Palestinians, and little trouble for the Israeli Defence Forces responsible for their security. There were, however, several Israeli settlements outside the bloc, some next to huge refugee camps, whose inhabitants had to travel through densely populated Palestinian areas in order to reach Israel proper or their schools in another Gaza settlement. Some prominent Labour Party leaders pleaded with Rabin to evacuate the whole Strip and save the expense and dangers implicit in the administration of the convoluted maze

– also called "the Swiss cheese". But Rabin would not stray from the Oslo script. Settlements and their possible evacuation were not to be discussed until the permanent settlement talks. The most vulnerable of all the nearly forty crossings, check-posts and junctions required to patrol, defend and escort Jewish colonists was the Netzarim intersection, less than a mile southeast of the isolated settlement of Netzarim. (A few miles further south, similarly cut off, was the Kfar Darom settlement, the only one with a pre-1948 history.)

Netzarim lay close to two small refugee camps, el-Bureij and Nuseirat, both with a history of fierce resistance and extremist politics. When the first Palestinian revolt began in late 1987, life at Netzarim became more and more complicated. By 1992, the nervous tension, and some ideological quarrels, had emptied the settlement. Housing Minister Ariel Sharon, who – still – believed that no settlement must be allowed to fall into neglect, drew up an ambitious plan for 2,500 new apartments in Netzarim, a whole new Jewish town, larger than anything ever seen in the Strip. Then came Labour's and Yizhak Rabin's unexpected election victory in June 1992. A clarion call was sounded by the settlement organisations: "Return to Netzarim!" Volunteers were rushed there in order to block any plans to cede it to the Palestinians.

The exposed Israeli position became a favourite target of Islamist fighters during the Oslo years. Twenty Israeli soldiers died and hundreds were wounded by car bombs, bicycle bombs, donkey-cart bombs and live fire. Each time, the Israeli government reacted with closures which deprived Gazan labourers of their income and eroded the support for Arafat and the peace process – just as intended by the attackers. The Netzarim-type junctions were a godsend for Hamas and Jihad fighters – indefensible, isolated positions tied directly to the big political game. The traffic of Israeli soldiers to and from the outposts was also a comfortable target. Every day, several roadside bombs exploded or were discovered.

Both Rabin and Arafat accused the Islamists and the Jewish extremists of "acting together" to derail the Oslo Agreements. Arafat even claimed to have evidence of such collusion. Original Israeli ID-cards were found during a raid against a Hamas office in Gaza City. But during 1995, Arafat became increasingly convinced that Iran played a central role in the efforts against the PA. At the beginning he lashed out at "outside meddlers", but after the massacre of Israeli soldiers at Beit Lid in January 1995, he openly warned Iran and its "lackeys": "I will personally cut off the hands of anyone taking a cent of Iranian money".

For journalists, intellectuals and social critics, Palestinian self-rule was not the yearned-for new dawn. But to the modern, secular life-style, which had been on the defensive, not to say hibernating, since the Islamist advances during the first Intifada, Arafat was a redeemer. Just a year after his arrival, the change was obvious at a glance: bars, beer, cultural evenings on daring subjects and, above all, an impressive return of Western dress among young women. The big-bearded, Saudi-styled commissars of public morale, who had scanned the street-corners with menacing glances, disappeared. To leftists and Fatah secularists, the jazz-concerts and high-brow French films displayed at newly-built foreign cultural centres were welcome harbingers of normality; to the Islamists, they were proof that the peace process was not merely a political sell-out, but a moral and cultural surrender. The Islamist mouth-piece *al-Watan* and the neighbourhood preachers fought fiercely against this modern avalanche. Jazz and rock music were scientifically developed in order to lure young women to sin, they warned. Poor Gazan children, starved of entertainment, were enchanted by the visiting Russian circus. But the circus, according to the Islamists, was the work of the devil; the acrobats and clowns were all carriers of AIDS, and spectators went there at their peril. Another undesirable side-effect of the new order was the rise in fraternising between local Gazans and the many foreign advisers, experts and aid bureaucrats now in residence among them. Many lived a rather sheltered life, in the well-guarded Greenacres apartment complex, but there was ample opportunity for cultural contamination during work, at the beach – where the Islamic bans were again ignored – and during the modest but growing night-life activities.

# 19

# Exit Rabin, Enter Likud, 1995–1999

*The extremists in Netanyahu's camp hoped he would drop the Oslo process altogether. But Netanyahu was eager not to appear as the guilty party, especially not in the eyes of President Bill Clinton, who had invested heavily, politically and personally, in the process. On September 4, 1996, at the Gaza–Israel checkpoint at Erez, Netanyahu met and shook hands with Yasser Arafat, the man he had branded as "master terrorist". Two days later, as if frightened of what he'd done, Netanyahu vowed never to allow the establishment of a Palestinian state.*

The murder of Yizhak Rabin by an Israeli ultranationalist in November 1995 shocked Arafat no less than it shocked Israel. A few days later he paid his condolences to Rabin's widow Leah at her home north of Tel Aviv. Apart from fedayeen incursions in the 1950s it was Arafat's first, but not last, visit to Israel. The fears that the Oslo process would be shelved were not realised immediately. In fact, the Oslo road to peace would never look more promising than it did at New Year's Eve 1996. The Israeli opposition, facing a storm of popular indignation for its incitement campaign the months prior to Rabin's assassination, lay low. The number of Palestinian workers allowed into Israel reached its highest number in years. Palestinian police returned large numbers of stolen cattle and cars to Israel. The peace project won record support in both Israeli and Palestinian polls. It seemed inconceivable that Shimon Peres, Rabin's successor and the prime mover behind the Oslo accords, should fail to carry the approaching elections. Arafat had already won his first elections in a landslide in January, securing a massive majority in the new Palestinian parliament. Peres' Labour Party even dared to remove its traditional opposition to a Palestinian State from its new platform.

On January 5, 1996, Yihya Ayash, one of Hamas' foremost explosives experts, was killed in Gaza when his mobile phone exploded in his face. It was the work of the Shabak, possibly with some assistance from Arafat's secret services. Ayash was a popular hero among the Islamists, and the outcry stunned Arafat. Hamas swore revenge and kept its word. After a series of suicide bombings in Tel Aviv, Jerusalem and Ashdod the political map had been re-edited in favour of the radicals on both sides. The Israeli opposition got wind in its sails anew and huge demonstrations under banners like "Not this kind of peace" began to eat away at Peres' comfortable lead. Likud's election propaganda revelled in gory footage. Closures, more hermetic than any ever seen, were imposed on the territories.

The panic of the Israeli government was shared by Arafat and by Washington. High CIA operatives led by George Tenet arrived in Gaza with anti-terror equipment for Arafat's forces. Both Peres and Arafat blamed Teheran, and US Secretary of State Warren Christopher said he had proof that Iran was spending millions in order to clinch the elections for Benjamin Netanyahu, the Israeli nationalist opposition leader. The EU sent large shipments of food-aid to Gaza to mitigate the misery brought on by the closures, and the highest ranking international conference ever was convened in Egypt under the banner "No to terrorism!". The US, Russian and French presidents, along with a host of Arab leaders, tried to shore up the peace efforts, and Arafat rounded up hundreds of Islamic militants. He even managed to convince Hamas founder Ahmad Yassin, in an Israeli jail at the time, to go on TV and ask his followers to refrain from attacks at this stage.

But the decisive event in the downward spiral which would bring Oslo's enemies to power was not of Hamas' making. During a large-scale offensive against Hizbollah in Southern Lebanon the Israeli Air Force bombed a UN compound in the village of Kana. A hundred civilians who had sought shelter there died. Outraged by the killing of innocents, many of Israel's Arabs, who would normally have voted for Peres, stayed home on election day, May 29.

Netanyahu's election victory stunned the world – and the Gazans. The extremists in Netanyahu's camp hoped he would drop the Oslo process altogether. But Netanyahu was eager not to appear as the guilty party, especially not in the eyes of President Bill Clinton, who had invested heavily, politically and personally, in the process. On September 4, 1996, at the Gaza–Israel checkpoint at Erez, Netanyahu met and shook hands with Yasser Arafat, the man he had branded as "master terrorist". Two days later, as if frightened of what he'd done, Netanyahu vowed never to allow the establishment of a Palestinian state.

Few of the central issues during Netanyahu's three years in power concerned the Gaza Strip directly. The first big drama occurred a few weeks after Arafat's and Netanyahu's first meeting, when the latter, egged on by Jerusalem mayor Ehud Olmert, opened a two-thousand year old tunnel near the Temple Mount for tourism. The event became an escape valve for pent-up Palestinian frustrations and deteriorated into a mini-war, with nearly a hundred Palestinian and fifteen Israeli fatalities. In the Strip the most intense fighting took place in Rafah, where Palestinian police overran an Israeli position and killed an Israeli colonel. It was the first time Israeli helicopters were called in to fight regular PA forces. In other parts of the Strip Palestinian forces exerted themselves to block angry crowds of civilians who tried to march on Jewish settlements.

The Israeli decision, in August 1996, to speed up settlement activity, mainly in the West Bank, cast a shadow on the peace process. But Israel carried out several further redeployments on the West Bank, and turned over most of the city of Hebron and several other areas to Palestinian control. In March 1997, after an angry letter from King Hussein of Jordan to Netanyahu, Israel agreed to Arafat's partial use of the new airport Dahaniye south of Rafah. A year later Prime Minister Bernie Ahearn of Ireland was the the first foreign dignitary to land in Gaza after a direct flight.

Arafat quietly consolidated his rule in Gaza. His methods were pragmatic, ceding to the Islamists on non-crucial issues and hitting them mercilessly when they went too far, "an iron fist inside a silk glove". He renamed a street in Gaza City after Hamas bomber Yihya Ayash, but sentenced Hamas and Jihad members to death when it suited him. Hamas' leadership in exile pressed hard for further suicide actions inside Israel, but with some notable exceptions Arafat's intelligence services kept the Islamists on the defensive. Three young women were killed by a bomb in a Tel Aviv café in late March 1997, which rendered Arafat Israeli accusations for having given a green light to terrorism. Ariel Sharon and other hawks claimed that the PA was stockpiling weapons in Gaza in violation of the agreements.

But Arafat kept his head cool and for most of Netanyahu's rule he managed to prevent actions which would have served the Israeli nationalists as pretexts for abandoning the process. Netanyahu's Defense Minister Yizhak Mordechai conceded that Arafat was "doing a reasonable job in fighting terrorism". On one count Benjamin Netanyahu, without intending to, intervened deeply in the affairs of the Strip. After two bloody Hamas attacks in Jerusalem in the summer of 1997, the Prime Minister, pressed by the hawkish wing of his Likud party, wanted resolute action against the Hamas. On September 25, 1997, on a street in Amman, Jordan, a team of Israeli agents managed to spray poison into the ear of Khaled Mash'al, the most influential Hamas leader outside Palestine. The Mossad agents were arrested shortly afterwards and the affair snowballed into a huge international impasse. Netanyahu, who had been advised against the attack by the Mossad, was now confronted by a furious King Hussein of Jordan, who regarded the assassination attempt in his capital as a personal affront. In order to salvage the peace treaty with Jordan Netanyahu was forced to humiliate himself doubly: by rushing a doctor with an antidote to Mash'al's bedside; and by releasing Hamas founder and supreme leader Ahmad Yassin from the prison where he had spent nearly a decade. Yassin was not only set free – along with forty others – he was allowed to return to Gaza where he was given a messianic reception by his followers, much to President Arafat's displeasure. Arafat knew that with all the means at his disposal, he could never have drummed up anything like the euphoric welcome given Yassin by the Gazans.

The atmosphere was not improved when Sheikh Yassin took to criticising Arafat's rule in foreign media in a manner no other Gazan would permit himself. Yassin was always courteous in his choice of words, and avoided the standard epithets of the Hamas grafitti – "traitor" and "collaborator" – but he got the wounding message through. Yassin, often harangued and pampered by Arafat in the past, could not be dealt with the in way the president usually handled dissidents. The paraplegic preacher was on his way towards becoming an international star, in his own way as emblematic to the Palestinian cause as Arafat himself. Yassin was considered beyond arrest or intimidation, but when he felt his position threatened the conciliatory Arafat became ruthless: In the autumn of 1998 Sheikh Yassin was put under house arrest for the first time. Arafat also worked hard to convince his friends abroad to downgrade their red-carpet receptions of his rival. After Yassin's trip to Iran, where he was fêted like a world leader, Arafat managed to get Saddam Hussein and Nelson Mandela to cancel planned visits by Yassin.

Yassin-Arafat relations soured further after Hamas' key explosives' expert on the West Bank, Mohieddin al-Sharif, was killed in Ramallah on March 29, 1998. Israeli sources claimed he had suffered an accident while working on a car-bomb. The Hamas spread leaflets which tied Arafat's forces to al-Sharif's death. The dispute went on for months and led to mass arrests among Hamas sympathisers, including the Gazan closest to Yassin in the Hamas hierarchy, Dr. Abdelaziz Rantisi.

At the beginning of 1999 Arafat's rule in Gaza was solid, if not uncontested. Bill Clinton's visit to Gaza in December 1998, during which the President spoke warmly of Palestinian independence, was a feather in Arafat's cap. But the real purpose of Clinton's visit had been to back Arafat in his bid to get the Palestine National Council to revise those clauses in teh National Covenant which called for the destruction of Israel. The revision was not popular in Gaza, and in order to placate the critics Arafat released a long list of hard-core Islamist prisoners.

Arafat's opponents still fetched less than 20% in public opinion polls. But the peace process had been gradually hollowed out of much of its content, amid land confiscations, house demolitions, restrictions on movement and a torrent of colonisation projects in the West Bank. In the Gaza Strip the endless squabbles over the roads to the settlements remained the main bone of contention. The Israelis would open up, and close, the coastal road between Gaza and Deir al-Balah; the Palestinian police would block, and then be forced to open, the roads to the Netzarim and Morag settlements; and Palestinian civilians would block the access to the Katif settlement bloc.

The only person in the Israeli government with a real interest in the peace process, Defense Minister Yizhak Mordechai, had excellent relations with the Fatah strongman in the Strip, the head of Preventive Security Muhammad Dahlan. But Mordechai, not least for that reason, was gradually falling out of favour with Netanyahu, who fired him in February 1999. Shortly afterwards, President Bill Clinton put aid to Israel on hold after Netanyahu had reneged on promises made in the Wye River Memorandum. In response to Israeli foot-dragging Arafat threatened to declare Palestinian statehood unilaterally. Netanyahu warned him that he would regret such a move, and Clinton held him back, begging him to wait for the result of the May 1999 elections in Israel.

The Gaza Strip, the peace process and Arafat's rule would get one short lease on life before being hurled down the abyss of death, destruction, civil war and repression where it has languished for the past decade. During the drama performed by Ehud Barak and Arafat they rushed Israelis and Palestinians between peaks of expectation and pits of disappointment. The complex events culminating in the ill-fated Camp David summit in July 2000 have been scrutinised, fought over and and revised with nearly the same ferocity as the true reasons for the outbreak of the Great War in 1914. In retrospect Barak's and Arafat's choices during that stage have assumed such grave import that some feel that their failure still cast a shadow over future attempts at peace for years to come.

In late May 1999, when the Israeli Labour party and its new leader Ehud Barak defeated the scandal-ridden Netanyahu governement at the polls, the Gaza Strip would have struck a visitor absent since 1993. There were tree-lined boulevards, curbs, painted lanes, even pavements and street-lights in many places where until recently cars, trucks, carts and pedestrians had negotiated dusty, unpaved crossings without a semblance of rules. The flat skyline, not only of Gaza City but of the southern urban areas as well, was assuming a second dimension, with multistorey apartment blocks rising, even inside the refugee camps. In many areas the sanitary infrastructure, teetering for years on the verge of collapse, had been salvaged by donations, and in parts of the Shaati camp by the beach the ever-present stench from the open sewers no longer overwhelmed the salty Mediterranean breeze. Small bars and eateries, driven out of business by Islamist pressures, made their return and there were evenings when the city of Gaza assumed a semblance of its traditional self: garrulous, carefree and Mediterranean. But in the realm of economic and social imponderables there was little to match the outward signs of improvement. Gradually – the most recent Hamas suicide attack had taken place in September 1997 – more and more Gazans were allowed to resume work in Israel. But most applicants were turned down for security reasons. Gazans were no longer allowed to apply at the Erez checkpoint. They first had to stand in line at an office in Jebaliya in order to get a clean bill of trust from the Palestinian security authorities. Some were allowed to work in the West Bank. Israel charged fifteen shekels for each "safe passage" permit to travel through Israel between the Strip and the West Bank. But the price charged the Palestinian worker depended on where he acquired it, and from which of Arafat's fourteen security services. It could be double or three times the original price. Corruption was no longer exceptional, it was the system.

The PA public sector was bloated with security officials. Of the 110,000 PA employees 43,000 were policemen, gendarmes, intelligence agents, marines and other armed personnel. There were few Gazan street-corners without armed official presence. Most of these security officials were poorly paid, between two and three hundred dollars a month, and few of them declined opportunities to milk the citizenry for more. Two-thirds of the Palestinian budget of 650 million dollars came from taxes, VAT and customs levied by Israel and transferred to the PA. Foreign aid and local tax-collection made up the rest.

Thousands of Gazan bread-earners were kept busy sweeping streets or white-washing walls, their wages paid by foreign governments or NGOs. The Palestinian dream of independence from the Israeli economy did not materialise. After almost four years of peace negotiations the bulk of the bilateral trade-volume consisted of Israeli exports to Palestinian territories. Even so, Israeli sales to the territories – 1.6 billion dollars – comprised only 8% of its total exports. The imports from the territories, 280 million dollars yearly, made up 2% of Israel imports. Some Israeli companies, like the Tnuva dairies, enjoyed virtual monopoly status in Gaza.

Like many dictators Yasser Arafat regarded an independent economy, capable of generating better times without his involvement, with mixed feelings. In its attention to detail and its indifference to overall growth, his hands-on centralism came close to Fidel Castro's. Whatever did not emanate from him would be kept in check. When the Islamists of Gaza presented plans for a residential area with clinics, child-care centres and other utopian extras laid on, Arafat vetoed it. When the Qatari Crown Prince Omar bin Khalifa arrived in August 1999 there were tough wranglings over Doha's donations to the rapidly growing Islamic University of Gaza – they would have to be presented as an official contribution from a friendly government, not as a reflection of Hamas' status in the region. On the other hand Arafat was not averse to explore new economic venues with Gazan Jewish settlers in order to discuss possible joint ventures in tourism and manufacturing.

# 20

# Barak's Gamble and the Second Palestinian Uprising, 1999–2001

*In late June 1999, President Clinton suggested that Barak and Arafat could only cobble together a peace agreement if they were locked up in a remote locale for days. On July 5, he announced a summit meeting at the Camp David retreat in Maryland. Nearly a hundred Palestinian and Israeli experts and advisers met up to chase the elusive peace. It was to be now or never. Failure would bring back the Likud and its new leader, Ariel Sharon – a sworn enemy of the Oslo concept; it would also be an encouragement to Arafat's Islamist rivals. The battle of nerves enveloping the event generated a sinister and menacing atmosphere.*

Ehud Barak – like many Palestinian critics – regarded his predecessor Shimon Peres' visions of a "New Middle East", based on economic cooperation, as so much romantic verbiage. The route to peace, in Barak's view, went through separate economic development. Cooperation would be the result of peace, not its main vehicle. Barak sought a deal with the Palestinians, but he had been, like the Palestinian radicals, against the piecemeal appoach of Oslo from the start. The Rabin–Arafat formula of postponing all difficult decisions to a distant and mythic final-status stage appeared to him a hazardous wager which played into the hands of extremists on both sides.

There was much to say for Barak's analysis, but the new game-rules which he proposed would prove no less perilous. Barak was no politician. His model of doing things was the military one, of defining goals and executing plans. He wanted a deal with Arafat which would put the whole Israel–Palestine issue behind both peoples for good, including all of the volatile and daunting issues at the heart of the conflict. Barak had no patience for managing the conflict, he wanted to resolve it. The infernally complicated re-drawings of the West Bank map in three stages, with 27% of the West Bank changing status in six different redeployments in Areas A (Full Palestinian control), B (mixed control) and C (Israeli control), agreed by Netanyahu and Arafat at Wye River, seemed a waste of time to

Barak. He wanted to wriggle out of the Oslo provisions and jump straight to the final status talks, and in his enthusiasm for redefining the Oslo formulas he managed to sweep most world leaders off their feet. "America will walk with you towards peace", declared Bill Clinton after meeting with Barak in July 1999. There was a world-wide feeling that the conflict was coming to an end and Barak was beleaguered by world leaders, like Spain's José Maria Aznar or Russia's Boris Yeltsin, who demanded or pleaded for a "role" in the imminent historical developments.

But Arafat resisted. The Wye memorandum, he said, was a test case of intentions and results and must not be skipped. He stood his ground and Barak had to carry out the second withdrawal stage according to Wye. But he insisted that Arafat keep his part of the bargain and supply lists of all his armed personnel, collect all unauthorised weapons and purge anti-Jewish matter from Palestinian school books. At the Sharm al-Sheikh summit in Egypt, staged by Clinton at Barak's insistence in September 1999, it seemed that Arafat was moving closer to Barak's vision of a comprehensive settlement soon. It was proclaimed with great fanfare that the parties would present a framework for a definite peace settlement as early as February 2000; and that a Palestinian state would be established in September 2000.

It is not our task here to account for the vicissitudes of the Israel-Palestine peace process, but in order to understand the tragedy which followed Barak's hyperactive efforts one must try to recreate the giddy atmosphere created, among both peoples, by the bombardment of promises, deadlines and millenarian pronouncements. Israeli government spokesmen already calculated the volume of future Syrian–Israel trade, and Barak promised a reduction – never implemented – of compulsory military service from three years to 30 months. Expectations grew wildly, while the core issues of the conflict remained as knotty. During his first months Barak's optimism was contagious. No one, from Clinton to Syria's wily Hafez Assad, was impervious to it. Even those who doubted that Barak was the wizard come to untangle the primordial knots of the Middle East with one magic slash, found it awkward to question his plans.

But as time wore on and the sanguine timetables had to be revised the frantic expectations fanned by Barak began to work against him. His "the sky is the limit" rhetoric was often at variance with his deeds. During autumn 1999 he okayed 5,000 new settlement homes in the West Bank and still refused to let foreign vessels anchor at Gaza harbour. Many Gazans felt that their imminent needs were constantly put on the back burner while huge assemblies of experts and jurists pored over maps of West Bank, its roads and its subtle subdivisions into A, B and C areas. Gaza was still the de facto capital of the embryonic PLO state, and the Gazans had urgent problems which were rarely addressed. Their chief grievances concerned the Salah al-Din highway, the main north–south throughfare of the Strip, which was dotted with Israeli checkposts and watchtowers, kept there to ensure safe movement for the 6,000 Israeli settlers. More important still, in Gazan eyes, was the need to remove the Israeli settlement enclaves altogether. According to the Beilin–Abu Mazen plan from 1995, the Katif Bloc, which contained most of the Israeli settlements in the Strip, would remain in Israeli hands, and the Palestinians would receive the Halutza area in the Negev desert in return. But neither side had accepted the proposal, and now, in order to push for concrete action on the issue, Palestinian civilians and security personnel began to prevent Gazan labourers from working in the Israeli settlements, mainly at the greenhouses of the Katif bloc. Some Palestinians were shot at, most probably on Arafat's orders, as they tried to sneak past the pickets. Barak's response was drastic – all Palestinians, some 2,500, residing inside the Israeli enclaves, were refused access to the rest of the Strip.

On May 15, 2000, when Palestinians commemorated the 1947–49 refugee catastrophe, the *Nakba*, violent confrontations between Palestinian civilians and Israeli soldiers took place all over the occupied territories, and also by the Netzarim junction in the Strip. Soon afterwards Arafat proclaimed several "days of rage", during which hundreds were wounded in similar incidents. Israeli intelligence reports noted that Arafat had tried to control the level of violence but failed. Barak warned Arafat not to speculate in violence and urged Bill Clinton to "get Arafat moving" towards peace. By then Barak's coalition was ridden with crisis, and both public opinion and the media wanted to cash in on his generous peace promises bandied about for almost a year. Barak had pulled Israel out of Lebanon on May 24, 2000. The majority of Israelis had wanted out of Lebanon, but the implementation, celebrated by Shi'ite Hizbollah as a fateful victory "on the way to Jerusalem", did not bring Barak much glory at home. Both Barak and president Clinton had invested heavily in the Israeli–Syrian negotiations, which had stalled. Clinton's term was nearing its end, and Barak's coalition was crumbling. Both of them urgently needed success on the Palestinian track.

In late June, President Clinton suggested that Barak and Arafat could only cobble together a peace agreement if they were locked up in a remote locale for days. On July 5, he announced a summit meeting at the Camp David retreat in Maryland, to begin in a few days. Nearly a hundred Palestinian and Israeli experts and advisers met up to chase the elusive peace. It was to be now or never. Failure would bring back the Likud and its new leader, Ariel Sharon – a sworn enemy of the Oslo concept; it would also be an encouragement to Arafat's Islamist rivals. The battle of nerves enveloping the event generated a sinister and menacing atmosphere. Israeli security sources leaked "reports", real or imagined, about a new Intifada being prepared in case of failure. Chief of Staff Shaul Mofaz predicted, during a visit to Gaza, that tanks and planes would be used against the

Palestinians if they turned their weapons against Israel. Around the Netzarim junction, the eternal flashpoint of the Strip, Israeli soldiers built grenade-proof roofs above the observation towers, and the Palestinians sandbagged their positions at the other side of the road. The apocalyptic mood was further worked up by pompous and self-pitying rhetoric on both sides – Barak spoke of the future of the Jewish people weighing heavily on his shoulders. In the refugee camps of the Strip and elsewhere people marched in thousands, ostensibly to strengthen Arafat, but really to warn him against any concessions on the issues of Jerusalem and the right of return.

The dramas and the eventual failure of the two-week long Camp David marathon has become a fertile battle-ground for scholars and partisans, often with simplistic apportioning of blame to either of the two sides. Even if Barak (on settlements and Holy Places) and Arafat (on the right of return) had ceded enough to clinch a deal, it is extremely doubtful that they would have overcome the furious opposition brewing within their respective constituencies.

On their return, both leaders presented themselves as stalwart patriots who had stood firm and refused to haggle about sacred principles. When Arafat landed at Dahaniye airport in the Strip he received a hero's welcome. Dark predictions of failure being followed by a slide into a bloody abyss were put to shame – for the time being. Arafat did not carry out his threat to declare statehood unilaterally and Barak, ceding a little more ground, said he did not rule out handing over the Holy Basin in Jerusalem to international control. Talks never stopped, in fact there were more than sixty high-level contacts during Barak's last six months in office, but as Barak's public support plummeted such contacts lost their relevance. Clinton did not give up, and in early September he gave peace one more shove, as he shuttled between Barak's and Arafat's hotel rooms in New York.

By then the unofficial Israeli election campaign was in full swing. In August, extremist Israelis had been turned back as they tried to pray on the Temple Mount. Barak's adversary, Ariel Sharon – who had been his patron during his army days – made much of this, and of the reports that Barak had been close to ceding the area. When Sharon, surrounded by a thousand policemen, entered the Haram al-Sharif temple area on September 28, he had no idea that the visit would pave his way to power and spell the destruction of the Palestinian Authority. The Palestinian reaction was not immediate. The Israeli policemen on the mount had been forced to hold back and concentrate on their defensive duties as young Palestinians taunted and tried to stone Sharon. On the next day, September 29, the police hit back with a vengeance and things got out of hand, as Palestinians all over the territories marched on Israeli checkpoints and bases and were met with live fire on a scale they had never experienced before.

Israeli plans of how to counter a new Palestinian rising had been prepared long in advance, by chief of staff Mofaz and his deputy Moshe Ya'alon, both future Likud politicians. During the first days of clashes, Israeli soldiers fired 1.3 million rounds. Attack helicopters fired rockets against official PA targets in Ramallah and Gaza. As usual, the focal point of violence in the Strip was the "Martyr's junction", which connected the isolated Jewish settlement of Netzarim with the Karni crossing into Israel. Thousands of Palestinians hurried to Netzarim from nearby Gaza City. Some of the Palestinian policemen on the spot tried to keep the protesters away from Israeli positions, but heavy Israeli fire from towers inside the settlement turned the crowd against the PA men: "Shoot at the Israelis instead of pushing us back!"

In the crossfire between Palestinians and Israelis at Netzarim, the emblematic tragedy of the second Palestinian rising took place – the heart-breaking death of 12-year old Muhammad al-Dura. His father Jamal, recovering in a Jordanian Army hospital, told me how he had tried to shelter his son from automatic fire by using his own body as a shield. Much of the drama was captured by a French television crew, which broadcast an edited version of the event. Little Muhammad's death etched itself onto the memory of millions of viewers around the world, and became a powerful asset in the Palestinian effort to portray Israeli violence as blind and disproportionate. The issue of whether France 2 TV doctored the footage in order to besmirch Israel has been the subject of a bitter decade-long French court battle, not yet laid to rest. But whichever bullets killed al-Dura, there was powerful evidence for Palestinian claims that Israeli soldiers had orders to use live ammunition against civilian demonstrators even when not in real danger. During the first six months of the first Palestinian uprising, December 1987–May 1988, the average daily death toll (in the Strip and the West Bank) was 1.1 Palestinians and 0.1 Israelis. During the first four months of the second Intifada, Palestinian fatalities stood at almost four a day, while Israel lost 0.3 a day, mostly army personnel and settlers. Among the Palestinian victims, many were between 12 and 18 years old, and many were shot from a distance of more than 100 meters.

But the character of the conflagrations changed markedly as the conflict wore on. At the outset, the crowds of Gazan civilians who confronted Israeli soldiers at junctions and settlement gateways had been unarmed, and PA forces had often made genuine efforts to temper them. Gradually, however, armed PA men were drawn into the conflict. In Israel, this fact was often presented as the result of Yasser Arafat's duplicity. Even while declaring cease-fires, it was claimed, he egged his men on. But from what I saw in Gaza, the PA units were pushed into active fighting by different factors. Firstly, by the Palestinian demonstrators, who would not accept that "their" forces turn the other cheek while Israeli fire was directed against them. Secondly, Israeli fire was increasingly directed at the armed Palestinians. To be sure, some PA gendarmes and policemen eagerly turned their AK-47s against Israeli targets, but many others tried desperately to keep up coordination with their Israeli counterparts and halt the downward slide. In the polarised frenzy, anyone questioning the wisdom of armed defense against Israel was sure to be labelled a traitor. The head of the Department of Political Science at Bir Zeit University, Salah Abdul Jawad, was brave to write in the Jerusalem paper *al-Quds*: "The participation of armed elements in popular demonstrations, and the fire directed against Israel soldiers and settlers must cease, even though such actions take place within a framework of self-defense. The long-range shooting is futile."

In Gaza, as in Israel, endless debates raged over Arafat's role in the unfolding drama. Was he, as he himself and Israeli nationalists liked to think, the Palestinian mover behind the scenes, or was he trying his best to hide his impotence by holding on for dear life at the back of the beast of popular fury which had been unleashed? It was telling that even the Israeli security services couldn't agree. Aman, the military intelligence service, thought Arafat was in control, while Shabak, the general security service, regarded him as a powerless reed, swayed by circumstances beyond his control.

The Fatah militia Tanzim was not officially part of the PA security setup. But it was the most active and combative armed body during the fighting, and it enjoyed Arafat's protection without making it a habit to consult him before its operations. The distinction between Tanzim and the even more mercurial al-Aqsa brigades, another Fatah outgrowth, was often difficult to fathom. In late October 2000, Israel killed the Tanzim commander, Husein Abayat, in Bethlehem. Some days later, four Gazans died when their car was hit by a helicopter-launched missile. Israeli military spokesmen claimed they had been Tanzim operatives, which was fiercely denied in Gaza. These were the first of the helicopter-launched targeted killings which would become such a controversial part of everyday life in the Strip during the years to come. It is true that many highly placed Palestinian leaders and commanders were killed in such attacks, but there was also a tendency, in both camps – to promote victims posthumously. Hamas bureaucrats and neighbourhood activists with no military past were routinely presented to the Israeli public after their demise as being among "the top leaders of Hamas' military wing".

# 21

## The Return of Sharon

### The Destruction of Palestinian Self-Rule, 2001–2003

*Anyone arriving in the Strip in late 2003, having been absent during the first years of the al-Aqsa Intifada, as it was now called, had to struggle to get his bearings. Many of the landmarks and familiar points of reference had been destroyed or revamped beyond recognition. Foliage had been uprooted, trees cut and buildings flattened, partly by the actual fighting, more often as a security measure by Israeli troops, who wanted no orchards, houses or other hiding-places along the roads where they convoyed settlers to their fortress-like colonies. The ground overlooking checkpoints, main junctions and entrances to settlements was levelled and bare. The inner landscape of the Gazans was taking a similar pounding.*

On December 10, 2000, Ehud Barak gave up attempts to keep his coalition afloat and called new elections. By then, the Gaza Strip had become a place of urgent and extreme danger, to its inhabitants and to foreign correspondents, who were used to roaming the area without plans or precautions. Israeli artillery fired straight into refugee camps and villages, something unheard of until then. After the Palestinians began to use shoulder-borne missiles, the work of camera-carrying personnel became an ordeal. Several of them were shot after having been mistaken for militants, and some were shot for no discernible reason at all.

During the 2001 election campaign, Ariel Sharon vowed never to evacuate the Katif settlement enclave in Gaza. He fulminated against the plan to swap the Katif area for the Halutza bloc in Israel. To scupper the idea of turning Halutza over to the Palestinians, he promised to build a new town there. The election campaign was accompanied by countless ceasefires, promptly broken by one side or the other, and growing disillusionment everywhere. The ideas of the Israeli peace camp fell into disrepute and the Gazans, who until September had backed negotiations with Israel, swung abruptly in favour of armed struggle.

Sharon's stunning election triumph, 62.3 per cent over Barak's 37.7 per cent, struck fear far and wide. Sharon's loathing of Arafat personally, as well as of the Oslo process, boded ill for both. The official PA newspapers, *al-Ayam* and *al-Hayat al-Jadida*, called upon Palestinians to carry out civil, not armed, protests. But Sharon's ambition was to delegitimise Arafat and his rule, and events would play into his hands. The first game-changer occurred on March 18, 2001, when a mortar shell, launched from Beit Hanun in the north of the Strip, wounded an Israeli soldier in the kibbutz Nahal Oz. Shells had landed before, in Israeli colonies inside the Strip, but firing such weapons across the border was crossing a red line, in Sharon's eyes. During April, tens of mortars fell around the Israeli town of Sderot. Israel responded by re-occupying large swathes of autonomous Palestinian territory around Beit Hanun in the northeastern end of the Strip. There was a great international outcry, the US included, and after a few days the forces were pulled back. But the uproar caused in Israel by the inaccurate mortars was a revelation to Hamas, whose options for striking at Israel had been severely limited by the fencing in of the Strip. Two leading weapons' experts in the Islamist camp, Nidal Farhat and Adnan al-Ghoul, were told to speed up the development of Hamas' first real rocket, the Qasam. In September 2001, Farhat, whose mother Mariam was a well-known Hamas figure and member of parliament, went to see Hamas' highest military commander in the Strip, Salah Shehade. Farhat announced that he had made a rocket. Shehade was impressed but sceptical. Half a year later, the first Qasam landed in Sderot. Hamas possessed a weapon Israel could not, and still cannot, defend itself against.

Another watershed was September 11, 2001. Until then, relations between Ariel Sharon and US president George W. Bush had been frosty, at times outright unpleasant. US leaders had been unhappy with Israel's "disproportionate use of force" during the second Intifada, and vice president Dick Cheney had warned Israel that use of F-16 fighters and other American war materials for riot control violated the terms of sale. The Islamist terror attacks in America played into Israeli nationalist hands in more than one way. The news footage from Nablus and other Palestinian towns, where America was jeered by people carrying Osama Bin Laden's picture, were unhelpful to the Palestinian cause. (A survey showed that most Palestinians were really against the attacks; 64 per cent of them regarded the attacks as "un-islamic".) Above all, American shock and fears became fertile ground for Sharon's message: that Palestinian violence in the territories was really just another aspect of the terrorism which had risen to destroy America.

Arafat immediately understood the danger. He condemned the attacks and issued draconian orders to quell all outbursts of sympathy for the al-Qaeda. In Gaza, police fired live ammunition against pro-Taliban demonstrators, and there was a temporary drop in the general level of violence. But the circle of attacks, vengeance, diplomatic efforts and quickly-forgotten ceasefires was soon resumed. During December 2001 there was further escalation, after three large suicide attacks inside Israel. Arafat's forces in Gaza locked up hundreds of Islamists. Doing so had been much less difficult before September, 2000, when a popular majority supported Arafat's foreign policy choices and regarded suicide bombings as sabotage against their own interests.

But now, after more than a year of fighting and suffering, the tide of opinion had turned. Strong-arm measures against the Islamists did not go down well in Gazan neighbourhoods where buildings had been razed by Israeli bulldozers and bystanders killed during missile attacks on assassination targets. Arafat, humiliated by Sharon's constant "terrorist" taunts, was now disgraced from the opposite direction, by his own people. When PA police came to put Hamas leader Ahmad Yassin under house arrest, gun battles broke out between them and Yassin's bodyguard. Thousands of civilians rushed to the spot and surrounded Yassin's home. A few weeks later, when PA agents arrived in the Sheikh Radwan quarter of Gaza City to take Yassin's second-in-command, Dr Abdel Aziz al-Rantisi, in for questioning, a minor war raged for almost a day, resulting in seven deaths. PA forces again returned empty-handed, and observers in Gaza and abroad took notice of the embarrassing fact that Arafat was not in full control, even militarily. A host of Hamas institutions were banned and their offices boarded up and, after much brow-beating, Arafat extracted a moratorium on suicide attacks from Hamas. But Hamas only pledged to let Israeli civilians inside Israel alone, not settlers and not soldiers. On January 9, 2002, a Hamas unit attacked an Israeli infantry platoon on the Gazan border and killed four Bedouin trackers.

Israeli commandos immediately destroyed ships and installations in Gaza port. The government set aside nearly a hundred million dollars for improved security fences around the Strip. Those were "standard" measures. But the principal act of retaliation stunned even Hamas, who usually bargained for drastic Israeli replies – they were the most expedient way of eroding support for Arafat and undermining faith in his policies. Without warning, fifty civilian buildings in the Rafah refugee camps were flattened by Israeli bulldozers. Five hundred people were made homeless.

Assassinations, by drones or helicopters, of Islamist bomb-makers, real or imaginary, were not popular in foreign capitals, but they could count on a certain degree of understanding after the horrendous attacks on Israeli civilians. The destruction in Rafah took collective punishment to a degree not yet seen. Israeli house-demolitions until then had befallen relatives of suicide bombers or other terrorists. This time, those selected for retribution had no relation whatsoever to the deed in question. The condemnations were universal. Israel's leading columnist on strategic matters, Ze'ev Schiff, who rarely raised his voice, called it "an act of undisguised ruthlessness, devoid of military logic". Yosef Lapid, the veteran newspaperman who led the Shinui party, said "It makes us look like Huns, vandals, in the eyes of the world."

While Israel bombed Palestinian areas and Israeli busses exploded with record frequency, there were still constant talks between the parties, declarations of cease-fires, American and other envoys arriving, each with a new plan. Egypt and Saudi Arabia implored Arafat to do something about the suicide bombers. Foreign Minister Shimon Peres still dreamed of salvaging something of his life-work from the wreckage which piled up ever higher. Old formulas, like the "Gaza and Jericho First" plan, were discussed with PA officials, many of them as eager as Peres to turn the clock back. But gradually Peres began to suspect that Sharon was playing a double game: going through the motions of talks and diplomacy, while really taking care to foil initiatives for restoring the political process. As soon as things began to calm down, there was an Islamist attack or an Israeli bombing. On February 4, 2002, on the eve of a new US effort, both Foreign Minister Peres and Defence Minister Benjamin Ben-Eliezer, who often blocked Sharon in the security cabinet, were out of the country. Sharon gave the green light for a missile attack on a car full of Gazan fighters from different movements, all of them insignificant. The diplomatic initiative fizzled out. The only one of the countless peace plans to survive was the Saudi one, which got Arab League support and is still considered a serious venue.

By now, Arafat spent less and less time in the Gaza Strip, and during the remainder of his life he only visited the Strip on a handful of occasions. In February 2002, Israeli tanks surrounded the PA government compound in Ramallah, the Muqata, turning Arafat into a prisoner. Sharon was now telling foreign leaders openly that if they'd only help him exchange Arafat for another leader, "good things would take place".

The siege around the Muqata was lifted after some weeks of international protests, but then resumed, time and again, after attacks against Israelis. Sharon wanted to prove his point: either Arafat was responsible for Palestinian actions, or if not, he was unfit to be their leader. President George W. Bush was gradually won over to this point of view, and did his part in eroding the Palestinian president's standing, by declaring, "I am disappointed in Arafat".

Sharon had his old *bête noir* prostrate, almost at his mercy. But his own standing was only a little more enviable. In March, 2002, the Arabs and the Jews of the Holy Land were dying and bleeding at a rate not seen since the 1947–49 war. Close to 2,500 people died during the first two years of fighting and terror, and 25,000 were injured. The proportion of Jewish victims was much higher than during any earlier confrontations, more than a third of the total. The Palestinians in Gaza were scoring points which must have infuriated the Prime Minister, such as knocking out several of the celebrated Merkava tanks and killing their crews. Sharon, who had come to power on a law-and-order, let-me-deal-with-terror ticket now bore the brunt of Israeli frustration. Sickened by the abuse hurled at him by voters and citizens, he even stopped attending the events of his own Likud party.

At the end of March 2002, Sharon decided to expel Arafat from the country. He was blocked during a stormy government session. But after 30 people celebrating Passover at a Netanya hotel were killed by a Hamas suicide bomber on March 27, Sharon declared: "We are at war!". He gave the green light for a long-planned operation, "Defensive Shield", an attack against the cities of the West Bank, with much destruction in Jenin and Nablus. The declared aim – which failed – was to uproot terrorism. The presumed real goal, to crush Palestinian self-rule, was achieved. On April 15, the Fatah–Tanzim leader on the West Bank, Marwan Barghuti, was caught by the Israelis after a two-year manhunt. Hundreds of Palestinians were killed and thousands jailed. Israel's international standing took another nosedive and Yasser Arafat's influence over the course of fighting diminished further as regular units split up into local gangs. When the operation was over work began in earnest on Sharon's brainchild – the separation barrier.

During the Defensive Shield operation Palestinian self-rule areas marked "B" and "C" on the maps reverted to A-status, to total Israeli control. Gaza was different: its Oslo-map had only had two area categories, "white" and "brown" – Palestinian and Israeli – no intermediate B-zones of mixed control like the West Bank. There was some gruesome fighting in the Strip during the bloody spring of 2002, there were casualties in the hundreds when Israeli missiles went astray, and there were several Hamas terror attacks against Israel from Gaza, but there was no Israeli attempt to take over the Strip. In the West Bank, Arafat's kaleidoscope of security services was torn apart as its leaders, until recently Israel's partners, became wanted men and fled for their lives. The most useful of Israel's allies in the West Bank, Jibril Rajub, the ruthless head of the Preventive Security Services, the PPS, was attacked and humiliated.

Gaza was different. Its PPS leader, Muhammad Dahlan, was still in charge and many of his units intact. Not even Sharon, who had pacified Gaza with ruthless force in 1971, felt like trying to do it now. In January 2002 a senior Israeli commander had said that fighting terror in Gaza was like emptying the ocean with a tea-spoon. Dahlan, instead of being crushed, was about to be promoted in a new American-Israeli effort to elbow out Arafat from centre stage. The dissatisfaction with Arafat among those closest to him grew incrementally during the fighting. "Abu Ammar" was not so much indecisive as capricious. Orders given with much fanfare one day were silently reversed soon afterwards. One week he would wink at the irregular al-Aqsa "brigades" to attack Jewish settlers. Then, facing Israeli thunder, he would send his regulars to discipline the mavericks. All these machinations were so subtle and so hard to interpret that it often seemed that only Arafat himself knew which was the Palestinian strategy of the moment. Mistrust and confusion flourished. Even among his closest associates there were some who became convinced he had to be dropped. By the autumn of 2002, Sharon's and Bush's refrain – "Arafat must go" – had found echo within Arafat's own inner circle. The first dissident who dared to stand up and be counted was Mahmud Abbas, "Abu Mazen", who told the Ramallah daily *al-Ayam* in November: "The militarisation of the second Intifada was a total mistake. It located our struggle against Israel in the arena where they are strongest and we are weakest – the military arena."

It was a sign of the times that the near-official *al-Ayam* dared to publish such thinly veiled criticism against the leader. Muhammad Dahlan in Gaza had resigned in October, after having denounced the lack of "reforms" and "reorganisation" within the PA. Arafat had always valued loyalty more than competence, a weakness easier to forgive in a guerrilla chieftain than in a head of state. When Abbas carried on with more pointed barbs, such as "we want negotiations, not war", Arafat knew he faced the most dangerous internal threat ever. One after another of his most trusted protégées took up the rallying cry of "reforms" (less discreet terms like "corruption" and "misrule" were out of the question.)

The first concrete reform to be suggested was the re-organisation of the jumble of Palestinian security services whose commanders were accustomed to taking orders from Arafat alone. The new service would be organised and run by Dahlan, the Fatah leader from the Khan Yunes refugee camp. Arafat, as predicted, welcomed the reform proposals, but immediately set about pulverising them. The neutral term "reform", Arafat understood only too well, was mere courtesy. The idea was to chip away at his authority, wrest control of the armed forces from him and invest a prime minister – a post created for the first time, with those functions.

On April 29, 2003, Prime Minister Mahmud Abbas's cabinet was finally approved. An earlier attempt had been rejected by Arafat, who called its reform-minded set of ministers "an outright provocation". At the time, Arafat was again temporarily imprisoned in his compound by Israeli armour, while the Palestinian Parliament in Ramallah voted to beef up the Prime Minister's authority by transferring several functions to him from the President.

It is a testimony to Arafat's skills that he single-handedly subverted the carefully laid American–Israel–Abbas plan. The Tanzim and al-Aqsa hit squads in the West Bank continued to take orders and money directly from him, not from the heads of the reformed services. Abbas's attempts at disarming them were blocked. This meant that when Abbas promised the Israelis and the Americans calm and cease-fires, he could not deliver. While outwardly observing forms and treating Abbas courteously, Arafat paid street-mobs to throw rocks and shout insults for days on end outside

Abbas's villa in the Bala'a quarter of Ramallah. Abbas was particularly vulnerable, since he had no power-base outside the PLO. He had left his native Safed in northern Galilee as a child. He had no clan, no village, no party (except the Fatah, where Arafat prevailed) to back him up against the more abrasive egos of Arafat and the leaders of Arafat's irregular units.

In his desire to expose his Prime Minister as a powerless stooge, the jealous Palestinian president had a queer ally: Ariel Sharon was also keen to discredit Abbas. After years of Israeli nationalist claims that Arafat was the heart of the problem, one would have expected them to lend a hand and shore up the fledgling Palestinian Prime Minister, who spoke so courageously against armed violence. The day after Abbas's inauguration he prepared to fly to Gaza, the intended power-base of the regime he hoped to establish. At dawn, Abbas's men in Gaza called and asked him to postpone his visit. There had been a large Israeli commando operation in the Sajaiya neighbourhood during the night. Nine people had been killed and many metal workshops, suspected of participating in Hamas' rocket programme, had been destroyed. This was not the time to face the Gazans with talk of a peaceful turn.

Abbas understood the dynamics of how Palestinian armed actions played into the hands of Israel. His plan was to enforce enough calm to deprive the Israelis of their pretext for not negotiating seriously over the new American peace plan, tailored specifically for Abbas: the Road Map. But Ariel Sharon's real problem was not Arafat. It was the idea of Palestinian self-rule and statehood. In fact, Arafat's capriciousness and aversion to serious planning had been a huge asset for Sharon. The last thing he wanted now was for the battered, moribund PA to be brought back to life by a clear-headed diplomat who enjoyed the trust of Europe and Washington.

The claim that Israeli targeted killings during Abbas's six months in office were largely designed to undercut the reforms of the Prime Minister and Muhammad Dahlan cannot be scrutinised until the 2050s, when historians gain access to the relevant documents. But the suspicion that *hisulim* – "eliminations" in Hebrew – of Gazan Islamists were becoming a foreign-policy tool was difficult to keep at bay. There was a simple formula by which Sharon could regulate the intensity of diplomatic movement: the more killings, and the more innocent victims, the less traction for Abbas's reform attempts and the less international pressure for Israeli concessions. Of course, the air-to-ground killings also carried a price tag, if only in cases of widespread civilian damage. When a one-ton bomb was dropped on Hamas supreme military leader Salah Shehade in July 2002, fourteen civilians, most of them children, died in the blast, which made a deep crater in a densely built-up part of the old Daraj quarter of Gaza City. "Shehade was soon replaced by Ahmad Ja'abari, a much more competent man", an Israeli officer told me. The international outcry was so intense that Israel, in order to placate it, let several thousand Gazans return to jobs in Israel. In October 2003, after a wayward missile killed twelve civilians in Gaza, the Israeli peace-camp politician Yosi Sarid, known for his excellent intelligence sources, caused great embarrassment to the military spokesmen by showing that the official version concerning the "pin-pointed" air attacks was tainted by disinformation.

Anyone arriving in the Strip in late 2003, having been absent during the first years of the al-Aqsa Intifada, as it was now called, had to struggle to get his bearings. Many of the landmarks and familiar points of reference had been destroyed or revamped beyond recognition. Foliage had been uprooted, trees cut and buildings flattened, partly by the actual fighting, more often as a security measure by Israeli troops, who wanted no orchards, houses or other hiding-places along the roads where they convoyed settlers to their fortress-like colonies. The ground overlooking checkpoints, main junctions and entrances to settlements was levelled and bare. The inner landscape of the Gazans was taking a similar pounding. The sounds of gunfire, explosions, aircraft and humming drones accompanied the lives of most people in Gaza City, Khan Yunes and Rafah. Gaza, where a visit to the psychologist had been regarded as an admission of madness, saw mental problems and sleep disorders proliferate, not least among children in the bomb-intensive areas. Dr Eyad Sarraj from Gaza City is a pioneer in many fields in his society, not least human rights. But the way he has managed to change attitudes to psychiatric treatment is equally impressive.

For most Gazans the horrors of the fighting were compounded with the stress brought about by economic decline. In May 2001, after eight months of violence, less than half the number of trucks were entering the Strip than a year earlier. There was a corresponding drop in outgoing traffic, as thousands of tons of Gazan fruit and vegetables, produced for the Israeli market, rotted and dried. Supplies and spare parts imported by Gazan businesses or donated by foreign governments also became hostage to the political developments, as Israel held up shipments in the port of Ashdod pending good behaviour from the Palestinian government.

In addition to the tangible hardships there was the growing insight that all this was not a momentary failure but a total breakdown of the political process. Even though most Palestinians still favoured a mutual cease-fire – 71 per cent in April 2003 – the PLO was constantly losing support to the Islamist camp. At this time, Hamas' top leader in Gaza, Mahmud al-Zahar, declared that Hamas was now ready to challenge the PLO for the leadership of the nation. His words drew furious reactions from PA officials, which only served to underscore their truth. The reforms of Mahmud Abbas's new "clean" Palestinian government were meant to restore public faith in the secular leadership. But the PA government's new star, the economist Salam Fayad, was too righteous for the taste of most establishment figures. Only weeks after being named minister of finance, Fayad had mobilised US and Swiss contacts to help him trace a large part – almost $700 million – of the "disappeared money" which Arafat's *eminence grise* Muhammad Rashid had stuffed away in secret accounts. The news should have redeemed the PA in public eyes, but it was used skilfully by Hamas to stain it further.

# 22

# The Death of Yasser Arafat

## The Evacuation of the Strip, 2003–2005

> *If any Israeli leader was personally identified with the settlement project in the occupied territories, Israel's most ambitious and most costly national endeavour since taking control over all of historical Palestine in 1967, it was Ariel Sharon. To him colonisation had seemed an imperative, not a tactical matter linked to expedience and political circumstance . . . it was not only Sharon's world-view which was transforming, but the country's, when in 2004 Sharon spoke openly about "a Gaza Strip without Jews", and cracks began to open up all over the Israeli political system.*

Mahmud Abbas's main effort as head of government was the proposed "*hudna*" (truce) between, officially, the PA and the Islamist movements; and, unofficially, between Israel and all Palestinian armed forces. It ended in failure. But the way Abbas, with the help of Washington, managed to goad both Islamic extremists and Israeli nationalists into accepting the scheme was a diplomatic masterpiece. The *hudna* went into effect in late June 2003, and for a short spell there was a genuine feeling of recovery. Israeli forces were pulled back from most PA areas and for a couple of months things looked hopeful. There were a few incidents, but both sides kept their cool until August 19, when a Hamas preacher from Hebron blew himself up on a Jerusalem bus, killing 23 people. Abbas's main ally in the PA, Muhammad Dahlan, implored Sharon not to overreact, promising him to hit Hamas hard. But Sharon did not wait. Two days after the Jerusalem bomb, a helicopter-fired missile killed one of Hamas' top leaders, Isma'il Abu Shanab, as he travelled in a car with two colleagues in Gaza City. Two large retaliation attacks over the next weeks returned everything back to "normal". Abbas realised that there was no real space for him to carry out any reforms. After a few weeks of renewed bloodshed he resigned, in late September 2003. His reform project was the most sensible and most rational way out of the woods, but it faced the resourceful coalition Sharon–Arafat–Hamas, all determined to see him fail. Each of them put a different spin on Abbas's failure: to Sharon it was conclusive proof that the Palestinians could not reform themselves; in Arafat's eyes Abbas's surrender underscored his favourite axiom, that nothing could be achieved without the old boss; while Hamas triumphantly pointed out that accommodation and compromise with the Israelis was futile.

If any Israeli leader was personally identified with the settlement project in the occupied territories, Israel's most ambitious and most costly national endeavour since taking control over all of historical Palestine in 1967, it was Ariel Sharon. To him colonisation had seemed an imperative, not a tactical matter linked to expedience and political circumstance. In the late 1990s, when many in his Likud party had quietly shelved their grandest expansion dreams, he still called upon nationalist youngsters to illegally occupy and settle desolate hilltops along the Judea–Samaria ridge in the West Bank. During his successful election campaign in 2001, he thundered against those spineless defeatists in the Labour Party who called for an evacuation of the Gaza Strip. Consequently, when Sharon, in December 2003, first hinted at the uprooting of the Gazan settlements, Israel-watchers realised that it was not only Sharon's world-view which was transforming, but the country's. A little later, on February 2, 2004, Sharon spoke openly about "a Gaza Strip without Jews", and cracks began to open up all over the Israeli political system. A year later, when Sharon had already committed himself to the unilateral withdrawal from the Strip, his party refused to follow. In a complicated upheaval, which cannot be detailed here, Sharon's Likud–Labour coalition came apart, and so did those two parties, the pivots around which Israeli politics rotate.

Interestingly, part of the Israeli peace camp, led by Oslo negotiator Yossi Beilin, was largely opposed to Sharon´s plan to evict the settlers and move out of Gaza no matter what. To carry out such momentous change without any coordination with the Palestinian authorities, Beilin claimed, was a way to further humiliate and marginalise the battered PA – Israel's only conceivable partner for peace.

The Islamists were bound to claim an Israeli evacuation as a victory for its militant line. The Hamas–Fatah struggle for Gaza began in earnest a year and a half before the Israeli retreat, at a time when Sharon's declarations about withdrawal were still met with disbelief among Palestinians. On January 14, Re'em Riyashi, a young mother from Gaza City, managed to deceive the soldiers manning the metal detectors at the Erez crossing. She told them she had a platinum insert in her leg and was let through without a check. She killed four Israeli soldiers and became an instant celebrity. Her funeral was a mass event and her act even brought about a theological revision by Hamas supreme leader Ahmad Yassin, until then a fierce opponenent of female self-immolation. One difficulty with such attacks was that the would-be *shahida*, female martyr, had to spend time unchaperoned in enemy territory awaiting her opportunity. But now Yassin joined in the chorus of praise and even claimed that women, no less than men, were obliged to wage jihad.

Sharon was not going to help Arafat take credit for him pulling Israel out of the Strip. But the alternative scenario, with Hamas getting the credit, was equally abhorrent to him. It was not only Hamas who was taunting him, claiming that he was folding under their pressure. Large segments of his Likud party, lead by Benjamin Netanyahu, accused Sharon of having gone soft on terrorism. Sharon felt he did not have his party behind him. To silence that criticism he had to put a stop to Hamas' swaggering. His choice of method stunned all concerned. It is probable, but not known for certain, that the decision to kill Hamas founder and revered leader Ahmad Yassin was taken by Sharon after two suicide bombers killed ten Israelis in the Ashdod port area on March 14, 2004. On March 22, as Yassin exited the Mujama' mosque in the Sabra quarter in Gaza City, missiles hit his entourage, killing him and several others. The reaction in Gaza was earth-shaking, and had barely subsided when, just three weeks later, Yassin's successor and closest collaborator, Dr. Abdulaziz Rantisi, was killed by an Israeli missile aimed at his car.

The following months were among the bloodiest and most dramatic in the annals of the Strip. Yasser Arafat, who had named Ahmad Qurei'a, "Abu 'Ala", as his new Prime Minister after Mahmud Abbas, had recovered much of the authority stripped from him when the Palestinian parliament endorsed Abbas as Prime Minister. It was infernally difficult for Arafat to style himself as the undisputed ruler of the post-withdrawal Strip. He feared that Sharon's refusal to discuss the Gaza issue with any Palestinians was aimed at fomenting internal Palestinian violence, thus underlining the "lack a partner for peace" which was the cornerstone of Sharon's unilateral doctrine. Arafat needed Hamas cooperation, but the Quartet – the USA, the UN, Russia and the EU – warned him not to bring the Hamas into his government. After large-scale suicide attacks in Jerusalem and Ashdod in early 2004 the PA response was less resolute than on earlier occasions, earning Arafat the usual accusations from Sharon of being soft on terrorism.

On May 3, 2004, in the Likud party's internal vote on Sharon's Gaza evacuation scheme, 62% of the voters went against him. The vote was carried out in an atmosphere most detrimental to Sharon's designs, hours after news arrived from the Strip about a settler mother and her four daughters who had been gunned down and killed in the Katif settlement bloc south of Khan Yunes. At their memorial service the mourners were attacked by Palestinian gunmen.

A week later, during an offensive inside the Zeytun neighbourhood of Gaza City, an IDF personnel carrier hit a mine and Israel was forced to bargain with Hamas to get the fragmented body parts of six soldiers. Next day five soldiers were killed along the Philadelphi route on the Gaza–Egypt border, again by a shoulder-carried missile brought in from Egypt via underground tunnels. Operation "Rainbow", designed to clear populated areas along the Philadelphi, was launched on May 18. At this time it was still assumed that Israel would keep the Philadelphi stretch even after leaving the Strip, in order to be able to act against the smuggling tunnels connecting the Egyptian part of Rafah with the Palestinian one.

On May 19 Israeli television reporter Shlomi Eldar brought back shocking footage from Rafah. Houses were being razed by IDF bulldozers and dynamited by engineering corps. Hundreds of Gazans, perhaps more, had become homeless overnight. One sequence, of a blind old woman in the Brazil refugee camp rummaging through the rubble of her home in search of her heart medicine, made waves around the world and caused a furious row between Sharon and his Justice Minister (and friend) Yosef Lapid, who said he was reminded of his own grandmother during the Holocaust. In addition to the IDF surge in the tunnel area, another part of Rafah, Tel Sultan, which lies too far from the border fence to serve as a tunnel terminus, was sealed off. Tel Sultan was a comparatively tranquil part of Rafah, compared to the Shabura and Brazil camps where the armed resistance is usually concentrated. On May 20 several Israeli Human Rights' bodies petioned the Supreme Court to intervene against atrocities allegedly committed in Tel Sultan.

Of the 24 who died in Tel Sultan, two were unarmed teenagers, a brother and a sister, shot by snipers. More than a thousand were left homeless. During the operations inside Tel Sultan Israeli tanks fired a shell against demonstrators marching from Rafah in the direction of Tel Sultan. Ten people died and the Israeli government was forced to bend to international pressure and call off Operation Rainbow. On May 28, 2004, the Hamas-made rockets claimed their first fatalities among Israeli civilians, a child and a man in the town of Sderot. Large parts of the northern Gaza Strip, almost reaching the Jebaliya refugee camp, were invaded in yet another operation, "Front Shield". The Israeli forces, it was declared now and during countless subsequent efforts, would remain until the Palestinian rocket threat against Israel had been removed. But it was never removed, and the Israeli public, as well as the Gazan one, slowly realised what the IDF was reluctant to spell out in so many words: Israel's mortal enemy has finally achieved a kind of balance of terror; a weapon difficult to find and neutralise on the ground and impossible to intercept in the air. In October 2004, after more rocket attacks, hundreds of Israeli elite troops were sent into the Jebaliya area, killing 159 people, a third of them civilians, but without uprooting the Qasam rocket infrastructure. All metal workshops, including innocent ones, had long since been destroyed. This was a heavy burden on the local economy, but not on the rocket business, which somehow kept thriving, even though its resourceful leader Adnan al-Ghoul was killed in the attack.

The Hamas, still dazed by the loss of its two principal leaders, was content with developing and firing rockets. It accepted, for the moment, Arafat's rule in Gaza and even took his side during the serious challenges mounted against him inside his own Fatah movement. On July 17, 2004, Arafat carried out a mini-coup in Gaza, overseen by his relative Musa Arafat. Media outlets and police bases were secured by Musa Arafat's "Fatah Hawks". At the bottom of this lay the personal grudges festering between Yasser Arafat and his one-time protégée Muhammad Dahlan. Dahlan and the other Gazan natives wanted their share in Fatah's decision-making bodies, which were dominated by the "Tunisians", the bureaucrats brought back by Arafat from exile. Against Dahlan's Preventive Security – now run by Dahlan's crony Abu Shbak – Arafat fielded Musa Arafat, corrupt, tough and infinitely reliable. The streets of Gaza City filled up with demonstrators, thousands in favour of Dahlan; hundreds in favour of Musa Arafat. The two factions began to shoot, and then to kidnap eachother. On August 1 Dahlan gave Arafat an ultimatum: "You have ten days to dismiss Musa Arafat!" No one had ever spoken to the President in such a tone. The Egyptians forced a meeting between Arafat and Dahlan, with outward manifestations of reconciliation but with none of the underlying issues resolved. On October 12 Musa Arafat survived a bomb-attack against his convoy in Gaza, and a week later there was a regular battle, with hundreds of participants, between Dahlan's and Musa Arafat's forces in the Sajaiye quarter, with 65 wounded. Sharon, predictably, pointed to the Gazan strife as ample justification for his refusal to deal with Arafat and the remnants of the PA.

On October 27 Arafat lost consciousness. He was flown to Paris after Sharon had promised not to block his return. On November 11 he died after several days in coma. During his memorial service in Gaza his loyalists from the al-Aqsa Martyr's faction of the Fatah shot at his successor Mahmud Abbas and at Muhammad Dahlan outside the mourner's tent.

Sharon wanted Arafat to be buried in Gaza, and Israeli spokesmen pointed to the fact that his family owned a burial plot in Khan Yunes. The Palestinians, naturally, had hopes of laying their leader to rest in Jerusalem, but Sharon told them to banish such thoughts. In the end Arafat's remains were brought to Ramallah, to be enshrined in a Pharaonic mausoleum.

When Mahmud Abbas took over after Yasser Arafat his initial prospects were slightly more auspicious than they had been two years earlier, when his reform projects had been blocked by Arafat. This time around Ariel Sharon was not interested in seeing him fail, and several times his pleas with the Americans sufficed to avert expected Israeli invasions into Gaza. On January 9, 2005, Abbas was elected president by 62.3% of the voters.

But there were still the Hamas and the internal Fatah opposition to give Abbas sleepless nights, especially the al-Aqsa Martyr's Brigades. The Brigades, Abbas's old Nemesis, had largely been hunted down and disarmed by the Israelis in the West Bank, but in Gaza they were a force to reckon with. Only days after his ascension to power they carried out an attack specifically designed to embarrass him. A truckload of dynamite was brought inside the Karni checkpost between the Strip and Israel and killed five Israelis, several of them Israeli Arabs working to ease the plight of the Gazans. Israel immediately prepared for a new Operation, called "Eastern Step", but big-power pleas managed to contain it. Abbas vowed to let 8,000 PA policemen crack down on Hamas rocket facilities.

At the end of January 2005 Hamas took part in its first election ever, to some municipal councils. It did well, and during the Islamists' celebration clashes erupted in Gaza City between them and Fatah groups. On February 8 there was an unexpected breakthrough during Israeli-Palestinian talks in Egypt. Sharon promised to coordinate the pull-back from the Strip with Abbas, to release eight hundred prisoners and to give wanted militants in the West Bank an opportunity to turn in their weapons and return to civilian life. Abbas promised to seal Hamas' weapons tunnels under the Philadelphi route (he lacked the means to do it and the Israelis knew that.). Hamas, without signing any papers, let it be understood that it would respect an inofficial truce as long as Israel did so. To sweeten the deal Egypt agreed to return its ambassador to Tel Aviv after four years' absence. So eager were the parties to preserve the agreement that two weeks later, when an Islamic Jihad suicide bomber killed five in Tel Aviv, both Israel and the US blamed the Syrians, the patrons and hosts of the Islamist movements, rather than the PA.

More necessities were let through into Gaza by the Israelis, but there was still wretched bureaucratic tangles each time goods bound for Gaza had to be cleared from Ashdod port. Three hundred thousand Gazans, according to the Israeli Human Right's group B'Tselem, now lived in "dire poverty". In another round of local council elections, in May, Hamas carried three large constituencies of the Strip, the town of Rafah, the refugee camp al-Bureij and the village of Beit Lahiya. The results frightened the PA leadership, and Abbas decided to postpone the legislative elections until 2006.

The approaching evacuation of the Strip cast a shadow over all other concerns in Israeli politics. Sharon, barely keeping control over his settler-friendly party, wanted international recognition for having ended the occupation of Gaza. His legal experts told him he would only get it if Israel let go of the Philadelphi route between the Strip and Egypt. For the Israelis, the twelve-kilometre route, or rather a crucial one-kilometer stretch of it, was a constant headache and source of bad news. During their search for new tunnels, many soldiers were killed by booby-traps. As soon as a tunnel was dynamited, little boys with buckets were sent in to repair them. In spite of all these efforts the underground traffic flourished and huge stocks of weapons reached Gaza. The slowdowns and queues at the crossing points into Gaza also made cheaper goods, like canned food, worthwhile to bring in. In the coming years, this would grow into a multi-million racket: Sardine tins, powdered milk, any food with passed expiry dates, from

Egypt, Turkey, Denmark and India, found a new market in Gaza. The special Quartet envoy to the region, economist and former World Bank head James Wolfensohn, was furious at the Sharon government's tactic of using the import–export entry points at Erez and Karni as valves which opened and shut according to the number of rockets falling over Israel. One acute problem was the large greenhouse areas of the evicted Jewish settlers, which had been purchased by the Palestinians for huge sums. Its harvest of tomatoes and strawberries for the Israeli market would be a dead loss if the Karni crossing was not kept open. "Israel", said Wolfensohn "acts as if there was not going to be any disengagement at all."

During late summer 2005 thousands of Israeli ultra-nationalists streamed into the Strip, hoping to obstruct the eviction of the Gaza settlers. The Hamas informed, via its senior Gazan leader Mahmud al-Zahar, that it would keep fighting Israel even if it left Gaza. On July 14, after a Hamas rocket killed a woman in an Israeli village, President Abbas declared a state of emergency. Three persons were killed and more than 40 wounded as the PA police went after the Hamas rocket squads. Leaflets and mosque loudspeakers heaped vitriol over Abbas and his no-nonsense Interior Minister Nasser Yusef – they were nothing but Zionist lackeys. Hamas' principal message was that the Israeli exit was not the achievement of the PLO, but of Hamas. Walls were covered with posters showing masked Hamas fighters expelling frightened, black-caftaned, ultra-orthodox Jews from the Strip. (There were no such Jews among the Gazan settlers.)

At midnight August 14–15, the Israeli Army sealed off the Strip and began to empty it of Israelis. A week later there were no Israeli civilians left in the Strip. Only soldiers remained, loading military supplies onto trucks, dynamiting houses and uprooting trees. Public buildings and synagogues were left intact. On September 12 Israel declared an official end to its occupation. Large crowds of Palestinians marched on the settlements to celebrate. During one of those celebrations there was an explosion in the Jebaliya camp near Gaza City, and nineteen people were killed. It was an accident, caused by careless handling of explosives by the Islamists, who claimed that Israel was behind it and quickly "retaliated" by its most massive Qassam barrage to date, 35 rockets against Israeli targets.

On December 25 the new border crossing at Rafah was opened. On the Palestinian side PA police handled incoming goods and travellers, with 50–70 European Union supervisers keeping watch. Israel's security services were supposed to monitor the proceedings via closed-circuit television, with an option to object to the entry of undesirables. But in practice this routine did not work, and the main responsibility for the movements between Egypt and Gaza fell on the Egyptian border personnel, known for their venality, and the PA. At times Israel would paralyse the Rafah crossing by keeping the observers from getting to work.

# 23

# Sharon's Departure

## The Hamas Election Triumph, 2005–2006

*After the Hamas election victory, from the very first moment, President Abbas made it clear that he was not going to cede the prerogatives of power. All armed personnel of the PA would remain under his command. "Don't worry, I'll call all the shots", he told Israeli Foreign Minister Tsipi Livni soon after the results were in. Hamas' designated head of government, Isma'il Haniyeh, advised Abbas "to respect the results and remember that we, not he, got rid of Israeli occupation".*

Hamas knew well that the Gazan public was more repelled by Fatah–PLO corruption than it was attracted to Hamas' core ideology; and that two-thirds or more of all Palestinians still favoured mutual cease-fires and a two-state solution.

From the moment Hamas entered the political process, in early 2005, it generally left attacks against Israel to the smaller organisations. The Israelis regarded this as a ruse, since the infrastructure used by Islamic Jihad and dissident Fatah gunmen was largely owned and maintained by Hamas.

Within the framework of his sanguine vision of a democratic Middle East, President George W. Bush had pushed for fair and open Palestinian elections. But as the date drew near, his new secretary of state, Condoleezza Rice, began to regard this policy as a monumental mistake. She became convinced that Hamas had already made a strategic decision to aim for both political and military dominance of the Strip, regardless of the election outcome. This was the view of Israeli security insiders. The Shabak secret service chief, Yuval Diskin, reported to Ariel Sharon that a Hamas takeover was imminent. The head of military intelligence concurred, coining a new term for Gaza which would gain much currency later on: "Hamastan".

On November 21, 2005, Ariel Sharon broke away from Likud to form a new party, Kadima, made up of Likud and Labour Party defectors. After Hamas did well in yet another round of municipal elections, there were clear signs of panic both in Washington and within President Abbas's inner circle in Ramallah. Sharon declared that unless Hamas renounced violence and erased the anti-Semitic paragraphs from its charter, Israel would not cooperate with the PA during the January elections. Many, both inside and abroad, were disappointed with what they regarded as Sharon's insipid statement. They had wanted him to give the PA a clear ultimatum to keep Hamas out of the political process. Abbas came close to doing just that, but in the end he decided that such measures would be devastating to the standing of PLO–Fatah. At this time, Abbas and the PLO were worried about a good Hamas showing, not about being voted out of office. Their complacency was one reason for the senseless proliferation of Fatah lists, which would squander many thousands of votes.

The first days of 2006, the most dramatic for years, changed Palestinian and Israeli politics deeply. On the evening of January 4, Ariel Sharon, whose new party looked poised to make a clean sweep in the next elections, suffered a brain haemorrhage. The magnitude of the stroke was such, said his doctors, that it was unlikely that he would ever regain his mental faculties. The news reached Gaza in the middle of the election campaign, and was immediately incorporated into it. There were huge celebrations in the Gazan refugee camps, with parades of children carrying hastily printed placards which read *Sharon ila-l-Jahin*, "To Hell with Sharon!" and setting off fireworks. Sharon's exit undoubtedly served Hamas' cause. The Abbas government and PLO officials could not publicly rejoice in the demise of Israel's leader, while nothing prevented the other factions from doing so.

Hamas had been forced by the PA to accept tough constraints on their campaigning: no electioneering from mosque pulpits, no foreign funding, no threats of burning in hell for those who voted Fatah. The results, nevertheless, stunned the world and set the Palestine-Israel conflict on a new course. Hamas not only won. It secured a comfortable absolute majority, 74 seats against Fatah's 45 in the legislative council.

From the very first moment, President Abbas made it clear that he was not going to cede the prerogatives of power. All armed personnel of the PA would remain under his command. "Don't worry, I'll call all the shots", he told Israeli Foreign Minister Tsipi Livni soon after the results were in. Hamas' designated head of government, Isma'il Haniyeh, advised Abbas "to respect the results and remember that we, not he, got rid of Israeli occupation". Haniyeh, 43 years old, was born in the Shaati camp on the beach of the Mediterranean, and his family hailed from al-Jura, the home village of Hamas founder Ahmad Yassin and many other Islamist luminaries. If he talked tough to Fatah, he was almost conciliatory in his statements directed at Israel and the rest of the world. In an interview with the *Washington Post* he said that if Israel returned to its 1967 borders, "a peace in stages" would be possible. The new spokesman of the legislative council, Hamas' Abdul Aziz Dweck, a town-planner from Hebron, went even further in his inaugural address, and came close to hinting that Hamas would honour previous agreements between the PA and Israel.

It was obvious that Hamas was exploring ways to gain international legitimacy – something it had taken little interest in until now. But with some exceptions, notably Russia and South Africa, few countries and international bodies were ready to deal with Hamas. President Bush warned that there would be no aid without the recognition of Israel. NATO and the EU also declared that they would have no diplomatic contacts with the new Palestinian government, and that aid would be channelled in ways designed to bypass Hamas officials.

Israel instructed its diplomats to lobby hard abroad to help isolate Hamas. Three days after the elections, the Karni goods terminal began to reduce its opening hours, and the money transfers from Israel to the PA – VAT, customs and other indirect taxes levied by Israel on goods consumed in Palestinian territories – were suspended. This was a violation of the 1994 Paris agreement and met sharp criticism from the EU. President Abbas was no less firm. He declared that the peace negotiations, which were anathema to Hamas, would continue as before. Israel's caretaker Prime Minister Ehud Olmert, who, unlike his predecessor Sharon, was genuinely interested in strengthening Abbas, promised further pullbacks on the West Bank if he won the March elections. On the eve of the Israeli elections Isma'il Haniyeh, without compromising on the issue of recognition of Israel, again made an effort to placate Israeli centrist voters: "We don't want a bloodbath," he declared.

But the Islamic Jihad was on a different track. On Israeli election night it fired its first Katyusha rocket, much more powerful than the standard Qassams. Kadima, the party Sharon launched two months before leaving the scene, had enough wind in its sails left to win the elections even under the unpopular Olmert. Two days after his victory, large areas in the Qassam-firing zones – Beit Lahiya, Beit Hanun and Jebaliya – were attacked in massive aerial, naval and artillery bombardments. In a spiral of vengeance and retaliation, the small Jihad militia managed to compromise the new Hamas government and turn the world against the Islamist movement like never before. On April 10, 2006, the EU decided to cut aid to the PA. The US, which had already done so, outlawed private donations to the PA. The economic punishment worried Hamas more than the Israeli bombing. President Abbas's money men had been busy since Hamas' election victory funneling millions from the official PA coffers to accounts where Hamas could not reach them. The new Palestinian foreign minister, Hamas' hardliner Mahmud al-Zahar, went to Cairo to plead with his Egyptian colleague Ahmad Abu al-Gheit. But Abu al-Gheit refused to even see him, a veritable slap in the face.

We know now – from what took place during the Hamas–Israel truce in the second half of 2008, and from the situation after the 2009 Gazan War – that Islamic Jihad is unable to carry out any meaningful shooting at Israeli targets without the permission of Hamas. It is a fact that Hamas refrained from attacking Israel during the spring of 2006, but then gave the Jihad *carte blanche*. That was a gross blunder, considering that the weak, unmartial Olmert was much more sensitive than Sharon had been to public pressure demanding action against the rocket fire, and also considering that many of the international actors who opted for the embargo were ready to be swayed by concrete Hamas steps against violence. It is unlikely that Hamas, given a chance, would ever have become "domesticated" or weaned away from Iran and Syria. But it is certain that no serious attempts were made to drive a wedge between Prime Minister Haniyeh's camp, which was obviously eager to break the cycle of violence, and the fanatics in Hamas' exiled leadership and its Iran-trained military commanders. No attempts were made to take Haniyeh up on his word and offer incentives in return for the curbing of the Jihad artillerists. In Israel, some of the most respected strategic analysts – such as former Mossad boss Ephraim Halevy and general Giora Eiland, head of the National Security Council – warned against gambling on regime change in Gaza. According to them, Israel should shelve all emotions in dealing with Hamas, and offer it non-intervention in return for cessation of attacks. Perhaps, if Israel had suggested such a deal to Haniyeh, he would have been, as usual, overruled by exiled leader Khaled Mash'al. But instead, Israel kept insisting on something Hamas couldn't deliver – recognition of the Jewish state.

Israel's undeclared but systematic policy was aimed at getting Hamas into a diplomatic corner. It marched willingly into that corner. An example of Hamas' unimaginative way of doing things, while the whole world was looking, was its reaction after an Islamic Jihad terror attack in Tel Aviv, which left eleven dead. While Abbas and Fatah condemned the attack, Hamas refused to do so, deliberately squandering diplomatic points and attracting hatred and condemnation for an act it hadn't committed. Hamas, battered from all directions, turned its attention to the only task left, consolidating its hold over Gaza. Its interior minister Siyad Siyam announced that since President Abbas was not ready to cede control over the existing security services, Hamas would have to set up its own ones. In late May, 2006, an embryonic Hamas police force, the *tanfidhiya* – "executive" – corps, paraded through Gaza City for the first time, equipped with automatic rifles and armour-piercing shoulder missiles. It was a show which drew indignant protests from the Fatah camp, and after some weeks Hamas agreed to pull its forces off the streets. It was a sly move. The rapid and highly efficient upgrading, by instructors trained in Iran, now took place out of public view. Interior Minister Siyam, who was killed by an Israeli missile in the 2009 war, was a dynamic and single-minded organiser. The 30,000-strong Fatah security establishment had some well-trained units. But many of its men in arms were over sixty years old. Others had reached positions of command through friendly cousins or string-pulling. But in Hamas' fighting units there were no slump postures and no potbellies, and some of them had gone through specialised training unknown even to the elite Fatah bodies, now given crash courses in counter-insurgency by the US General Keith Dayton.

The job of running and coordinating the fledgling forces of Hamas was given by Siyam to Jamal Abu Samhadana, a former Fatah man who had set up a small movement called the Popular Resistance Committees. The PRC was – unlike Islamic Jihad – closely linked to Hamas and never went its own way. President Abbas annulled the appointment of Abu Samhadana, while Hamas upheld it, and on June 8 the dispute was settled by an Israeli missile, which killed Abu Samhadana and three of his men. Hamas was torn by internal debates on whether to resume attacks inside Israel.

Two weeks later, on June 25, 2006, a joint Hamas–PRC commando team carried out a spectacular operation against an Israeli position inside Israeli territory. Via a tunnel, dug from inside the Strip, an armoured unit was attacked, two soldiers killed and one, corporal Gil'ad Shalit, was abducted. Apart from the embarrassment, the Israeli government, which had concentrated its attacks on Islamic Jihad for more than a year, was now pressured by the public outcry to end the 18-month quasi-truce with Hamas.

On June 28, Israeli forces poised themselves inside the Strip, ready for a three-pronged assault: 65 Hamas members in the West Bank were rounded up and jailed without trial, among them eight government ministers, 20 legislators and several mayors. The only power station in Gaza was destroyed and entry points into the Strip sealed. The following day, Israeli forces entered Gaza from several directions, concentrating on Rafah and Khan Yunes, where Shalit was thought to be held.

The abduction of Gil'ad Shalit was a tactical feat, but it would prove a flagrant strategic blunder. Prime Minister Haniyeh understood this and tried to get the affair over with. But, yet again, his hand was stayed by the Syrian-based exile leaders. The Israelis, who initially refused even to consider Hamas' demands, gradually began to negotiate an exchange of prisoners via Egypt. On October 2, Egyptian Foreign Minister Ahmad Abu al-Gheit revealed that Hamas had turned down an Israeli offer to release a thousand prisoners, chosen by Israel, for Shalit.

Before the 2006 war in Gaza was over, nearly 400 Palestinians had been killed. But the suffering of the Gazans received scant attention, because of the war between Israel and Lebanese Hizbollah which broke out on July 12. During the following autumn, Israel's policy in Gaza was characterised by the extreme contrast between its dovish defence minister, Amir Peretz, the first person from the Israeli peace movement ever to hold that post; and the head of Southern Command, the pugnacious Yo'av Gallant. The general was, not without reason, obsessed with the flow of ever-heavier war materials brought into Gaza through the underground tunnels. He wanted free hands to strike harder against both the tunnels and the rocket workshops. Peretz, appalled by the heavy toll of civilians, alternately unleashed Gallant and reined him in. In November 2006, operation "Autumn Cloud" left 60 people dead, a figure which included a larger proportion of civilians than the usual one-third. In one strike, on November 7, 18 Palestinians from one family were killed. One Palestinian operation during this round of fighting quickly took on the aura of legend: Palestinian women brought in female dresses under their skirts to fighters holed up and surrounded by Israelis in a mosque in Beit Hanun. The men, dressed up as women, filed past the unsuspecting enemy.

Hamas, deprived of taxes as a source of revenue (income tax was negligible; the only taxes which made any difference were the indirect ones collected by Israel), and unable to carry out international bank transfers, now had to carry cash across the border in suitcases. Several high-level Hamas officials were caught by Egyptian customs men at the Rafah crossing and relieved of bags bulging with bills. No one was too important to shirk this duty. On December 14, Hamas Prime Minister Haniyeh returned from a trip to Iran and the Gulf states and was forced to part with $30 million. From then on, cash transfers were mainly carried out via the tunnels.

Haniyeh's hurried return from abroad was provoked by what was, to ordinary Gazans, the most disturbing incident yet in the burgeoning factional war. Three small children were murdered on their way to school, only because their father was a Fatah intelligence colonel, Baha Balusha. Considering the dispersion, the political fragmentation and the divide-and-rule tactics of Arab leaders, the Palestinians have been remarkably apt at avoiding internal fighting. Refugee camps swarming with mutually hostile and armed gangs have rarely been seen fighting to the death. But the killing of the Balusha children, and some other cold-blooded killings of non-combatants, set the ball rolling. Bombs, missiles, drive-by shootings and murders started to tear neighbourhoods and families apart. Civil war, interrupted by short and brittle cease-fires, raged during the spring of 2007 throughout the whole Strip, mostly in Gaza City, Khan Yunes and Rafah. As militants kept up the fire from street corners and rooftops, residents scurried from doorway to doorway, dodging snipers and cross-fire on their way to shops and markets. During the last week of January 2007 more than 60 people were killed and hundreds wounded, many of them civilians. Schools closed down. When someone in either camp was abducted – forty a day was not an uncommon number – the first place his family went to look for him was the morgue, not the hospital. Most Gazans with a foreign passport, or with some skill marketable abroad, prepared to leave. Some who had neither paid dearly to get their families out via the tunnels to the Egyptian part of Rafah.

# 24

# Civil War and the Hamas Takeover, 2007

*As Israel allowed President Abbas's forces in the West Bank to rearm and take over the large towns, and Hamas quickly consolidated its hold over the Strip, two quasi-states took shape. No aspect of life in either territory – be it security, justice, education or public morals – escaped the violent polarisation initiated by both camps. You no longer had to be a militant to be dragged away for questioning; it was enough to be a sympathiser. Yellow Fatah flags in Gazan demonstrations provoked the same brusque police intervention as green Hamas banners did in the streets of Ramallah.*

The Palestinians have a special standing in the Arab world. Everyone realises that Nasser's pan-Arab vision will never come true. The Arabic-speaking lands will not be united into one polity. The only real pan-Arab concern alive in Arab hearts and minds is the Palestinian issue. The sight, therefore, of Palestinians murdering each other and gearing up for civil war was much more than a tragedy to other Arabs, it was an assault on their pride and self-esteem. If they couldn't rectify the results of the 1948 and 1967 fiascos, at least they had to stop the most emblematic of all Arab peoples from destroying itself. In February 2007, after firm inter-Arab prodding, President Abbas and Hamas' Khaled Mash'al promised King Abdullah of Saudi Arabia to stop shooting – which they did not – and to form a government of national unity, which they did.

The Fatah–Hamas détente was greeted with much relief, not least by the Strip's inhabitants. Some of the sanctions were lifted, and the Israelis were forced to let more provisions through, but state-employed Gazans' wages were still in arrears of several months.

The unity government of Hamas–Fatah was, however, a mere paper construction. There was no trust, no reconciliation, and the countless truces were interspersed with violent incidents. President Abbas refused to pay the price Hamas demanded for a real truce: an end to the relentless Israeli–Fatah assault on Hamas members and institutions on the West Bank.

Mahmud Abbas and his *de facto* defence minister, Muhammad Dahlan, pleaded desperately with the US, Israel, Jordan and Egypt to disregard the old rules and get them arms and ammunition. There was some loosening up of regulations, and several thousand automatic rifles from Egypt and Jordan were let through. The Fatah–PLO camp had much less access to the underground smuggling tunnels into Gaza than their adversary. Hamas had learned to bring in the money and the weapons it needed even when Israel shut the entry points. The Israelis were furious about the slack routines on the Egyptian side of Rafah, where hundreds of trucks laden with civil and military material arrived daily, bound for the Strip via the tunnels. The venality of the underpaid Egyptian soldiers is well-known, but any open reference to this problem was an insult which made official Egypt bristle with indignation. Israel tried everything to block the tunnels, but failed in spite of years of experience. The tunnels became big business. A share in a tunnel was a lucrative investment, and the Hamas government registered and taxed the passages. During periods of relative calm, when the Israelis opened up the overland traffic of goods, the hourly rate for using a tunnel plummeted. It was said that the tunnel owners would pay freebooting rocket squads to shot rockets at Israel in order for her to retaliate, seal the borders for imports and push the tunnel-rates up again.

Meanwhile, the helplessness of their high-tech army in dealing with the low-tech Gazan rockets infuriated the Israelis in affected areas, especially the town of Sderot, which more and more people now began to abandon. The Air Force took out rocket launchers and killed their operatives in large numbers, but they were all replaced within hours. Russian oligarch Arcadi Gaydamak, who wanted to run for mayor in Jerusalem, denounced the "spineless government" and spent millions on bussing the citizens of Sderot to "quiet weekends" at Tel Aviv hotels. The rockets may have fallen at the perimeter of the country but the fallout was becoming a matter of national politics. The indignation at Israel's perceived impotence had the potential to decide a national election.

With Hamas and Fatah busy with their all-emcompassing feud, lawlessness flourished in Gaza. New, clan-based militias appeared. Often these players were mere mafias masquerading as political movements. The most notorious of these gangs was Jeish al-Islam, "the Army of Islam", alias the Dughmush clan from the Sabra quarter of Gaza City. The Dughmush's compound, comprising the better part of a block, was defended like a fortress, and its chieftains did not take orders from anyone. The Dughmush, said to have arrived from Morocco a century earlier, sported full Islamist beards but their only gods, according to a friend of mine who knew them, were power and booty. Some believe that it was they who killed Musa Arafat, the PA police chief in Gaza and a Hamas scourge, in September 2005. When BBC correspondent Alan Johnston disappeared in March 2007, he was the 12th or 13th journalist to be abducted and held for ransom. In most, if not all, those operations, the fingerprints of the

Dughmush were visible. They even had a hand in the raid which brought Israeli soldier Gil'ad Shalit to Gaza. One explanation for the bogged-down negotiations on Shalit is that the Dughmush regard Shalit as an insurance policy. Israel will surely exact vengeance for the Shalit's ordeal once he is repatriated, and the only known accomplices to his abduction are the Dughmush. "Once Shalit is back in Israel, the Dughmush compound in Sabra will be flattened", a source of mine has confided.

The most remarkable thing about the Hamas takeover of the Strip was its brevity. Rather than the epic battle the Gazans had feared, raging for months in alleys and street corners, the 13-year PLO rule over Gaza ended with a five-day whimper. The rout was comprehensive, humiliating and more brutal than anything ever seen between Palestinians. PLO leaders and commanders with distinguished records fled for their lives – in fishing boats to Egypt, or into Israel via the Erez crossing, where they were taken to the West Bank. Not a few of those denied entry by the Israelis were murdered in cold blood by Hamas, "to our eternal shame", in the words of Israeli veteran politician Yosi Sarid.

Gazan Fatah strongman and presidential adviser Muhammad Dahlan, the man entrusted with the defence of the PLO in Gaza, was abroad for medical treatment, rather than leading his men. For all his protestations, his absence ruined his reputation. He had, it was believed, realised that the struggle was futile, saved his own skin (he would surely have lost it had Hamas got hold of him) and left the men who trusted him to the wolves. (The hatred of Dahlan in Hamas circles is of a Biblical nature, and impervious to the passing of time. In July 2009, at the wedding of a relative, Mahmud Dahlan, a bomb went off and injured 63 people, some of them seriously.)

Dahlan and a hundred faithful followers ended up in Ramallah, another five hundred Fatah fighters made it into Egypt, and close to two hundred defected and joined the Islamist forces. Some policemen with explicit Fatah records were weeded out, but most remained in the service. Immediately after the Hamas takeover, the Rafah crossing between Egypt and Gaza was closed down, because its complicated arrangements – with PA–Fatah, Egyptians, EU observers and Israelis all in delicate roles – could not be maintained. The only crossing kept sporadically open was Karni, the entry point for Israeli goods coming in, and Gazan agricultural produce going out. The inscrutable ways of the Israeli crossings had been a calvary for years to Gazan businesses. But now, without declaring it unequivocally, it dawned upon them that the Israeli government was closing down all economic interaction with Gaza. Israeli producers of consumer goods, for whom the Strip was a 5–10 per cent share of the market, lost half a million dollars a day, while Gazan growers and subcontractors lost almost everything. Necessities and money can be brought in via tunnels, but their goods, even if smuggled out to Egypt, could find no markets there. Most state employees continue to receive – reduced – salaries from the PA coffers in Ramallah, on condition that they did not show up for work in the Hamas ministries. (Some were forced to do so.) But as Gaza lost most donor funding and all Israel-collected revenue, the municipal workers in the Strip went for months without seeing any paychecks.

As Israel allowed President Abbas's forces in the West Bank to rearm and take over the large towns, and Hamas quickly consolidated its hold over the Strip, two quasi-states took shape. No aspect of life in either territory – be it security, justice, education or public morals – escaped the violent polarisation initiated by both camps. You no longer had to be a militant to be dragged away for questioning; it was enough to be a sympathiser. Yellow Fatah flags in Gazan demonstrations provoked the same brusque police intervention as green Hamas banners did in the streets of Ramallah.

Until the Israeli withdrawal in 2005 there was an electronic fence, 63 kilometres long, separating the Strip from Israel. Palestinian fighters cut through it and dug tunnels under it to get at the Israeli border settlements, whose inhabitants had lived in fear ever since the abduction, by tunnel, of Israeli soldier Gil'ad Shalit in the summer of 2006. Now a new, double-lane patrol strip was added, with additional mine-fields. Still, with all the efforts of the militants, most Gazans who make it through the formidable obstacle-course are not terrorists, but people looking for work.

Hamas has worked swiftly. They have set up roadblocks, Israeli-style, in the Strip, collected arms from Fatah people, and rushed Iranian cash, flour and tinned food through the tunnels to stave off a food emergency. Without being told (they would soon be told) all but a few indomitable activist women donned the hijab. Jazz, dancing, drinking, and kissing in cars went from being unwise to dangerous as Hamas built up its own judicial system. When the defeated Fatah camp found a legitimate pretext to take to the streets – such as the third anniversary of Yasser Arafat's death in 2007 – the dreaded "Executive Force" of Hamas fired live rounds into the crowd. The following year Arafat commemorations were banned in the Strip.

After only two weeks in power, Hamas joined the smaller fighting groups and resumed rocket fire against Israel. The Israelis began to ramp up military pressure against the Strip, hoping that a popular outcry inside Gaza would bring down the shooting. In mid-September 2007, the Israeli cabinet declared the Strip "enemy territory" and announced that electric power would be cut off. The Strip was blacked out several times, but Defence Minister Ehud Barak's plan to bring the Hamas to its knees this way was foiled by interventions of the Israeli attorney general and the Supreme Court. Barak then cancelled all exit visas for Gazans studying abroad. Pumps, engines and other spare parts of vital importance for Gaza's sorely tested sanitary infrastructure gathered dust awaiting clearance at Ashdod harbour.

Considering these, and all the other impediments in its way, Hamas has done an impressive job of cementing its authority. But there is one irksome challenge to its dominance that it has not managed to come to terms with. The large number of Gazans who provide the Israeli security service Shabak with information is an embarrassment and an acute danger to Hamas leaders. Each time a car with Islamist leaders or rocket personnel is pinpointed and turned into a smoking hulk by Israeli missiles, the operation has been preceded by a discreet phone call from a neighbour or colleague or even family member of the targeted ones. Cell-phones and internet connections make it much easier than before for the *jawasis* – collaborators – to cover their tracks. The feverish suspicions set in motion have become a fast-track option for personal vengeance. To report a fellow citizen as a possible collaborator has become a sure way to get him in trouble. But in spite of all the Hamas efforts, spying hasn't diminished. During November and December 2007, the Israelis stepped up their air attacks against objectives in the Strip. The accuracy of the missiles steadily increased, and the number of non-combatant victims fell sharply, from over a third to less than 10 per cent. There was no technological breakthrough to explain this. It was the result of better real-time intelligence. (Note that the accuracy of mortars, tank-guns and heavy artillery, often used close to populated areas in Gaza, is much inferior to the guided air force ordnance.)

But Hamas is also making headway. The Qassam rockets, if not stored in cool places, have had a tendency to ignite themselves, causing great damage and exposing arsenals. Rocket production never ceases in the Strip. During the times when Hamas is bound by a truce or a promise to the Arab League not to fire, it has let the smaller fighting groups make use of the new pieces. "Hamas rockets are like fresh bread, they have no shelf-life", an Israeli rocket expert told me. But towards the end of 2007, Israeli military sources revealed that Hamas had managed to create a stable rocket fuel which stored safely for long periods. If this was correct, and it proved correct during the 2009 war, Hamas, like Hizbollah in Lebanon, could stockpile rockets in order to keep up sustained bombardment for a long period, even as it was under heavy attack.

Apart from independent-minded women and Fatah members, the group most vulnerable to Hamas' strong-arm rule were Gaza's few thousand Christians. Rami Ayad, a Baptist bookseller, accused of missionary work among the Muslims, was taken away and shot and several Christian shops were torched. Preparing for Christmas in 2007, Gazan priest Issam Fares told the foreign press that he had deep misgivings about the future of Christian life under Islamist rule. Islamic Jihad fired a missile against a group of Gazan Christians as they waited to cross Israel for the Christmas celebrations in Bethlehem. Many of those who received transit permits to attend the Bethlehem celebrations did not return. There is a lively and growing Gazan community in the "Christian triangle" of Bethlehem, Beit Jalla and Beit Sahur.

During the first half of 2008, the immediate interests of Hamas and Israel steadily converged. Both needed a respite. Farmers were shot at from the Israeli side because militants dressed up as farmers often approached the fence to shoot at the Israeli farmers on the other side. Most inconvenient to Hamas, the regime which condemned materialism, was the material misery in Gaza. It did not help to bring in suitcases of dollars when there was nothing to stock up the shelves with. The typical Gazan street-corner grocery was beginning to resemble its Zimbabwean counterpart. Hamas was not amenable to arm-twisting, but several of its local leaders had a pragmatic side, and this unwinnable shooting contest with a better-armed enemy looked like squandering popular support for no good reason.

The Israelis were equally helpless. Hamas' artillery had come a long way from the pathetic, sputtering basement contraptions which exploded in the faces of its makers a decade earlier. By now, Soviet-designed, Chinese-made and Gaza-assembled Scuds and Katyushas were falling over the city of Ashkelon and rapidly improving its range in the direction of even larger targets like Ashdod and Beersheba. Israeli real estate and farmland prices plummeted in an ever widening semicircle around the Strip.

During the cold January of 2008, the lack of fuel and other basics became urgent in Gaza. In what looked like an unplanned thrust of popular rage and need, the Palestinians overran the high metal border fence and streamed by the tens of thousands into Egypt, buying everything in sight. During a week-long bonanza, merchants and truck-owners in Cairo kept up a constant train of deliveries to Rafah and el-Arish. The joy of the confined Gazans was spontaneous enough, but the tumbling of the hated wall had been carefully prepared by Hamas for weeks. Its foundations had been perforated at strategic points with or without the connivance of the Egyptian border-control units.

During the spring of 2008, Prime Minister Olmert and Defence Minister Barak, whose personal relationship was plagued by mistrust, agreed that there was only one choice open to them: a truce or a war. Carrying on the tit-for-tat rocket/air strike duel only underscored their impotence in the eyes of the Israeli public. In Gaza too there was much – discreet – scorn of the rocket policy. It was a common view that a rocket which could cause real destruction in Tel Aviv would be a strategic weapon worth having, but that rockets which mainly terrorised Israelis in the periphery invited and justified, in European and US eyes, the heavy Israeli retaliation.

Olmert, whose indecision had bungled the ground effort in Lebanon in

2006, refused to go to war unprepared again. On June 19, 2008, a six-month Egypt-brokered *tahadiya*, "calm", went into effect. The government was roundly abused by the nationalists for having "given in to terrorism", but the Israelis living in the southwest of the country returned to normal life and the rocket craters disappeared from the front pages. The Gazans were equally content to be able to sleep at night, but no normality awaited them. Fuel, flour and medicines were let through, but only the bare necessities. The contents of the truckloads entering Gaza were meticulously examined and "forbidden" goods, such as sweets or novels, were impounded.

As the end of the "calm" approached, tension arose. In each camp the pros and cons of renewing the agreement were reiterated over and over. Israeli military planners were frustrated at not being able to attack the smuggling tunnels, which they claimed Hamas was using to stock up on new weapons, especially shoulder-carried anti-tank missiles. But some generals baulked at the dangers and pitfalls of a Gazan operation, where there is little elbow-room to display Israel's tactical advantages. They tried to cool off the politicians by reminding them that occupying the Strip would cost $4 million a day. Hamas was split. It had made good use of the lull, but there was a strong feeling that Israel must be pushed to pay a higher price for the calm, either by calling off the ruthless campaign against Hamas charities and organisations in the West Bank, or by an unconditional and complete opening up of the import–export channels between Israel and the Strip.

On November 4, Israel broke the truce and entered the Strip to blow up an underground tunnel dug near the Kissufim junction. Seven Palestinians militants were killed. The rocket and mortar fire against the Israeli border towns was taken up again and went on for two weeks. But the situation slowly stabilised. On November 9, Amira Hass, one of only two Israeli reporters inside the Strip – the other one was Suleiman al-Shafi, from the Bedouin township of Rahat – reported that Isma'il Haniyeh said Hamas "would accept Israel within its 1967 borders" in return for a *hudna* (a long-term, binding truce). A little later, Israel transferred a hundred million shekels in new bills to relieve the cash-crunch of the Gazans, whose Israeli notes were crumbling from overuse, a move interpreted as an olive branch.

In retrospect, both sides accused the other of never having had any real intention of keeping the peace, but of having utilised the breathing space to develop new and even bloodier schemes. On November 24, Ehud Barak lashed out in the Knesset against "ranting war-mongers". Some days later, an Israeli soldier lost a leg to a Hamas mortar shell and there were some air strikes against targets in Gaza. There were agonised debates within Hamas, about which we still know very little. Few of those who resisted extending the truce wanted war. They assumed that the parties would return to the *status quo ante*, and that Israel, after a few weeks of rockets and popular outcry, would be ready to discuss a renewed *tahadiye* with improved terms for the Hamas. On December 14, Haniyeh said that Hamas would not extend the truce, but that it would not shoot unless attacked. Three days later, 21 rockets fell over Israel. On December 18, Haniyeh gave formal notice of the end of the *tahadiye*. Foreign Minister Tsipi Livni was called to Cairo by the Egyptians for emergency talks. Hamas Foreign Minister and local Gazan strongman Mahmud al-Zahar said prolonged calm would require food, fuel and relief for Hamas members in the West Bank, on the run from the united efforts of Israel's and Ramallah's special forces.

The day before Livni's arrival in Cairo, 70 rockets – an all-time record – were launched towards Israel. On the 26th, this reporter saw large troop movements converging around the Strip and the roads nearest to the Strip were closed off to civilian traffic.

# 25

# Operation "Cast Lead", 2008–2009

*What stunned Hamas, more even than the unexpected ferocity of the attacks, was the international reaction . . . clearly discernible beyond a smoke-screen of dutiful condemnations, was Egypt's stance. "This war is only superficially about Gaza. It is really about defending the Egyptian regime against its internal and foreign enemies, about sending a message to Iran: 'We have been slow to react but here it comes.'"* (Basem Eid, Palestinian human rights activist)

Rarely has an expected military operation caused such a surprise in all quarters: on the side of the attackers, the attacked and the bystanders. Some Hamas spokesmen hinted later that they had been mislead by the Egyptians to discount the possibility of an Israeli government consisting of ultra-orthodox parties ordering an attack on the Sabbath. The three-minute air-strike, which killed several hundred Hamas men (if one counts several dozen freshly graduated police cadets as such) and at least twenty civilians, took the wind out of Hamas for a brief spell, but it soon got its rocket forces in place. They kept up a steady barrage during the whole war. The Grads, Katyushas and Qassams caused considerable damage, loss of life and general disruption in southern Israel, but the political fall-out was much smaller than Hamas had hoped. Normally, during rocket attacks from Gaza the inhabitants of the attacked towns and the tabloid press would raise hell, denouncing the government which had deserted them and demonstrating outside the government compound in Jerusalem. But this time, the Israelis on the receiving end of Hamas' fire did not trouble the government at all. In fact, they specifically implored Israeli leaders to carry on the attack on Gaza regardless of how many rockets fell on them. A few days after the outbreak of the war, I was with a photographer in the southern Israeli city of Ashkelon, with the task of making a street-level survey of hearts and minds. We spent hours trying to find at least one person opposed to the war, but in the end we had to give up.

On the Gazan side, the reactions were much less unanimous than claimed by most foreign media. It was stated with much confidence that the Israeli onslaught would now bring Gazans of all hues rallying around Hamas. It was even said that Gazans hostile to Hamas were now coming over to its point of view. This view of Palestinians, as people incapable of critical judgement of their own leaders, driven only by indignation, hatred and gut-reaction to events, is an invention. I spoke to several Gazans on the phone during the war, most of them sworn opponents of Hamas, and I heard many cool-headed assessments of the misfortunes which had descended upon them. I did not hear, from anyone but Hamas people, any conciliatory remarks about the Gazan leadership and the way it conducted its affairs.

Defence minister Ehud Barak stated his objectives early on: "To change the situation fundamentally, until there is no rocket fire". Many Israeli decision-makers had far higher ambitions. General Yo'av Gallant, who had planned the operation and now commanded it, wanted to "Damage Hamas' smuggling routes, its leadership and its tactical options" – goals which were only partly realised, if at all.

What stunned Hamas, more even than the unexpected ferocity of the attacks, was the international reaction. In time, when the details about the types of weapons used and the amount of damage caused surfaced in several human rights reports, Israel would pay a price in good-will and sympathy. But during the initial stages of the war, and indeed until the end, Israel drew much less diplomatic flak than expected. European understanding was much more substantial than anything seen in recent years, but the real novelty, clearly discernible beyond a smoke-screen of dutiful condemnations, was Egypt's stance. Basem Eid, the Palestinian human rights activist, an astute observer of the below-surface dynamics of the regional power game, told me on the third day of the conflict: "This war is only superficially about Gaza. It is really about defending the Egyptian regime against its internal and foreign enemies, about sending a message to Iran: 'We have been slow to react but here it comes.'"

Eid's hunch was borne out by events. There was a concerted Israeli–Egyptian–American effort all through the war to block any ceasefire initiatives or mediation efforts led by countries not hostile towards Iran, such as Syria, Qatar and Turkey. Such policy motives and calculations are unmentionable in the Arab world, both in official rhetoric and in the press. But the Egyptian foreign minister, Abu al-Gheit, no doubt with the full understanding of his boss, came close to breaking the rules. He openly accused Hamas of causing the war by breaking the truce, and Iran for plotting against Egypt. Of course, official media branded the Israelis as murderers and President Mubarak called on their Israeli colleagues to "stop the madness". But, for all that, Egyptian forebearance remained Israel's trump card during the conflict. As long as Hosni Mubarak did not recall his ambassador from Tel Aviv, Israel could take any abuse.

There have been cases in the past when Israeli tanks and snipers have fired intentionally against unarmed civilians. But not following standing orders. During Cast Lead, it appears that few, if any, of the ground troops who entered the Strip were aware of any restrictions on when and against whom to open fire. It does not appear a great exaggeration to describe the common procedure thus: leaflets were dropped from the air with orders to the inhabitants to get out. Half an hour later, all incoming Israeli troops regarded anyone present in the area as a combatant, regardless of age or sex. Built-up areas were attacked by artillery and aircraft long before any foot-soldiers reached it. Some of the weapons used were notoriously inaccurate, such as mortars fired from tanks.

The Israeli tactic had two objectives: to bring down the number of Israeli fatalities by assuring that no armed resistance came within range of the soldiers, and to establish a new "price tag" for the firing of rockets against Israel. In other words, the blurring of the civilian/combatant distinction and the overkill volume of fire seem to have been the plan, not an unintended consequence. In some of Israel's previous campaigns, costly efforts have been made to bring down civilian casualties and muffle the international outcry. There is little evidence of that ever happening during Cast Lead. None of the compilers of foreign investigative reports on the war – Amnesty, Human Rights Watch, the UN – had access to Israeli fighting personnel. They could only speculate as to Israeli intent and standing orders. But the Israeli organisation *Shovrim shtika*, "Breaking the Silence", did supply revealing evidence on this score in its report on the war (www.breakingthesilence.org.il).

*Shovrim shtika*'s reports are based on the testimony of combat soldiers, interviewed by other combat soldiers. It never publishes allegations unless it has two independent sources for an event. While foreign studies are often shrugged off by Israeli authorities as biased, one-sided and based on hearsay, the *Shovrim shtika* results could not be dismissed as hostile or unpatriotic. For that reason, they were furiously condemned by Israeli spokesmen, who even accused the compilers of siding with the enemy. The government even managed to frighten the Dutch government into cutting off its support for the Israeli NGO.

There were instances of common theft and wanton destruction by Israeli soldiers who took up positions in abandoned Gazan homes. These crimes, reported by soldiers, were condemned by Israeli spokesmen, who insisted they were a marginal phenomenon. Hamas war crimes during the fighting, apart from shelling civilian areas in Israel, included the killing of at least 35 people, most of them Fatah-related, for alleged spying.

Very few Israeli soldiers found themselves face to face with a flesh-and-blood enemy during the war. In fact, many returned home without having laid eyes on a Hamas fighter. The much feared anti-tank weapons of Hamas were rarely used to any effect. Conventional heroics, on either side, was absent, including assistance of wounded civilians. Rather than entering a building to check for enemy presence, a "neighbour", i.e. a Palestinian civilian, was sent in to attract possible fire. (A practice forbidden by Israel's Supreme Court.) If "neighbours" were not available, the house was shelled, dynamited or bulldozed without checking it. Few Hamas men confronted the Israelis. They all shed their uniforms and withdrew to their tunnel warrens below the town centres. Only if the Israelis entered, would there be any hand-to-hand fighting.

Many Gazans died needlessly. Except for Shifa in Gaza City, the hospitals in the Strip were incapable of handling the avalanche of wounded. There were intense humanitarian efforts to bring Gazans to Israel for treatment. When, after several frustrating days, the Israeli Army's resistance to the idea had finally been overcome, Hamas vetoed the initiative. It was not going to give Israel any opportunities to look good.

Israel sent ground troops into Gaza a week after the air attack began. Part of Hamas, mainly the leaders inside Gaza, were ready for a negotiated truce by then. The Israeli leadership was also split. The commander of Cast Lead, general Gallant, wanted to carry on into the Hamas underground "fortress". Asked when the war should end he said: "It shouldn't end until Ahmad Ja'bari [the Hamas supreme commander] gets a shot in the neck in the middle of Meidan Filastin [Palestine Square in Gaza City]."

But there were strong incentives for Israel to call off further operations. In spite of Ban Ki Moon's general friendliness towards Israel, relations between Jerusalem and the UN soured dreadfully after several Israeli hits on UN installations, including its main storage facility, which burned down. Elections were drawing closer in Israel, and its leaders were receiving signals from Washington that the incoming president would like to see the Gazan misery exit the front pages before his inauguration on January 20. More than a thousand Palestinians had died, and the figure was bound to rise when the rubble was examined. In Egypt, where the main opposition group, Hamas' mother organisation, the Muslim Brotherhood, made productive use of the situation, the government had also had enough.

On January 17, Israel began to pull out unilaterally, without any deal or even understanding with Hamas.

# Epilogue

## Post-War Gaza: An Uneasy Stalemate

> *One day, if not in our time, Gaza will again become a land-bridge between Arabia and the sea, between Egypt and the Levant, free to prosper and plan without the crippling interference of outside and home-grown despots. When that day arrives, Gazans old enough to remember will most likely regard this moment, the summer of 2010, as the worst in living memory.*

A hundred years ago, the eminent orientalist Richard Gottheil foresaw great things for Gaza: " . . . as the eastern shores of the Mediterranean are opened up to the commerce of the world, and as the projected railroads bring the inner parts of hither Asia into direct connection with the sea."

There was good reason to be optimistic. With 40,000 inhabitants, Gaza was one of the largest towns in the Levant. From time immemorial, its annual fairs, weekly markets and maze-like bazaars had been an entrepôt for goods produced in three continents. During times of strife, Gaza City lived dangerously in the shadows of big powers; during stability it prospered as if by default. The stability brought by British rule, first in Egypt and then in Palestine, got Gaza back on track towards recovery of its ancient position. The steamship traffic, which ended the reign of pirates in the Eastern Mediterranean, turned local plants like the bitter watermelon and barley into boom-products coveted by commodity dealers in Hamburg and London.

The Gaza region was designed by geography to accumulate wealth, home-grown and foreign, and to connect lands separated by oceans of sand or water. This book is largely a catalogue of reasons why this has not happened in our time. The Israeli government controls much of the Strip's access to water, limits the use of the land closest to the separation fence and the use of all but a small stretch of Gaza's traditional fishing waters. Israel also controls the airspace of the Strip, its import and export terminals, and the possibilities of its inhabitants to travel. Even without those impediments, it would be a challenge to achieve sustainable development with a such a vulnerable environment and such a population pressure on limited resources.

There were hopes of improvement after the 2009 war. The Egyptians put great efforts into a Hamas–Fatah deal which would have enabled reconstruction in Gaza without allowing imported building materials to be used for military purposes by Hamas. But Hamas could not accept a new order in Gaza which opened up the way for a Fatah come-back, not unless a symmetrical deal was struck on the West Bank, to allow for renewed Hamas operations there. It seems now that Egypt, Hamas and Fatah have given up all hope of reconciliation, though they keep up a show of trying.

A year and a half after the war, much of the rubble remains. Many of the damaged homes have been repaired, but few of the 4,000 destroyed homes have been replaced. Thousands still live in tents. Parts of the fresh-water distribution and wastewater treatment networks are still out of order.

When more than five billion dollars in Gaza reconstruction aid were pledged by donor nations outbidding each other at the posh Red Sea resort of Sharm al-Sheikh – all concerned knew it was an empty charade. Even if the contributors had made good on their promises, which they haven't, there was the added challenge of preventing any cash from reaching Hamas coffers or being spent on war materials or fortifications. Egypt, Israel, the Fatah government in Ramallah and many donors were adamant about this condition, which was well-nigh nigh impossible to meet. "Getting things done and launching projects in a territory run by a totalitarian government without involving that government is a contradiction in terms", a Scandinavian aid person involved in the effort told me. Business ventures and plans are also stalled by the requirement of keeping Hamas out of the profits. In 2000 British Gas discovered substantial offshore gas deposits north of Gaza and received the concession to drill and market it from Yasser Arafat. Israel's Prime Minister at the time, Ehud Barak, did not dispute the Palestinian's claims to the find. But now the extraction efforts remain bedeviled by politics, with Israel and others demanding that the Palestinian share of the proceeds, above a billion dollars, does not reach Hamas.

Goods enter the Strip from Israel, to the tune of less than a hundred trucks a day – a third of the demand. The restrictions on goods allowed into Gaza via Israel are wide-ranging. Among the banned products are diapers, poetry books and candy. Israel thereby stimulates the tunnel traffic under the Philadelphi passage, along the Egyptian border, and strengthens Hamas, which farms taxes and fees from that trade. In August 2009, Israeli Prime Minister Benjamin Netanyahu allowed the delivery of a substantial amount of reinforced concrete. But he stressed that normal trade, in either direction, would not be resumed until Hamas releases Gil'ad Shalit, abducted in 2006. It is often said that Gaza is a prison and the Gazans are prisoners, but it would be no less correct to describe them as hostages; sequestered hostages in an ideological war of nerves between Israel and Hamas. At the time of writing the tension is centered on the fate of the soldier Shalit, but it will hardly subside even when that issue is resolved.

During Hamas' most creative and successful decade, 1997–2007, the Iranian connection was an unqualified blessing. But, as with Hizbollah in Lebanon, it has discovered that there comes a time when the aims of the sponsor and the sponsored begin to diverge. If Hizbollah insists on the role of Iranian spearhead against Israel, then – because of Israeli attacks and retaliation – it will hurt its own chances to win Lebanese elections. Likewise, it was one thing for Hamas in Gaza to be regarded as an Iranian battering-ram against the Egyptian regime *before* it ascended to power in 2007. Once in control, the stakes and the comparative benefits were redefined. If Hamas manages to unite Egypt and Israel against itself, then it is gambling with its own primary interest, which is to hang on to power in the Strip. Some of the local Hamas leaders would prefer to reassess the ties with Iran and improve relations with Egypt, and there are heated debates in the secretive *Shura* council, Hamas' supreme decision-making body, both about the degree of dependence on Iran and about the ties to Egyptian organizations odious to official Cairo.

The expanded Israeli–Egyptian collaboration in the attacks on the "Persian caravan" – the missile route from Iran to Sudan via Sinai through the Rafah tunnels – is a genuine setback for the Hamas maximalists, i.e. those who believe in acquiring a Hizbollah-like arsenal of rockets with Tel Aviv within its range. The details of this anti-Hamas effort are largely unknown, but the steady traffic of Israeli war-ships through the Suez Canal, without any Egyptian complaints, is surely a worrying sign for Hamas. In January 2010 Mahmud al-Mabhuh, the Gazan in charge of the Iran–Gaza connection, was assassinated in Dubai, apparently by Israeli agents but probably with the assistance of Palestinian-Fatah and perhaps other Arab intelligence services.

There are interesting, if uncertain, signs that Iranian influence in the region has peaked. If Iran should be weakened by internal strife and international sanctions, there will come a time when Hamas in Gaza will be forced to realign itself diplomatically. The hatred and fear of the Egyptian leaders against Hamas, especially after the discovery of a daring Hizbollah-run spy effort in Cairo in the spring of 2009, bodes ill for Hamas in the long run. The Egyptian press has standing orders to blacken the reputation of Hamas and to portray it as an enemy of Egypt and its people. So do the state-employed imams, who regularly preach the word against Hamas in their sermons.

There are Palestinian refugee camps around several Arab capitals, just as there are camps outside Gaza City. But the similarity is superficial and illusory. Hundreds of thousands of refugees have made it out of the camps of Amman, Beirut and Damascus, with hard work, luck and initiative. In the past, Gazan emigrants supplied several Arab countries with white-collar labour, but today there are no escape hatches from Gaza's misery – other than flight through the tunnels and the nerve-racking life as a paperless alien in Cairo. While the growth forecast for the West Bank in 2009 is among the highest in the world, Gaza continues to fall behind. To achieve growth without either trade or industry would be to defy nature but, on top of the obvious handicaps, Gaza is also cut off from the clearing mechanisms of international banking; it is dependent on Israeli currency but rarely supplied with banknotes. The agriculture of the Strip is also a victim of the conflict. Hamas' constant attempts to dig tunnels under the border in order to take Israeli hostages has made the Israelis extend their "exclusion zone" for Gazan farmers; 24 per cent of the Strip's arable land now lies too close to the Israeli border to be worked.

In addition to the external burdens, Hamas ramps up the pressure on the Gazans from within. Since there are no elections in the offing, and no struggle for the hearts and minds of the Gazans, Hamas can give free rein to its inclinations. The ubiquitous guardians of public morality are getting more intrusive by the day, pouncing on couples in parked cars or strolling on the beach and physically enforcing the ban on unchaste attire. In February 2010 the Hamas government ordered the largest Palestinian mobile telephone operator Jawal to hand over lists of all calls made between Gaza and the outside world, in order to monitor contacts between Gazans and the Israeli and the PLO secret services. The company first refused, but complied when faced with a closure order.

Privacy, never an abundant good in Gaza, is well-nigh eradicated. But there is what totalitarian regimes do provide: order. Even during the 2009 war there were few instances of looting. The infamous chaos, *al-fawda*, of the pre-Hamas years, where gangs and clans robbed and terrorized at will, is a thing of the past.

The military situation a year and a half after the 2009 war has temporarily changed in Israel's favour. Deterrence keeps rocket fire down, but underground communication tunnels are being expanded and new and better missiles are being stockpiled by Hamas for the next round of fighting. Israel views these as offensive preparations, but it is also a life-insurance for the Hamas leadership. Regime change in Gaza, whether by Israel, the Fatah or the Egyptians, would surely be fatal for all those now in charge.

Since the 2009 war both Hamas, Egypt and Israel face new and ominous challenges, which are bound to affect their Gazan strategy. There are now al-Qaeda-related networks and probably also embryonic al-Qaeda cells in the Strip. The Egyptians, who took tunnel smuggling rather lightly until the 2009 war, have began work on a huge metal barrier along the Philadephi tunnel zone. Even if it will not eradicate smuggling this obstacle will make it incomparably more costly and dangerous. The plans have caused great indignation in the Islamist camp and all over the Arab world Egypt is accused of teaming up with Israel in its squeeze against Gaza. During demonstrations against the new barrier Hamas gendarmes on the

Gazan side have opened fire on the Egyptian force on the other side and even killed an Egyptian soldier.

The motive behind the Egyptian wall is a genuine fear that subversive ideas, weapons and money reaching Gaza via the Persian caravan should spill over into the Nile valley. The Sinai desert is large and easy to infiltrate, as witnessed by the number of Sudanese and Darfurian refugees who are smuggled into Israel by Egyptian Bedouin. Rather than chasing after pack-camels in the Sinai vastness the Egyptians prefer to hit the Iranian connection where it is most localized and vulnerable, at the Red Sea ports and at its last link, the tunnels into Gaza. During its first year in power, the coalition government of Benjamin Netanayhu has enjoyed relative calm on the Gazan front. Hamas military activity is concentrated on two types of activity: the digging of tunnels into Israel and the laying of mines inside Gaza to prevent Israeli incursions. More troublesome, from Israel's point of view, is the so-called Goldstone Report on the Gaza war. The report, produced by the UN Human Rights Council, Israel's most relentless Nemesis in the international arena, is biased and inaccurate in many respects. But it provides incontrovertible evidence of Israeli human rights violations and war crimes committed during the war. Instead of swiftly investigating those instances and punishing offending soldiers, official Israel has countered by branding the findings as anti-Semitic drivel and Judge Richard Goldstone as a self-hating Jew. The US, Italy and some other nations have supported Israel in its wholesale rejection of the findings, but the EU parliament has adopted its recommendations.

In late May 2010, a flotilla of ships with hundreds of activists on board assembled in the Eastern Mediterranean. Its declared purpose was to break the Israeli naval blockade around the Strip and deliver aid to the Gazans. Its real aim was to mobilize world opinion against the Israeli–Egyptian control over all the points of entry into the Strip. Some earlier seaborne activists had been turned away, and some had been let through. But this time Israel decided to put an end to these voyages once and for all, by towing the ships to Israeli ports and arresting all aboard. The way it was done played straight into the hands of Hamas and Israel's critics. At dawn, May 31, Israeli commandos took charge of the five smaller ships in the convoy and escorted them to the port of Ashdod. But when boarding the main vessel, the *Marmara,* Israeli soldiers met fierce resistance. The Israelis responded with automatic fire, killing nine people and setting off an international outcry against the blockade.

One day, if not in our time, Gaza will again become a land-bridge between Arabia and the sea, between Egypt and the Levant, free to prosper and plan without the crippling interference of outside and home-grown despots. When that day arrives, Gazans old enough to remember will most likely regard this moment, the summer of 2010, as one of the worst in living memory.

# Gaza History Timeline

**3000–2000 BC** Repeated Egyptian conquests of Gaza. The local Canaanite peoples sometimes submit, sometimes resist.

**18th century BC** The Hyksos people, which ran most of Egypt for centuries, turn the towns of Sharuhen, in the southern Gaza Strip, and al-Ajul by the Gaza river, into massive fortresses.

**15th century BC** The Egyptians, eager to prevent assaults on its eastern frontier, erect a mighty fortress at Gaza, depicted on the friezes at Karnak.

**1457 BC** Pharaoh Thutmose III sets out to quash a rebellion by one of his Canaanite vassals, the King of Kadesh, and spends time in Gaza.

**12th century BC** The Philistines arrive from Crete and Asia Minor. Gaza becomes the most important centre in their five-city state.

**529 BC** Persian Emperor Cambyses fails to overrun Gaza. Only after a long siege do the Gazans hoist the white flag. The Persians turn the city into a vast fortress, mentioned by the Greek historian Herodotus, who calls Gaza *Kadytis*, "one of the greatest cities in all Syria".

**332 BC** Gaza is the only place in Palestine to offer resistance to Alexander the Great. He takes the city after a long siege and sells its inhabitants into slavery. Gaza, along with the entire Levant, rapidly assimilates Greek customs.

**96 BC** The Jewish king Alexander Yannay tries to storm Gaza, but only enters it after a year-long siege.

**61 BC** The Romans put an end to Jewish statehood. Pompey takes Jerusalem and annexes the whole country, including Gaza, to the new Roman province of Syria.

**34 BC** Anthony includes Gaza in his lover's gift to Queen Cleopatra of Egypt.

**30 BC** The Roman senate annuls the gift and Augustus gives Gaza to Herod, who rules in Jerusalem as a Roman vassal.

**4 BC** Augustus brakes off "the Greek cities", Gaza among them, from the province of Judea and makes them part of Syria again.

**1–2 centuries AD** Bloody persecutions of Christians in Gaza by the pagan majority, which worships a wide selection of Greek and Oriental deities.

**398** All pagan creeds in Gaza are outlawed by imperial decree.

**404–6** The Christians destroy the last pagan temples in Gaza.

**634** In their first important conquest outside of Arabia the Muslims defeat the Byzantine army outside Gaza. The Arabs develop the port Maioumas at the expense of Gaza City. Many Jews and Christians stay on.

**1100** Gaza falls to the Frankish Crusaders. Jews and Muslims are thrown out. A French chateau is erected at the summit of Gaza City and a European-type market town grows around it.

**1187** Islam's greatest conqueror, Saladin, crushes the Christian armies near Tiberias in the Galilee and regains most of the country for Islam.

**1191** Richard the Lionheart retakes Gaza, but is forced to abandon it and tear down its defenses a year later, when he strikes a peace deal with Saladin.

**1193** Saladin dies. During the following generation Gaza passes between Fatimids, Turks, Franks, Syrian Muslims, Caspian Tartars, the Mongols of Hulagu Khan and Egyptian Mamluks.

**1251** The Mamluks of Egypt begin their long reign over Gaza.

**1260** The feared Mongols arrive in Gaza. They are driven back and then beaten by the Mamluks at the battle of Ayn Jalut in the Jezreel Valley, their first military defeat ever.

**1516** The Ottoman conqueror Selim triumphs over the Mamluks at Khan Yunes, the new town founded by the Mamluks in the Strip, and puts an end to their long rule.

**1665** The Messianic claims of Shabtai Zvi, soon to wreak havoc all over the Jewish world, are announced in Gaza.

**1754** The yearly Meccan pilgrim caravan from Damascus is raided. The booty, loaded onto thirteen thousand camels, is sold in the Gazan bazaars.

**1799** The Bosnian Pasha Jazzar, the strongman of Palestine, leaves his coastal fortress in Acre to confront Napoleon at Gaza, but is thrown back, almost without a battle.

**1831–1841** Power-struggle in Gaza between the pasha of Egypt, Muhammad Ali, backed by the French, and the Ottomans, who get help from of British to cut short his expansion.

**1839** Thousands of Gazans die in the plague.

**1882** British *de facto* rule over Egypt begins and brings Gaza new trade opportunities. Gazan melon-seeds and barley are coveted by international markets.

**1890–1910** Schools, charities and hospitals are established in Gaza, mostly by Christian missions.

**1915, January–February** The Ottomans and their German allies fail to conquer the Suez Canal and beat a hurried retreat back to Gaza.

**1917** The first British attempt to drive the Turks out of Gaza, March 26–27, 1917, ends in failure. The Second Battle of Gaza, April 17–19, 1917, is an outright disaster, with more than six thousand British casualties. A new British commander Edmund Allenby, is put in charge of the Palestine campaign.

**1917, November 6** By a ruse of Allenby's, the German, Austrian and Turkish defenders of Gaza are defeated. Most of the City is destroyed by artillery fire.

**1920** The British Mandate over Palestine is established by the League of Nations.

**1925, February** The Muslim-Christian Association of Gaza protests against a Government go-ahead for the sale of Gazan lands to non-residents, i.e. Jews.

**1929** During country-wide riots the Jews of Gaza are saved by local Palestinians. The Jews leave the city forever.

**1930** The Jew Tuvia Miller buys a 60-acre citrus orchard a kilometre south of the village of Deir al-Balah, not far from the location of the ancient Hebrew town of Darom. It is the first Zionist settlement in the future Strip.

**1936–39** During the Arab Rebellion in Palestine, Miller's business in Darom is attacked repeatedly. In 1939 he leaves it, without selling the land.

**1946** Tuvia Miller sells his land near Deir al-Balah to the Jewish National Fund. In the autumn of that year, settlers from the national-religious Zionist movement Mizrahi establish a new colony there, named Kfar Darom.

**1947, spring** Britain gives notice it will return its mandate and transfer responsibility for Palestine to the United Nations.

**1947, November 29** The UN votes in favour of the partition of Palestine into a Jewish and an Arab state. Almost all of what would become the Gaza Strip belongs to the Arab state. Some Palestinians in the Tel Aviv–Jaffa area flee tension and violence for other cities, among them Gaza. It is the beginning of the *Nakba*, the Palestinian refugee disaster.

**1948, March** Egyptian leaders of the Muslim Brotherhood tour the Gaza area and call on the locals to join the struggle against Zionism.

**1948, April** Muslim Brotherhood forces begin their assault on Kfar Darom, the only Zionist settlement inside the future Strip. After losing more than a hundred men the Arab units force the Jews to flee.

**1948, May 15** The State of Israel is declared. Several Arab nations send troops into Palestine. Egyptian regulars and volunteers in the Gaza area.

**1948, December 22** the Israelis launches Operation *Horev*, destined to be the concluding round of fighting in the war.

**1949, January** Washington and London force Israel to call off its offensive against the boxed-in Egyptian forces in the south-western corner of Palestine. The Gaza Strip comes into being. US Quakers and, later, a new UN body, the UNRWA, provide food and shelter for the almost two hundred thousand refugees in the Strip.

**1950** Israel expels several thousand Palestinians from its southern coastal areas to the Strip.

**1956, October** Israel joins forces with Britain and France against Egypt. Israel occupies the Strip and intends to stay on.

**1957, March** The US forces Israel to withdraw from the Strip. A new UN force, the UNEF, puts an effective end to Palestinian raids into Israel from the Strip.

**1967, May 16** Egypt orders the UN forces to leave the Strip.

**1967, June 5** Israeli armoured forces cut the Strip in two. During three days of some of the toughest fighting of the Six-Day war, Israel conquers the Strip. The "open borders" policy of Israeli Defence Minister Moshe Dayan allows the Gazans to visit all parts of historical Palestine. Thousands of Strip residents begin to work in Israel.

**1970** The remnants of the Jewish village Kfar Darom, conquered by the Egyptians in 1948, is turned into a "Nahal" military outpost.

**1971, July** The head of Israel's southern command, general Ariel Sharon, gets permission to confront the vigorous Palestinian resistance inside the Strip with drastic measures. During his "dirty war" patrol roads are drawn through and around the refugee camps. The Palestinian fighting organisations are crushed and do not recover.

**1971, September** The pro-Jordanian Rashad al-Shawa, from the Strip's most powerful family, agrees to become mayor of Gaza City.

**1971, October** The Israeli authorities begin to set aside land in the Strip, 10% of the total area, for future Israeli settlements.

**1972** The PLO gives up trying to prevent Strip residents from working in Israel.

**1978–80** The later – famous – "Gaza First" formula is first suggested by Egyptian negotiators during the Camp David talks in 1978. PLO leader Yasser Arafat is tempted to explore the idea, but pan-Arab outrage against Egyptian President Sadat prevents him.

**1982, April** Israel returns the Sinai to Egypt and the new border fence cuts right across the town of Rafah. Twenty-thousand Gazans, mostly refugees from the "Canada" camp, end up on the Egyptian side.

**1987, December** The first Palestinian uprising against Israeli rule begins in Jebaliya in the Strip and spreads to all occupied territories. The Muslim Brothers in Gaza City launch a new movement, the Hamas.

**1988, March** Israeli commandos land in Tunis and assassinate Khalil Wazir, the PLO leader believed to coordinate PLO aid to Gaza and the West Bank.

**1989** Hamas, chided by other movements for avoiding confrontation with Israel, begin to abduct and kill Israeli soldiers.

**1990** After Yasser Arafat backs the Iraqi conquest of Kuwait thousands of Gazans lose their jobs in the Gulf states.

**1991** Israel starts giving visas to foreign workers to diminish its dependence on Gazan labour.

**1992, June** Yizhak Rabin is elected Prime Minister of Israel.

**1992, December** Secret negotiations underway in Norway between the PLO and Israel.

**1993, September** The "Oslo" talks lead to mutual recognition between Israel and PLO.

**1994, May** The Gaza–Jericho autonomy agreement is finalised in Cairo.

**1994, July** Yasser Arafat arrives in Gaza and takes charge of the PA (Palestinian National Authority). Donor nations spend millions in the Strip but quarrel with Arafat over lack of financial transparency.

**1994, November** PA forces fire into Islamist crowds in Gaza City.

**1995, November** Yizhak Rabin is killed by Israeli extremist. He is replaced by Shimon Peres who vows to carry on the peace process. Both Peres and Arafat denounce intensified Iranian attempts to derail the peace process.

**1996, May** The Israeli nationalists win the elections. Benjamin Netanyahu speeds up settlement activity and swears never to accept a Palestinian state, but meets with Arafat and withdraws Israeli forces from most of Hebron on the West Bank.

**1997, September** After a blundered assassination attempt against Hamas leader Khaled Mash'al, Israel is forced to release Hamas founder Ahmad Yassin and allow him to return to Gaza.

**1998, December** President Bill Clinton on official visit to Gaza.

**1999, May** The Israeli nationalists defeated in elections. Ehud Barak vows to finalise peace talks soon.

**2000, July** Clinton hosts Arafat and Barak at Camp David. The hopes of a final settlement are dashed.

**2000, September** The Second Palestinian rising begins. After a massive Israeli reaction PA forces are gradually drawn into the fighting.

**2001, February** Ariel Sharon elected Israel's Prime Minister. First Israeli victim of Palestinian mortar fire from Gaza.

**2002, January** Hundreds in Rafah made homeless by Israeli house demolitions in retaliation for Hamas attack.

**2002, March–April** Palestinian self-rule in the West Bank crushed by **Israel.**

**2002, July** A one-ton bomb, dropped on the home of Hamas supreme military leader Salah Shehade in the Daraj quarter of Gaza City, kills Shehade and fourteen civilians, most of them children.

**2003, April** After pressure from Gazan PA strongman Muhammad Dahlan, Arafat is forced to name Mahmud Abbas Prime Minister and to accept reforms. In November, himself humiliated and his reforms frustrated, Abbas resigns.

**2004, February** Ariel Sharon shocks his followers by speaking of a "Gaza Strip without Jews".

**2004, March** Hamas founder Ahmad Yassin is killed by an Israeli missile as he exits a mosque in the Sabra quarter of Gaza.

**2004, April** Yassin's successor, Abdulaziz Rantisi, is killed when an Israeli Air Force missile hits his car.

**2004, May** Over a thousand people in Rafah made homeless by Israeli house demolitions.

**2004, July** Mini-coup by Arafat in Gaza – his relative Musa Arafat confronts the old Fatah forces led by Dahlan.

**2004, October** 159 Palestinians in Jebaliya are killed during Israeli retaliation for rocket attacks against southern towns. The Islamist's foremost rocket expert Adnan al-Ghoul is killed during the fighting.

**2004, November** Yasser Arafat dies in Paris. Succeded by Mahmud Abbas as Fatah leader.

**2005, January** Abbas elected Palestinian president.

**2005, August–September** Israel evicts its settlers in the Strip and unilaterally announces the end of its occupation.

**2005, November** Denounced by his own party, Likud, for having evacuated the Strip, Ariel Sharon founds a new party, Kadima.

**2006, January 4** Sharon has a massive stroke and never recovers. Celebrations in Gaza, where people swing banners "Sharon on his way to Hell!"

**2006, January 9** Hamas wins landslide Palestinian vote. Abbas vows to retain control of armed forces. Israel restricts imports to and exports from the Strip.

**2006, April** The EU, following the US, halts aid to Palestinian Authorities in Gaza.

**2006, May** Hamas launches its own regular force.

**2006, June** Hamas and some smaller groups dig a tunnel into Israel, kill two soldiers and abduct corporal Gil'ad Shalit, whose fate will continue to dog Israel–Gaza relations for years. The unofficial 18-month truce Israel–Hamas breaks down and nearly four hundred Palestinians are killed during Israeli offensive operations in the Strip.

**2006–2007** The situation in Gaza slides towards civil war between the Hamas forces and those loyal to President Abbas. Widespread murders of Gazans and kidnappings of foreign journalists.

**2007, February** The Saudi Arabian king, backed by the Arab League, forces Hamas and Fatah to form a government of national unity. Both sides gear up for the Gazan endgame: Iranian weapons for Hamas arrive via tunnels, and Egyptian and Jordanian arms for Fatah via the Rafah crossing.

**2007, June** During five days of brutal fighting, Hamas overcomes all Fatah resistance in the Strip, and starts to impose its ideology on its inhabitants.

**2007, September** The Israeli cabinet, after intense rocket fire from Gaza, declares the Strip to be "enemy territory" and begins to cut power and fuel supplies.

**2008, June** An Egypt-brokered six-month *tahadiya* – "calm" – is established between Israel and Hamas. Both sides stop shooting and some supplies of necessities into the Strip are allowed by Israel.

**2008, November 4** Israel breaks the truce in order to stop the digging of an underground tunnel from the Strip to the Kisufim Junction. After two weeks of mutual firing, the *tahadiya* is restored.

**2008, December 18** Hamas declares an end to the truce. Wants the opening of the crossing points and an end to attacks against it in the West Bank in return for an extension of the *tahadiya*.

**2008, December 25** Hamas fires 70 rockets, an all-time record, against Israel.

**2008, December 27** Israel initiates Operation Cast Lead with the most massive air attacks ever against the Strip. Hundreds are killed, and most Hamas offices and command centres are destroyed in the course of minutes.

**2009, January 17** Leaving 1,300–1,400 dead; 4000 homes destroyed and 20,000 damaged, Israel calls back its forces without any deal with Hamas. After the war Hamas, for the first time ever, force all organisations in the Strip to stop firing rockets against Israel.

**2009, February–August** Egyptian-led negotiations about a Hamas–Israel prisoner exchange continue, without any progress. Israeli–Egyptian security cooperation against Hamas is stepped up. Egyptian attempts to reconcile Hamas and Fatah continue. In July Israel lets through some reinforced concrete, but reconstruction is still years from completion, and Israel says that the transfer of goods will not be normalised until the release of the abducted soldier Shalit.

**2010** Reconciliation talks between Fatah and Hamas break down. Egypt builds new metal barrier through Rafah in order to curb tunnel smuggling into the Strip.

**September 2009** The UN Human Rights Council publishes its investigation of the Gazan war, a scathing account of the civilian casualties of Israel's and – to a lesser degree – Hamas' warfare. The report, named after South African judge Richard Goldstone, who led the probe, is a severe diplomatic setback for Israel, which denounces it an anti-Semitic fabrication. Its content and its tendency remains the subject of heated debate.

**December 2009** Egypt, with American and EU assistance, starts construction of a new wall separating the Egyptian and the Palestinian parts of Rafah. Planned to run 18 metres deep and 11 kilometres long, the steel and concrete obstacle aims at blocking the smuggling tunnels supplying the Strip with food, consumer goods and weapons.

**January 6, 2010** Furious reactions on the Palestinian side of the border when the Hamas government discovers the Egyptian wall project. Tens are injured by automatic fire on both sides of the border during demonstrations. Egypt claims one of its soldiers is killed by

Hamas fire. Egyptian media and state-employed imams are told to step up the campaign portraying Hamas as enemies of the republic.

**January 20, 2010** Mahmud al-Mabhuh, the man who carried out the first ever Hamas attacks against Israel in the late 1980s, is killed by Israeli agents in Dubai. Al-Mabhuh, from the Jebaliya camp in Gaza, was the organiser of the intricate Iranian lifeline of weapons, cash and experts into Gaza via Sudan, the Sinai desert and the tunnels.

**February, 2010** The Palestine telephone operator Jawal is forced by Hamas' secret services to cede lists of calls between the Strip and other territories, notably the West Bank and Israel.

**March, 2010** A sharp drop in tunnel imports is noted in Gaza, brought on by the advancement of the Egyptian wall, which puts all but the very deepest tunnels in its way out of action. Tension with Israel mounts as maverick militant groups inside the Strip ignore Hamas' ban on rocket fire.

**March 25, 2010** Five Islamist fighters and two Israeli soldiers die in a shootout inside the Strip, after an Israeli unit is lured into an ambush by Gazans pretending to place landmines near the border fence. Neither side is eager for escalation and Hamas resolutely enforces the rocket-firing ban.

**April 15, 2010** International outcry as two Gazans, said to have collaborated with Israel, are shot without trial; 32 others met with the same fate during the 2009 war, and another 14 are awaiting the firing squad after summary procedures before a military court.

**May 31, 2010** A flotilla of six ships, bound for Gaza with aid and seven hundred pro-Palestinian activists on board, is intercepted in international waters by Israeli forces. The five smallest vessels are taken over by Israeli naval commandos and towed towards Israel. But while boarding the largest ship, the *Marmara*, the Israeli soldiers are met with fierce resistance by Turkish islamists and open fire, killing nine. Israel is roundly condemned and faces mounting pressure to end the naval blockade against the Strip.

# Bibliography

*Gaza ve B'noteha*: A collection of ancient and modern Hebrew sources on Gaza. Editor not stated. Jerusalem 1972 (in Hebrew).

Aburish, Sa'id K.: *Arafat – From Defender to Dictator*, London 1998.

Atrash, Imad: *Wildlife Field Guide of Wadi Gaza*, Beit Sahur 2003.

Aviad, Guy: *The Hamas Lexicon*, Tel Aviv 2008 (in Hebrew).

Avi-Yona, Michael: *The Holy Land*, London 1972.

Balawi, Hassan: *Gaza – Dans les coulisses du movement national palestinien*, Paris 2008.

Bartlett, Samuel: *From Egypt to Palestine*, New York 1879.

Butt, Gerald: *Life at the Crossroads: A History of Gaza*, Essex 1995.

Chamberlain, Michael. *The Ayyubids*, in *The Cambridge History of Egypt*, vol. I, ed. Carl F. Petry, Cambridge 1998.

Dowling, Theodore. *Gaza: A City of Many Battles*, London 1913.

Downey, Glanville: *Gaza in the Early Sixth Century*, Oklahoma 1963.

Eldar, Shlomi: *Gaza Like Death*, Tel Aviv, 2008 (in Hebrew).

Fosdick H.D: *A Pilgrimage to Palestine*, New York 1929.

Elpeleg, Zvi: *The Grand Mufti Haj Amin al-Husseini*. London 1993.

Fulton, John: *Palestine – The Holy Land*, Philadelphia 1900.

Gichon, Mordechai: *The History of the Gaza Strip: A Geo-Strategic Perspective*, The Jerusalem Cathedra, 1982.

Gazit, Mordechai: "The 1956 Sinai Campaign – David Ben-Gurion's Policy on Gaza, the Armistice Agreement and French Mediation", *Israel Affairs*, summer 2000.

Glaser, Eduard: *Reise nach Marib*, Vienna, 1913.

Horwitz-Mizrahi, Shira: *The Rate of Salination of Gazan Water Resources and the Implications for Argricultural Productivity*, Beersheba 1998.

Humbert, J-B: *Gaza Méditerranéenne*, in *Histoire et Archéoloie en Palestine*, Paris 2000.

Khalidi, Walid: *All That Remains*, Washington D.C. 1992.

von Lasaulx, Ernest: *Der Untergang des Hellenismus*, Munich 1854.

Levenberg, Haim: *Military Preparations of the Arab Community in Palestine 1945-48*, London, 1993.

Levontin, Zalman David: *Le-eretz avoteinu I–III*, Tel Aviv 1928.

Masriyeh, Norma: *Refugee Resettlement – The Gaza Strip Experience*. The Palestine–Israel Journal, 1995 (4).

Murado, Miguel: *La Segunda Intifada*, Madrid 2006.

Pritchard, James B (ed.): *Ancient Near Eastern Texts Relating to the Old Testament*, Princeton, 1969.

Milton, John: *Samson Agonistes*, in *Paradise Regained*, London 1671.

Morris, Benny: *The Birth of the Palestinian Refugee Problem Revisited*, Cambridge 2004.

Morris, Benny: *Israel's Border Wars, 1949–1956*, Oxford 1997.

Patai, Rafael: *The Children of Noah – Jewish Seafaring in Ancient Times*, Princeton 1999.

Porath, Yehoshua: The Emergence of the Palestinian-Arab National Movement, 1918–1929, London 1974.

Rikhye, Indar Jit: *The Sinai Blunder*, London 1980.

Rubinstein, Shimon: *Mabat al ha-Kehila ha-Yehudit be-Aza*, Jerusalem 1995 (in Hebrew).

Shmuel Segev (ed.): B'*Einei ha-Oyev*. Tel Aviv 1959 (in Hebrew).

al-Sharif, Kamil Isma'il: *Al-Ikhwan fi Harb Filastin*, Cairo 1954 (in Arabic).

Smith, George Adam: *The Historical Geography of the Holy Land*, London 1894.

Stark, K.B: *Gaza und die philistäische Kuste*, Jena 1852

Saliou, Catherine (ed.): *Gaza dans l'Antiquite Tardive*, Archeologie, rhetorique et histoire, Salerno 2005.

Swettenham, J.A: *Some Impressions of UNEF 1957 to 1958*, Ottawa 1959.

Tamari, Salim: *Mountains Against the Sea*, California 2008.

Tamimi, Azzam: *Hamas, a History from Within*, Massachusetts 2007.

Zohar, David: *Gamal Over Gaza – Egyptian Neocolonialism in Gaza*, Jerusalem 1968.

# Index